CONTEMPORARY SOCIA...
General Editor: MARTIN BULME...

14

Research Methods for Elite Studies

CONTEMPORARY SOCIAL RESEARCH SERIES

Research Methods for Elite Studies

Edited by
George Moyser and Margaret Wagstaffe
Department of Government, University of Manchester

London
ALLEN & UNWIN
Boston   Sydney   Wellington

Unwin Hyman Ltd
PO Box 18, Park Lane, Hemel Hempstead, Herts HP2 4TE, UK
40 Museum Street, London WC1A 1LU, UK
37/39 Queen Elizabeth Street, London SE1 2QB

Allen & Unwin Inc.,
8 Winchester Place, Winchester, Mass. 01890, USA

Allen & Unwin (Australia) Ltd,
8 Napier Street, North Sydney, NSW 2060, Australia

Allen & Unwin (New Zealand) Ltd in association with the
Port Nicholson Press Ltd,
Private Bag, Wellington, New Zealand

First published in 1987

British Library Cataloguing in Publication Data

Research methods for elite studies —
(Contemporary social research series; 14)
1. Elite (Social sciences) — Research
I. Moyser, George   II. Wagstaffe, Margaret
III. Series
305.5′2′072   HM141
ISBN 0-04-312035-0
ISBN 0-04-312036-9 Pbk

Library of Congress Cataloging in Publication Data

Research methods for elite studies.
(Contemporary social research series; 14)
Bibliography: p.
1. Elite (Social sciences) — Research.
2. Social sciences—Research.
I. Moyser, George.   II. Wagstaffe, Margaret.   III. Series.
HT608.R47   1987   305.5′2′072   86-14765
ISBN 0-04-312035-0 (alk. paper)
ISBN 0-04-312036-9 (pbk.: alk. paper)

Set in 10 on 12 point Times by Fotographics (Bedford) Ltd
and printed in Great Britain by
Billings and Sons Ltd., London and Worcester

Contents

Preface

Elites are a crucial element of modern society. Whether they are taken to be 'top people', the wielders of power or merely those whose opinions and actions count most, their presence can be felt in most aspects of life. It is in this context that the question arises of how one studies them – either directly as elites, or indirectly in pursuit of some other purpose. It is to this subject that the present volume is addressed and, as will be seen in the following pages, the issues and dilemmas involved can be varied and complex. Perhaps surprisingly, the same problems tend to arise in otherwise very different contexts.

The individual contributors, although obviously sharing a general concern for the methodology of social science, do not hold to any common substantive position. One does not have to be an 'elitist' in order to study elites. Indeed, being economists, political scientists and sociologists, their particular theoretical concerns, and the field locations of their research, cover a wide spectrum – the United States Congress, political leadership in Taiwan, and English bishops to mention but three.

To all of them, we, as editors, would like to extend our thanks. Without their insights and experiences this book would simply not have been possible. Needless to say, any imperfection of the whole is solely our responsibility. We also wish to thank the members of the workshop on 'Elite Interviewing', held at the Joint Sessions of Workshops of the European Consortium for Political Research in 1982, for providing the initial stimulus. It became very clear in those week-long discussions that here indeed was an important yet, in print at least, little considered topic that should be developed into a publication. Some of the members of that workshop are represented in this volume. To the others, whose papers are listed in the bibliography at the end, we also wish to extend our thanks for the part they played. Additionally, we wish to express our gratitude to Jean Ashton, Clair Dyson and Angela Jones for their endless patience in typing and retyping our manuscript, and to Kate Baker for her help with corrections.

The collection itself has been divided, somewhat heuristically, into three sections. The first, on 'conventional' elites, contains a set of essays covering a wide variety of definitional, operational and technical matters. Part 2 is concerned exclusively with economic elites, and again considers a number of approaches and analytic problems. Part 3 examines the sorts of elites who, for different and no doubt legitimate reasons, tend to make life difficult for investigative social scientists. They have, in consequence, been dubbed 'defensive elites' and throw into particularly sharp relief many of the difficulties and dilemmas that lie beneath the surface of all studies involving subjects who tend to be, almost by definition, somewhat larger than life.

Ultimately, of course, our collective endeavours must be judged by the reader. For our part, we hope that within these pages there is advice, guidance and stimulation to better research. It is to that goal that we as editors, and our contributors, are collectively dedicated.

George Moyser
Margaret Wagstaffe

1

Studying elites: theoretical and methodological issues

GEORGE MOYSER and MARGARET WAGSTAFFE
University of Manchester

1.1 Introduction: The Significance of Elite Studies

The central importance of elites in modern societies, indeed in almost all types of society, seems once more to be emerging as a major theme of social and political analysis. 'Elitism' or the 'elitist paradigm' is back on the agenda, so much so, in fact, that a new journal, *Power and Elites* (1984) and yearbook (Czudnowski, 1982) have recently been launched (see also Field and Higley, 1980). Not surprisingly, however, after decades of relative desuetude, the approach suffers from argument and confusion over key terms, a relative dearth of testable hypotheses, a failure clearly to separate normative from empirical theory and, not least, the lack of a firm data base in which the latter could be solidly grounded. This is not to imply that other theoretical frameworks, such as pluralism or Marxism, are free of such problems; but it is to say that those who wish to re-establish the significance of the 'elite' concept in social theory should (and do) recognize the large task that lies ahead.

A major part of that task is essentially methodological in nature; for if the elitist paradigm aspires to the status of a well-established social scientific theory, then the quality of the evidence on which it rests is critical. Progress in theory and method go together. It is in recognition of this that the present volume has been produced. It raises, in a wide variety of concrete contexts, the questions of method and technique that must be answered and the lessons that must be

The authors would like to thank Professor G. Parry for his comments and suggestions during the writing of this chapter. However, he bears no responsibility for any shortcomings.

learned if the study of elites is indeed to find a permanent place in our understanding of the human social, economic and political condition.

In that respect it is possible to identify a potential contribution in three related but distinct spheres. First, the study of elites raises a number of important normative issues and sheds light on such matters from a novel perspective. Indeed, the 'normative dimension' seems particularly salient in this field, involving challenges to some conventional and widely shared assumptions (or 'myths') about modern western societies and producing, in consequence, 'a polarizing, polemical style of discourse' (Marcus, 1983, p. 23). For example, Field and Higley (1980, p. 69) note that 'the existence of elites' has normative implications for judgements about 'the possible or desirable extent of freedom and equality' in society. Radical libertarianism and egalitarianism are both, in these terms, entirely utopian; freedom, liberty and equality must be set, and judged, in the context of hierarchy and specialization intrinsic to modern society. By the same token, Parry (1969, ch. 6) has discussed the problems and possibilities of reconciling elites and democracy. In part, it entails debate about the meaning of 'democracy'. This in turn requires evaluation of the arguments of 'conservative democrats' such as Schumpeter (1942), who value 'strong, authoritative government' (Parry, 1969, p. 144) in which astute leadership is of prime importance, and 'radical democrats' like Kariel (1961) and Bachrach (1967) who emphasize the ideals to be found in classical democracy. Should ordinary people be encouraged to share actively in the making of decisions that affect them? Or should society's leaders, as 'tough realists', be left to make the sometimes difficult choices from their informed vantage points, being held to account only from time to time by an arguably myopic electorate (but see Key, 1966)?

Clearly, therefore, the study of elites focuses attention on some fundamental questions about the way society ought to be organized, and the roles of the individuals who comprise it. Equally, however, it provokes questions which are capable, to some degree, of empirical verification. In that respect, we are dealing not solely with abstract and philosophical matters, but with real, historical situations: not so much 'who ought to govern?' as 'who governs?' (Dahl, 1961). In this way, the study of elites also throws light on the inner workings of societies: how they are stratified, how rewards are shared out; the criteria on which privilege is accorded and, above all, how power is exercised and by whom. All of this, it is argued, is in turn relevant to the persistence, peaceful adaptation or violent change of societies through time (Lijphart, 1968; 1977; Levine, 1978; Wilde, 1978; Purcell and Purcell, 1980). The most ambitious attempt to make such a connection is provided by Field and Higley (1980, ch. 2), who encompass within their remit virtually the entire experience of Western societies and Japan from agrarian to post-industrial times. This work was subsequently enlarged to a study of eighty one nations since the Second World War (Field and Higley, 1982). Both these analyses are bold and innovative. Nevertheless, they are only the beginnings of turning the thesis into an empirically sustainable account.

As the above comments imply, there is yet a third area in which the study of elites is particularly relevant – that of concrete and immediate issues of social engineering. There is a recognition that, in addressing urgent issues about peace and war, human rights, poverty, etc., elites at national, international and local levels have a crucial role to play. Their perspectives, the quality of their leadership, the immediate moral and political culture within which they operate and the social formations from which they are drawn are all part of the equation, and need to be taken into account in constructing policies that will be accepted and put into effect (Lindblom, 1968). This is the presumption, for example, of Arthur's contribution in Chapter 11.

In so far as the study of elites can also address issues and problems not strictly a part of the elitist perspective, the contribution of this volume is not one necessarily tied to that particular theoretical position. It has in this sense a much broader relevance. Thus, whereas Marxism and elitism have traditionally been opposed (see Binns, Chapter 12 this volume; Parry, 1969, pp. 27–9), Lenin's contribution is one which lays considerable stress on the need for a small, well-organized party acting as the vanguard of the proletariat. Hence, while Marxism does not find elites decisive in the march of history there is, nevertheless, a recognition of the significant role that effective leadership can play in bringing about or hastening revolutionary political change.

In more recent times, orthodox Marxists (and Soviet politicians) have continued to deride elite analysis (Poulantzas, 1969). Yet there are signs that elites are taken into account (Crewe, 1974, p. 9). This position has been taken both by revisionists (for example, Djilas, 1957) and by those seeking to synthesize the insights of both schools into the question of how leadership and power is exercised in modern industrial society (Burnham, 1942; Wright Mills, 1956; see also Parry, 1969, pp. 28, 50–4). For example, Miliband (1969/1973), in a relatively recent yet classic analysis, recognizes the existence of elites within advanced capitalist society whose views reflect genuine differences among 'members of the propertied classes ... over a multitude of specific policies and issues, not to speak of differences in religion and culture' (1973 ed., p. 43). However, as befits the Marxist perspective, such divisions within the bourgeoisie are ultimately subordinate to their overriding 'common interests and common purposes' (p. 45) as members of the dominant ruling class.

Pluralism also takes some cognizance of elites. In its 'extreme' form the emphasis is almost entirely on the behaviour of groups in the competitive political marketplace. However, this does at least beg the question of the extent to which performance and group preferences are the product of the group's leadership rather than of its social base or other external factors. Such a possibility is more explicitly recognized in the 'corporatist' model which some view as an extension or variant of pluralism, and others as a rival (Moran, 1985, p. 145). Though, as usual, the subject of different interpretations and analyses, at its core – at least as outlined by Schmitter's (1979) influential contribution – a place is explicitly reserved for the role of group leadership. Schmitter evokes an image of interests being organized into a limited number of hierarchical categories, with an emphasis on the control leaders exert over their members and on the relatively intimate links between these elites and the state authorities. It is this quality, the existence of limited network(s) of individuals who play a key role in national policy-making which is, of course, the starting point for an analysis founded on the concept of a 'political elite'.

The idea of elites as a part of the group life of a society, or as participants in a wider political process, introduces a second way in which the study of elites is broader than its associated paradigm. For these are both often instances where the researcher might wish to interview or utilize elites without their being the primary or ultimate research objective. They may, in other words, be contacted for the sort of advice, information or access that only they can provide. The relevant individuals could, for example, be party leaders best able to impart information about key decisions that affect the way a party system actually functions. They may be senior officials who have the sole authority to give access to governmental documents. Or they may be leaders of a trade union who can guide the researcher as to what questions should be asked, of whom and in what way. All of these activities require the knowledge and skills appropriate to elite study. They might not produce substantive information about elites *per se*, but they certainly will raise many of the relevant methodological issues and problems. This is not just a matter of access and interviewing technique but the whole question of assessing how the values of the individuals concerned, their positions, reputations and careers, etc., influence (or bias) the quality of the advice, information and access that is imparted. In other words, even in the role of experts and guides, rather than of leaders, elite individuals must be looked at through an almost equally sensitive methodological prism.

Having said that, it is, of course on the elitist paradigm that the study of elites mainly concentrates. (Not that the distinction is always clear cut; after all, Michels's study, one of the classics of the elitist genre, was also an investigation of the German Social Democratic Party, see Michels, 1959). Thus, many of those most closely concerned with elites look to the late nineteenth century and the early twentieth as the 'golden age' of elitism. Though earlier theorists back to Plato (Cornford, 1941) and Aristotle (Barker, 1946) were quite aware of the existence and importance of oligarchy in the societies of their day, it was not until Mosca (1858–1943) and Pareto (1848–1923) that a 'classical' elitist school emerged. In their work (Pareto, 1935; Mosca, 1883), a set of ideas emerged about the role of leadership in relatively modern societies. These ideas, allegedly less normative and more empirical than those of earlier theorists, in turn formed the basis for more recent research in this general tradition.

In what is essentially a book on methodology, it is not our purpose to review the substantive merits and demerits of this literature, not least because very thorough reviews already exist (see, for example, Parry, 1969; Putnam, 1976). It is perhaps sufficient to note that until the mid-1970s, according to Field and Higley (1980, p. 4), relatively little was done to follow up and build on the earlier foundations. There were, of course, some important studies (for example Burnham, 1942; Lipset, *et al.*, 1956; Wright Mills, 1956; see also Crewe, 1974, pp. 9–10). But the vogue and weight of research had shifted towards other paradigms, and especially towards the study of mass populations following the invention of the sample survey and opinion polling in the 1930s.

Since around the mid-1970s, however, the elite perspective has seen a modest revival in its popularity. This 'neo-elitist' persuasion is not quite the same as its classical antecedent, because of the subsequent impact by pluralists and Marxists on Western thought. The central difference revolves around views about the degree of autonomy exercised by elites in decision-making. Nowadays, there is widespread recognition that elites are to some extent constrained by external circumstances such as economic factors or mass opinion.

(Nordlinger, 1981; Burton and Higley, 1984). In this sense, 'neo-elitism' makes rather more timid claims for the central importance of elites but the gain, so it is argued, is a greater realism or empirical accuracy.

Whatever the reason, or reasons, for the revival, and several have been offered (for example Field and Higley, 1980, ch. 2; Marcus, 1983, pp. 3–4; Burton, 1984, p. 46), the result has been that its claims to credibility and respectability have been scrutinized in terms markedly different from those when it last achieved prominence. Since those days, the social sciences have changed considerably in their attitudes towards theory and research. In political science, for example, the 1950s saw the emergence of 'the behavioural era' (Seidelman and Harpham, 1985, ch. 5). This involved the acceptance of a neo-positivistic paradigm as the benchmark against which research tended to be judged, at least in the United States. Though characterized by some diversity, in general terms, this perspective placed emphasis upon the observed behaviour of people; the need for precise statements of hypotheses; the development of powerful and general conceptual tools; an emphasis upon empirical, as sharply distinct from normative, theory; the use of sophisticated methods of inquiry, and the rigorous ordering of evidence (see, for example, Seidelman and Harpham, 1985, pp. 151–2). Though later criticized by so-called 'post-behaviouralists' as being insufficiently sensitive to the urgent problems facing society (Easton, 1969), the commitment to such methods and approaches has since remained largely intact.

It is in these terms, therefore, that the elitist paradigm now tends to be judged – and found to be somewhat deficient. Indeed, the concepts and hypotheses of the elitist perspective on the one hand, and its methods and techniques on the other, have been quite heavily criticized. This has, of course, affected the whole climate in which the study of elites has been carried out. As this is also the climate in which the present volume has been produced it is important that we turn briefly to examine some of the main theoretical and methodological issues which seem to be at stake by way of 'scene setting' for the contributions which follow.

1.2 The Theoretical Context

By modern 'social scientific' standards, the theoretical and definitional content of elite studies presents a somewhat mixed record. Zuckerman caught the appropriate mood when he observed:

A paradox is attached to the concept 'political elite'. Few theoretical constructs can boast its obvious and powerful intuitive appeal. It is by now a commonplace to view societies as characterized by an asymmetric distribution of political power. Still, the concept's apparent ability to 'carve at a joint of nature' has run into peculiar difficulties. Attempts to locate its empirical referents and, thereby, to specify the occupants of the 'data container' political elite have led to a morass of conflicting definitions. Recent attempts to use the concept in powerful explanatory theories have been infrequent and unsuccessful. (Zuckerman, 1977, p. 324)

As he suggests, the idea of an elite, be it political or otherwise, is one that increasingly is seen as a useful conceptual tool in examining modern societies. For, as Stone remarked, 'contemporary society is complex society', a society characterized by bureaucratization, specialization and differentiation (Stone, 1984, p. 1). It is in this context above all that elites have traditionally been located. Indeed, elitists see them as an inevitable part of the way such societies are structured and of how they function. To understand the role of those who inhabit positions of institutionalized authority is to understand much of how society as a whole now operates. Yet, when it comes to making the term precise, and formulating some agreed procedures whereby it might be given concrete value, the 'inherent vagueness of the concept becomes a major difficulty' (Marcus, 1983, p. 7).

Within the political sphere, for example, definitions can vary to the extent of the criteria being so restrictive as to make the finding of an elite virtually impossible or, alternatively, so all-embracing as to make the category lose all sharpness and analytic value. Thus, in the former case, there are those who require elites to be 'unitary' (Burton and Higley, 1984, p. 3), that is, to exhibit group consciousness, coherence and conspiracy: a small number of individuals exercising power right across society (Meisel, 1958). In contrast, there are those who prefer 'minimal definitions' in which a 'wide variety of "established" and "dissident" groups' might be included (Burton and Higley, 1984, p. 5; see also Burton, 1984, p. 50-1). Suleiman is, perhaps, typical of this position. He says that 'All those who occupy positions of authority are part of the elite', (Suleiman, 1978, p. 4). This obviously could comprise a vast array of individuals from all walks of life, public and even private, depending upon how all-embracing authority is taken to be. Indeed, it is possible to argue that virtually all individuals in society exercise some authority at particular times and in particular situations. In this case, of course, the idea that such a group would be culturally, or socially distinctive, or that it would have some discernible and plausible effect upon political outcomes, is highly improbable. It is a definition, in other words, that is far too broad to have any analytic utility.

The definitional issue is further complicated when 'political elite' is linked, as is often the case, to some notion of political power (for example, Domhoff, 1967; 1979, ch. 1; Higley, Deacon and Smart, 1979, ch. 1). Power is notoriously illusive as a theoretical, let alone operationally definable, concept; it is a term of more than one 'face' or 'dimension' (Bachrach and Baratz, 1962; Mackenzie, 1967, ch. 14; Lukes, 1974). The consequences for the study of political elites are spelled out by Parry (1969, ch. 5). He points to the numerous difficulties and ambiguities involved: the failure by the 'power elite theorists' to include consideration of the scope of influence across particular policy areas; the role of perceptions – ideologies and images – in shaping power relationships; the complex problems of identifying 'big decisions' and 'decision-makers'; the highly consequential matter for a study's conclusions of the 'boundaries' of systems or subsystems within which power is held to operate; the 'costs' to elites of overcoming resistance to their rule. The result is an array of varied interpretations of what elitist theory should be taken to mean. The strongest is the image of an omnipotent elite in all issue areas and in all phases of decision; at its weakest and 'most banal it can mean merely the truism that in organized life fewer men issue commands than obey them' (Parry, 1969, p. 138).

The debates can be extended further in that 'elite' is not necessarily taken by all as synonymous solely with 'political elite'. Indeed, one of the classic authors, Pareto, held such a vision: the idea of an elite as 'a class of the people who have the highest indices [of capacity or performance] . . . in [every] branch of human activity' (Pareto, 1935, pp. 1422–3). This raises the possibility of 'elites' being those at the top of any socially significant hierarchy be it politics, sports, academia, religion or even beauty or crime. Certainly there are many instances of this idea of the elite as 'the best' from any walk of life being used (see Crewe, 1974, p. 34; Marcus, 1983, p. 8). For example, Domhoff examines 'the jet set' – 'rich playboys and movie stars' – as an elite, (Domhoff, 1971, ch. 3; see also Keller, 1983). Equally, Kelsall *et al.* (1972, p. 19) advance the idea of 'an elite . . . [as] essentially a social group of "chosen people" ' and, on these grounds, justify their study of all graduates from British universities (in 1960) as the study of an elite –'a select minority'. However, the more conventional idea of elite as in some definite if indirect way being part of a given society's power-holding circles is not entirely dispensed with. Domhoff's aim is to disprove Wright Mills' thesis that the 'jet set' is something apart from the 'power elite' (at least in the United States) (Wright Mills, 1956; Domhoff, 1971). Similarly, Kelsall *et al.* go on to argue that their pool of young graduates not only have high incomes and high status, but that their influence 'as a group . . . must be out of all proportion to their actual numbers in the population' (Kelsall, *et al.* 1972, p. 21). They are, the authors conclude, 'relatively elite'!

In part, the significance of the issue in research turns upon the theory being examined and the role played by 'elite' individuals in the particular study. We have in this volume reports of at least two projects involving elites (Chapters 4 and 5) where the research foci were not so much the leaders *per se* as the organizations within which they operated. In the first case, therefore, the theoretical context was one of the behaviour of political parties in varying strategic circumstances. The views of the top party people were obviously very important but whether they were 'powerful' or not, at least in a societal sense, could be left largely on one side. Equally, in the second case, whether or not bishops are part of some putative British political elite is an interesting question, but not one that necessarily required an answer within that study.

Having said that, it is certainly the case that the significance of elites *qua* elites largely centres around, or is based upon, the question of power and influence. As Crewe observed, 'No satisfactory theory of elites is possible without a prior theory of power' (Crewe, 1974, p. 34). In other words, the significance of studying elites as elites hinges primarily upon their links to the means whereby society as a whole moves in one direction rather than another. In this respect, Nadel's (1956) typology of elites has some utility. He distinguishes between 'social elites', 'specialized elites' and 'governing elites'. In the former cases, their influence arises not so much through overt political means as through far more subtle and indirect channels – their setting of standards for life-style, for example, which can affect the aspirations, values and behaviour patterns of the mass population.

The reality of such influence depends, of course, upon the extent to which the three Weberian pyramids of power, wealth and status interlock. In some societies, especially modern ones, as Parry (1969, p. 71) points out, there may be at best an imperfect correspondence. Wealth may not confer political power, nor social prestige (Kavanagh, 1971). Indeed, the powerful, in political terms, may consciously seek to undermine or reject the potential power of those with wealth or traditional status. The Russian Revolution was an extreme example but, even in Western societies, policies have been pursued from time to time whose effect at least was to limit the convertibility of status or reward into political clout. Even so, in both the United States and Western Europe there remains considerable evidence of the extent to which the three still go together (Putnam, 1976, ch. 2; Moran, 1985, ch. 6).

Ambiguities surrounding the term 'elite' also exist not only in 'horizontal' terms (i.e. the relative remoteness of given sets of 'top people' from the centre of power) but also in a 'vertical' way. Here we refer to the 'depth' of the elite stratum: at what point, definitionally speaking, does the top give way to the middle, or the bottom? Alternative images of such differentiations abound. The classical theorists, for example, tended towards a very simple model of 'rulers' and 'ruled', sometimes with a middle stratum interposed between the two. Since then, ideas have become more complex in order to try to capture more precisely the nuances involved. Thus, Putnam (1976, pp. 8–12) argues for a six-fold division of power. However, he also admits that deciding upon a cut-off point between the 'elite' and the rest is, in the end, a matter of *ad hoc* judgement.

In the light of all this, one may, perhaps, be forgiven for thinking that the term 'elite' ought to be jettisoned as too vague and problematic for use in modern social science analysis. However, while not ignoring the difficulties, they should not be over-stated. Indeed, this volume is itself a testament to the belief that the idea of an 'elite' is a very useful one; an idea that should be retained but clarified both theoretically and methodologically. Those who point to current confusions and ambiguities, therefore, are right to do so. But, in fairness, one must also point to the possibility, for some at least, of an emergent consensus concerning the definition of elites and, consequently, what the 'data-container' ought to comprise (Burton, 1984, pp. 51–2; Burton and Higley, 1984, p. 5). To that extent, progress has been made toward specifying a precise and agreed definition in recent years, but there is obviously still some way to go.

Perhaps the same might be said about the development of theory through which the concept might be seen fruitfully to be deployed. Writing as recently as 1984, Burton and Higley reviewed the progress, or lack thereof, in elite theory and saw only mixed results. They broke their review down into three major elements, reflecting the major 'contentions' of the neo-elitist perspective: questions relating to the inevitability of elites; the variability of elites; and, finally, elite and non-elite interdependence.

So far as the first is concerned they conclude that 'the sense in which elites always exist and the reasons for their universality remain murky issues' (Burton and Higley, 1984, p. 1). In part, this arises through the lack of a clear and agreed view of what elites are, without which, of course, it would be impossible to say whether or not they are inevitable. But, to the extent that elites are now widely thought of as 'arising from the structure and functioning of essentially bureaucratic organizations and institutions' there is now a basis whereby such a hypothesis can be tested out empirically (Burton and Higley, 1984, p. 5). 'It carves out a class of societies to which the theory applies' . . . sparing it from 'some unprofitable confrontations with other bodies of theory and at the same time giving it a less hazy rationale' (ibid., p. 8). Thus, on this front, they see the possibility of advance, but so far largely unrealized.

Similarly, in the crucial question of relating elites to social and political outcomes, they find 'only limited progress since Mosca and Pareto' (ibid., p. 10). Elite typologies or variables whereby differences in their structures or functions might be deployed in empirical theories have been few in number, only partially applied and open to criticisms of circular reasoning. Yet here too, they see an 'emergent classification' through which a cumulative stock of empirically-grounded theory might be developed. The typology relates essentially to the nature of 'intra-elite relations' (whether they are 'integrated' or 'fragmented') and the extent of a normative consensus amongst the individuals concerned (ibid., p. 11). Such a typology does, however, implicitly take a view as to whether ideological coherence or integration is separable from, or an essential part of, the definition of an elite. This is an issue we alluded to earlier and it is clear that, for Burton and Higley, integration should be treated as a variable rather than as a precondition. Whether they are right or not is, at one level, irresolvable as it is more a question of assumption or definition than of logic or explanatory power. On the other hand, in such situations, one definition often turns out to be more useful than another in helping to stimulate new theory and so better to understand reality.

In this respect, we might note the work of Giddens (1974) who clearly sees elite integration, both 'social' and 'moral', as something that varies and which can in turn help establish further theoretical distinctions. Set against differences in recruitment, for example, he develops four ideal types of elites: 'solidary', 'uniform', 'abstract' and 'established' (Giddens, 1974, fig. 1, p. 6). Though the terminology does not seem to have caught on, it does indicate one way in which substantive ideas can be developed. Indeed, this and the Burton–Higley contribution are only a starting point. Further refinements and theoretically significant properties need to be added (see Crewe, 1974). But, in doing so, one must continually pay heed to the central idea of 'elite'. The more the very stringent definitional criteria of Meisel (1958) are removed, the blunter the notion becomes as a tool of political, social and economic analysis. Thus, it may be that the trend away from his 'three Cs' entails a genuine cost if pushed too far. At present, however, it seems prudent to allow this to proceed if only to rescue the term for use in the real world where Meisel's elites are never in practice to be found. But, in the longer term, we must be prepared for a halt to be called and even for some retrenchment towards Meisel's position to take place.

Finally, we turn to the whole question of elite and non-elite relations. Again, progress is obviously dogged by the prior need adequately to demarcate the relevant strata. But beyond that, Mosca's and Pareto's original insight that elite and non-elite exist in a 'dynamic, interdependent relationship . . . has been the least understood and examined' by subsequent researchers (Burton and Higley, 1984, pp. 15–16). They have accepted this contention without, in Burton and Higley's view, trying to develop it into a more general and empirically robust theory. One example which seems aptly to illustrate this conclusion is a study of mass and elite interaction in the field of political participation (Verba and Nie, 1972). Some attempt was made to establish levels of agreement, or 'congruence', over issue priorities between local community leaders and citizenry and to show how this varied across different types of locality. As an exploratory exercise it threw up some interesting patterns. However, particularly from the elite side, it was methodologically very weak, a major drawback being that each local elite in their study comprised only seven individuals, and certainly would not permit any sub-elite analyses or measures of intra-elite consensus. Since then very little has been done to develop their ideas (but see Hansen, 1975; Hill et al., 1979) until a recent British study (Parry, Moyser and Day, forthcoming). In this project, on average over fifty elite individuals were included for each locality, a figure which allows more subtle analysis of elites and their linkages with non-elites (see also Parry and Moyser, 1983; 1984).

Besides lacking, as yet, a clearly developed body of testable propositions, the elite paradigm also exhibits shortcomings, by modern social-scientific standards, in not clearly demarcating the normative from the empirical. In this, of course, it is not exceptional:

Marxism and pluralism have also clearly mixed descriptive and prescriptive propositions. Perhaps with all political theory, based as it is on 'contestable concepts' (Gallie, 1955–56), this is inevitable. For example, Lukes argues that political power, on which all paradigms take a view, 'is one of those concepts which is ineradicably value-dependent' (Lukes, 1974, p. 26). 'Both its very definition and any given use of it, once defined, are inextricably tied to a given set of (probably unacknowledged) value-assumptions which predetermine the range of its empirical application.' But, in the case of the elitist paradigm, this merging of normative and empirical has been perhaps particularly salient and, in consequence, has given it a controversial character.

In the view of elitism's protagonists (a view seen as something of a 'straw man' by other theorists), the idea of 'fixed inequalities' being characteristic of modern as well as traditional societies became, in nineteenth-century Europe and America, 'an ideological unmentionable' (Marcus, 1983, p. 8). Hence, liberal and democratic thought could not easily reconcile itself with the existence of 'enduring groups of powerful and privileged individuals'. For their part, advocates of elitism see no incompatibility at all with liberal-democratic values (Burton, 1984, p. 49). Such a 'misunderstanding' or misrepresentation, if this is all it is, stems, they say, from two circumstances. First, they freely admit an incompatibility between elite theory and radical egalitarianism; society cannot be 'inevitably' unequal and yet accommodate a belief in the absolute equality of its members. Thus, radical ideas about democracy, to the extent that they are founded on such principles, are antithetical to the elitist position. Secondly, two of its classical advocates, Michels and Pareto, were in different ways supporters of Italian fascism. Here, too, controversy has raged as to whether or not there is a necessary and prescriptive connection. Burton is anxious to deny any such linkage: 'elite theory . . . is not linked to any particular ideology' and certainly not fascism (Burton, 1984, p. 49). However, Beetham (1977) argues to the contrary. It is not perhaps the position erected and 'disproved' by Bennett (1978) that 'elite theory is itself a brand of fascism', but rather, as Beetham later observed in replying to Bennett, 'that the character of elitist argument was such as to incline its proponents to support fascism in the particular historical context, and that its categories provided a convenient source of fascist legitimation' (Beetham, 1978, p. 489).

This chapter is not the place to try to resolve the issues at stake here. However, it is relevant to say that the empirical study and development of elite theory has gone forward within a visible and controversial prescriptive context. Indeed, Marcus claims that 'the inherent normative dimensions of elite research have often overtaken its modest, narrowly empirical goals' (Marcus, 1983, p. 9). Whether that is entirely fair is a moot point, but certainly the aura of elite studies is one that does not entirely evoke the approbation of those nurtured in a modern behavioural and social scientific ethos, supposedly so dispassionate, objective and 'purely descriptive'.

1.3   The Methodological Context

Modern evaluative criteria in the social sciences place as much emphasis upon the quality of the methods as on the theory. Certainly, the legacy of the behavioural revolution, so far as the study of mass populations is concerned, is one of great technical sophistication. Following the development of survey methods in the 1930s and of associated theories of sampling, selection of representative portions of large numbers of individuals, even of whole nations, has become relatively routine (Miller, 1983). Not that all problems have been solved, or that compromises with sound principles are not sometimes made in the interests of economy (see, for example, Goyder and Leiper, 1985). But by and large, relatively precise and sophisticated techniques for mass case selection are now available. The same can be said of analysis techniques. The widespread provision of computers since the 1950s has encouraged the development of a very considerable armoury of mainly quantitative analysis techniques. As a result, the image of contemporary social research on non-elites is one in which the methods deployed are generally and increasingly high-powered, thus allowing equivalently sophisticated substantive questions to be formulated and answered.

By these standards, the picture at the elite level is rather less rosy. Thus, so far as case selection is concerned, instead of precision and sophistication, there is argument and *ad hoc* procedure. The arguments have in part arisen through the linkage, already noted, between eliteness and power. Hence, the selection of individuals has depended upon choosing appropriate indicators of social, economic and political influence. Rival methods have been advanced in what Crewe calls an 'acrimonious and celebrated dispute since the 1950s' (Crewe, 1974, p. 34). Even more disturbingly perhaps, the alternatives (the 'reputational', 'positional' and 'decisional' approaches) have yielded rather contradictory substantive conclusions, demonstrating very vividly the interdependent nature of theory and method.

However, to the extent that there is some indication of a consensus developing around a definition of elite, so there is a seeming acceptance that a combination of these traditional methods may be necessary. An illustration of what is entailed is provided in the contribution by Hoffmann-Lange to this volume. But it is clear, both in this and in other similar research studies, that the procedures still involve a considerable amount of *ad hoc* choice in order to cope with the complexities of the real world. To that extent, a lot more work remains to be done in the development of indicators whereby the term elite can be effectively operationalized.

A brief example of the practical difficulties involved can be drawn from a recent attempt to identify a political elite for Louisiana (Kurtz, 1984), based, incidentally, entirely on a positional procedure. In many instances, the identification of the relevant individuals was simply ascribed to the 'judgement' of the researchers (Kurtz, 1984, table 1). This affected the inclusion of senior figures in eight 'metro daily papers'; fourteen 'civic and culture institutions'; members of five 'independent agencies and commissions' and 'major appointed officials' from the state executive. Even where a precise rule was used, such as the need for leaders drawn from manufacturing companies to each have a workforce of at least 750, it clearly is substantially arbitrary.

Furthermore, there was a major problem of system boundaries. The exercise of economic power in that state (as in the local economies of most other developed countries) was shared between 'domestic' and 'out-of-state' corporations. The dilemma that this porous boundary posed for case selection was very clear to Kurtz:

> In this sector, the leaders of many major institutions reside outside the state. Including them in the study would have resulted in a group of leaders who could not reasonably be considered a part of the Louisiana elite. Excluding them also would have created problems in that a large number of major institutions would not have been subject to analysis. A not entirely satisfactory but unavoidable compromise on this point was to include the out-of-state corporations and their resident managers. There can be little doubt as to the power and status differences separating resident managers from board members, but there seemed to be no other way to resolve the issue outlined here. (Kurtz, 1984, p. 52)

It should, of course, be emphasized that the Kurtz project is not exceptional. Every study that attempts systematically to identify an elite faces similar issues and problems. Equally, decisions about the procedures to be used then have a bearing on the results that subsequently emerge.

In such a situation, the goal of establishing a robust method for elite identification may seem distant. Not least, it is a question of the ground shifting under the researchers' feet: the criteria, to remain valid, vary both across time and across boundaries, especially national ones. So far as the former element is concerned, this is to note the important fact that the distribution of power across society has changed historically, and continues to change, possibly with increasing speed. It is possible to discern long term trends like the penetration by centralizing nation-builders of 'the periphery', industrialization and secularization, as having very significant effects upon indicators of power and therefore eliteness. Theorists have also pointed to the growing significance in more recent times of techno-cratic power – the control of knowledge – and to other features of post-industrial society (Galbraith, 1969; Ionescu, 1975). Finally the emergence (or re-emergence) of international agencies and trans-national interdependencies further complicates attempts to operationalize valid sets of national elite actors.

Similarly, as Galaskiewicz mentions in his contribution to this volume, cross-national variations also cannot be ignored. Clearly, in some countries, the military are all-important and yet in others almost totally insignificant. Every relevant institution, and the leadership positions within it, will vary according to local economic, political and social circumstances. Though attempts have been made systematically to tackle such issues (see Hoffmann-Lange) little progress has been made so far.

It should perhaps be re-emphasized, however, that such difficulties tend principally to reflect the fickle and elusive character of political power in modern society. To the extent that this is not a main focus or issue, the methodological problems are concomitantly eased. Thus, for many studies, it is not at all necessary to vindicate in any precise terms the basis for selection of elite individuals. It may be, for example, that in a particular research situation the elite suggests itself relatively unambiguously. We have in mind studies of relatively simple societies or of a particular locality or institution where power holding is perhaps more clear cut. Or it may be that, for the purposes of the research, questions of power and eliteness are at best a side issue. In this respect, a distinction has been made between elites *qua* elites and elites as experts or 'gate-keepers' (Moyser and Wagstaffe, 1985). In the latter two instances, it is more the quality of advice and guidance, or the degree of access to other data, which is of primary concern, and not so much whether the individuals are 'elites' or not – though this might be relevant.

If we wish to study elites as elites – their role in decision making processes, their recruitment patterns, their belief systems, etc. – then we are confronted both with a relatively wide diversity of methods or sources through which information can potentially be generated, as well as techniques for the analysis of that information. Indeed, it is a primary purpose of this volume to explore these alternatives, highlighting their virtues and their vices. It is, therefore, sufficient here merely to comment briefly on what might be involved; detailed examination in the context of concrete research problems can be found in the chapters that follow.

Traditionally, written or printed materials – speeches, articles, diaries, letters, autobiographies, etc. – as well as personal and biographical data often routinely collated and published by third parties, have formed the traditional staple diet of elite studies. While undoubtedly useful in exposing simplistic sociological accounts of elites, it has become increasingly clear that, methodologically, they have their fallibilities as well as exerting a certain constraining effect upon the kind of substantive questions that can be investigated (see, for example, Edinger and Searing, 1967; Crewe, 1974; Plummer, 1983 and Medhurst and Moyser in this volume). One problem is that they tend not to provide systematic evidence about elite behaviour which might then be scrutinized using sophisticated analytic techniques. This is a particularly trenchant criticism within the ethos of the behavioural persuasion. The response has been a growth of research methods designed to remedy this perceived deficiency.

One set of such methods relies upon the existence, at least for certain types of elites, of officially recorded behaviour patterns, normally concerning their formal decisional behaviour. Thus, for example, legislators, through having their votes on bills and motions, etc., put 'on the record', have provided the basis for a minor industry of elite research. In the main, such work has been based on the United States Congress and a systematic evaluation of what is involved is included in this volume (see Sinclair and Brady). However, it has been applied in other national contexts with varying degrees of success (see, for example, Moyser, 1979; Berrington, 1973; Wolters, 1980; Hagger and Wolters, 1981). Of a similar nature are the equivalent collections and analyses of 'judicial behaviour' – the decisions of judges on cases put before them. Again, this has been largely confined to the United States Supreme Court (see Schubert,

1964) but on a lesser scale reflecting, perhaps, the far fewer numbers of individuals and behaviours involved as well as the intrinsically more specialized arena.

Another relatively recent response to facilitate more direct study of behaviour has been the growth of 'elite interviewing'. One of its great merits is that it lacks the inflexibility and narrowness of decisional data methods mentioned above. Thus, 'behavioural' evidence can, potentially, be created not only to cover such behaviour, but also to reveal information about underlying attitudes, interactions and intentions. This, of course, speaks much more directly to the elitist agenda.

However, interviews are certainly not a complete answer in all situations of elite research. To that extent, we do not share Crewe's view when he claimed it to be 'surely superior to any alternative way of discovering what they (i.e. elites) believe and do' (Crewe, 1974, p. 43). It is made abundantly clear in the contributions to this volume that interviews pose considerable practical, methodological and analytic difficulties. They must only be used appropriately and judiciously; if necessary in combination with other methods of inquiry. Not least is this the case with 'defensive elites', as we call them, where such interviews, of whatever variety, are either not a possibility at all or, if they are, provide at best questionable evidence. Binns' discussion of attempts at elite interviewing in Eastern Europe and the Soviet Union (Chapter 12) is a sharp reminder of how much students of 'Western' or liberal democratic elites take for granted.

Elite interviewing is not, of course, one method or technique but a whole family comprising varied alternatives. One principal axis along which such alternatives differ is the degree of structure or directiveness employed by the interviewer (and/or researcher). This helps to identify three major variants: the fully structured, the semi-structured and the unstructured interview, the first two having been more extensively utilized in the study of elites than the last. The choice between them is ultimately a decision about which data-generation strategy best fits the particular research design and theoretical problems being addressed. For example, are these problems couched in phenomenological or positivistic terms? Are they a matter of certain 'variables' based on, say, elite behaviour or outlooks, putatively 'causing' certain measurable outcomes? Or are they more a matter of how different elite individuals subjectively see those outcomes and how they, as individuals, evaluate the circumstances in which they emerged? The first orientation tends to put a premium upon standardized and precise measurement and complex statistical analysis (e.g. causal modelling), possibly best served by the structured interview. The second orientation has a different priority, and a different stance towards understanding, more in tune with an interview format in which the respondent can set the agenda and terms of discussion (see Dexter, 1970).

Beyond that, there is a whole range of more practical constraints which also must be taken into account. For example, should the researcher depend on intermediaries to undertake the interviews? Is the agenda relatively straightforward and uncontroversial? Are the elite respondents tolerant of social scientific procedures, and sufficiently well-disposed to the researchers? All these, and more, bear on the matter making the choice very much one rooted in particular circumstances and situations (see Moyser and Wagstaffe, 1985, pp. 17–22).

Mention of the phenomenological perspective raises yet a third method which has been largely associated with it and, at the same time, also responds to the modern imperative of being close to actual elite behaviour. We refer to participant observation. This has been widely used to study individuals at the mass level (see Bogdan and Taylor, 1975) but, like the structured interview in the positivist genre, has been adapted to elite research. Indeed, the prospects and pitfalls entailed in this are the subject of Winkler's contribution (Chapter 7; see also Fenno, 1986). Now, participant observation can indeed include unstructured interviewing and the use of documents. To that extent, it is not an entirely novel approach compared with those previously discussed. But it does have some particular ingredients – observation *in situ*, extended contacts with 'subjects', etc. – that give it a distinctive style.

However, what is needed above all at the present stage of development is a more imaginative application of *all* these approaches in a variety of research contexts. Indeed, imagination might be applied to a consideration of yet other possibly more exotic procedures not discussed here, such as simulation, and experimental and projective techniques (Young and Mills, n.d.) to see if they too could be brought fruitfully to bear on the study of elites.

The same might also be said of forms of analysis, for here too there are under-exploited alternatives on offer. On the one hand, there are the well-established 'traditional' analytic and qualitative skills of historian, biographer and even journalist, sifting and assessing documents, papers and transcripts of informal interviews. What is involved, or can be involved, is well illustrated in Pridham's and Raab's contributions (Chapters 4 and 6). However, a wider range of typically more quantitative techniques are now becoming available which, although not yet widely deployed, might serve to complement and build upon those earlier techniques. Here, we will briefly mention two of particular relevance to elite studies. First, there is content analysis, a method, or rather set of methods, capable of throwing light on the ways elites use or manipulate symbols, and invest communicated messages with meaning. In fact, it has a relatively long history but only recently has it begun to make its presence strongly felt in the social sciences. There are now textbooks and computer software available to encourage its application (Krippendorff, 1980) but, so far as we are aware, little has yet been seen of it in the elite field.

The second technique, network analysis, certainly has begun to make its mark in this particular area. Indeed, Hoffmann-Lange's contribution shows how fruitful it can be in revealing characteristics of elite structures which other more intuitive or 'eyeball' methods might have left hidden. In this way, it is demonstrably of relevance to important substantive questions of elite theory. Some applications to elite studies have in practice been relatively simplistic (for example, Kurtz, 1984), but others have begun more seriously to exploit its potential (Bolland, 1984). Again, there is now a textbook available (Knoke and Kuklinski, 1982) although, in our experience, software availability is still relatively poor. What is needed, as with data generation, is its sustained and imaginative application which would undoubtedly throw up a more subtle and sophisticated array of empirical findings. This in turn would stimulate fresh questions and, not least, further development of the technique itself. Certainly, this has been the pattern with more 'conventional' analysis techniques associated with mass survey research.

Even a brief review of the methodological context surrounding the study of elites should not end without at least a mention of what comes after the analyses have been accomplished, the hypotheses tested, the results written up. For, perhaps uniquely with elite materials, ethical issues can emerge with considerable force. Information and knowledge, as we have noted, is a resource for power and influence in modern society. How it is presented, disseminated and stored is of interest to people involved in power, perhaps above all when it is information and knowledge about themselves! This delicate and potentially explosive situation imposes important obligations on the researcher and presents him, at times, with some difficult issues and dilemmas.

An indication of what is involved might, perhaps, best be given by briefly looking at the needs and responsibilities of those who are party to elite research, principally, the researcher, the elites themselves, other researchers (the 'social scientific community') and the wider audience of readers, media and the mass public. The latter group are likely to have a particular interest in the deeds, or misdeeds, of the 'high and mighty', an interest reflected in the extent to which the media may wish to disseminate the findings in their own way, and with their own gloss. How control of this is maintained by researchers once those findings have entered the public domain is sometimes a difficult matter. One spectacular example of how things can go awry is provided by Van Schendelen (1984) whose findings about the views of Dutch parliamentarians emerged in a newspaper report at a highly sensitive moment just before an election.

In this instance, the 'field' was changed, and future access by other social scientists compromised – at least momentarily. However, this is but part of the difficulty elite researchers have in handling their data. Often, particularly when obtaining interviews, guarantees of anonymity have to be given. This is a relatively, but not entirely, straightforward matter in the researcher's own publication pro-gramme, but a profound difficulty may arise in respect of the archiving and dissemination of the data themselves. For, unlike mass data, elite information tends to make the identification of individual names an easy matter. To make it impossible is often tantamount to destroying the value of that information. How, therefore, does the researcher reconcile the guarantees he may have given to respondents with the legitimate interests of fellow researchers who may wish to check his or her findings or to conduct their own secondary analyses? Not least, there may be those who hold different views about the appropriateness of such assurances, or about the role of social scientific evidence in wider debates. (The debate about the workings of the 'thirty year rule' relating to British Government files is a case in point.) Some discussion of the matter is given by Raab in this volume (see also Seldon and Pappworth, 1983, pt IV).

1.4 Conclusions and Overview

As this chapter has suggested, the study of elites is at a very interesting yet critical stage in its development both as a revived substantive perspective and as a setting for the pursuit of more methodological questions. However, if the potential is to be fully realized, then the substantive developments must be matched by, and harmonized with, methodological progress. This entails a profound awareness of what is involved – the whole gamut of particular pitfalls and dilemmas that elite studies represent. It also entails a recognition that studying elites is not the same as studying mass populations. There are, of course, some common issues and shared methods but there are equally many other respects in which elites are very different. Not least is this the case, for example, in the numbers of individuals typically being studied. On the one hand, systematic studies of mass populations tend to rely upon a thousand cases or more in order reliably to assess a particular research topic. Yet, almost by definition, elites studies involve relatively few people. There are instances, such as entire national elites, where potentially large numbers might be included, but, in the main, those included tend to be very restricted. All of this can affect the whole style of research, from data gathering to the precision and 'predictability' of results.

This, however, begins to raise issues for which detailed exemplification is best left to the contributions that follow. It is to those contributions that we now briefly and finally turn.

The remainder of the volume is organized in three sections, each relating to the methodological issues which arise when researching certain general categories of elites. Part 1 is concerned with political and social elites: Ursula Hoffmann-Lange describes, in considerable detail, the way in which a sample can be constructed for a large national elite survey and the problems such a venture may raise; Barbara Sinclair and David Brady offer a broadly based discussion of the relatively well-developed approaches and research tools which are available to the student of the United States Congress, approaches and tools which may have much wider applicability; Geoffrey Pridham reviews the very varied experiences he gained whilst working with party political elites in Italy; Kenneth Medhurst and George Moyser reflect upon their research into a major national religious elite, and Charles Raab discusses the virtues of oral history as a research tool. These contributions are all concerned with the kinds of elite personnel, i.e. party leaders, civil servants, bishops, legislators and other holders of high office, who are most often the targets of elite research. Less often examined, but in many ways of equal significance, are the elites which are the subject of the second section of the book: economic elites.

Thus, in Part 2, Jack Winkler discusses the need for, but also the difficulty of, participant observation in elite research. Many studies are based on what elites are thought to do, or what they say they do. However, it is essential, Winkler claims, for some effort to be directed to watching what they actually do, which may not be the same thing at all. A different rationale led Peter Brannen to choose a similar methodology in his work with an economic elite, and he makes some very pertinent observations on the problems encountered by researchers who choose to participate in the life-style of the elites they are studying. This, however, was not a problem which affected Galaskiewicz: he approached his subjects from the more detached position of the interviewer (rather than the participant-observer) and he explains minutely how he established his elite network. Galaskiewicz, Brannen and Winkler all encountered problems of access in some degree, as did most of the contributors to this volume. However, these difficulties were most marked for the authors of the remaining chapters of the book, and indeed it is this critical difficulty which provides a unifying theme of the final section: that of the 'defensive elite'.

Wagstaffe and Moyser, in their study of community elites, were confronted by some local leaders whose concern was more to protect their neighbourhood against what they perceived as unwarranted intrusions on its privacy than to help further yet another academic investigation. Also defensive, for complex historical and political reasons, were the elite persons with whom Paul Arthur worked in connection with his study of the problems of Northern Ireland. He too has words of warning concerning the pitfalls which await the unwary investigator who tries to work in a tense and emotive field. Another highly charged arena is that researched by Christopher Binns. His reminiscences concerning his efforts to interview elite personnel in the USSR are an object lesson in sheer persistence in the face of bureaucratic obstructionism. Equally, he provides an important perspective on how such individuals, and Marxists more generally, view the whole idea of an 'elite' in state socialist societies. Finally, there is the interesting experience of Moshe Czudnowski who studied the political elite in the one party state of Taiwan. Czudnowski has some salutory observations to offer to anyone proposing to survey an elite of a different (non-Western) cultural tradition.

Collectively, we hope all the essays included here will serve as a stimulus to methodological imagination, and as a basis for a more open discussion of the relevant issues. This might then act as an impetus to the development of new substantive questions and better research procedures and techniques.

Certainly, as we have repeatedly mentioned, the record so far has been rather patchy. There have been some developments but not enough to suggest that Crewe's gloomy conclusion of a decade ago

(Crewe, 1974, p. 10) that 'methodological innovations [have been] few and developments in elite theory almost nil' can now be considered out of date. The challenge, in other words, is still there. Thus, Marcus only recently suggested that 'what an elite is as a subculture in a mass liberal society such as America, what its practices, orienting ideas and intentions are, and in what sense it can be held responsible for events remain largely mysterious to both social scientists and [the] lay public' (Marcus, 1983, p. 4). Through a more careful concern for method, and a more imaginative application of analytic techniques, elites can be de-mystified and their study given widespread acceptance as a serious contribution to modern social scientific knowledge.

I

*Political and Social
Elites*

2

Surveying national elites in the Federal Republic of Germany

URSULA HOFFMANN-LANGE

Universities of Mannheim and Texas at Austin

2.1 Introduction: The West German Elite Study, 1981

Studies of national elites are concerned with the most powerful persons in a society, i.e. persons with considerable influence on collective decisions of central importance. This preliminary definition of national elites will be elaborated in a subsequent paragraph: before doing this, however, an overview of the theoretical approaches of elite research, as well as a short description of the research strategy used in the West German elite study of 1981, will be given.

In addition to providing essential descriptive information on the elites of a certain society, empirical studies of national elites can also be used to test theoretical assumptions about the relations between elites and society. Theories of elite recruitment and elite circulation constitute the oldest tradition in elite theory. They assume a relationship between the character of a society, the prevailing mode of elite recruitment and of the social characteristics of elites (Bottomore, 1966). Changes in the criteria of elite recruitment and, hence, in the social characteristics of elites, are taken as indicators of social change, and vice versa. In this vein, it is often assumed that the transition from traditional to modern industrial society has affected elite recruitment by substituting achievement criteria for the formerly prevailing ascriptive criteria.

Theories of conflict and consensus among elites assume, instead, a certain degree of independence of elites from societal restraints. They claim that elites can reach a consensus on procedural norms, the rules of the game, which allow peaceful conflict regulation even in societies with deep socio-cultural cleavages (Lijphart, 1977; Field and Higley, 1980).

The nature of the linkages between elites and non-elites (Putnam, 1976, ch. 6; Welsh, 1979, ch. 7; Stokes and Miller, 1962; Miller and Stokes, 1963; Barnes, 1977) in a society is a third major thread of theoretical thinking about elites. It is concerned with the responsiveness of elites to the demands of the general population, i.e. the representation of interests in elite decision-making. This can be studied by comparing values and issue attitudes of elites to those of the population at large. The degree of congruence among different elite and population subgroups is then used to test the adequacy of different models of interest representation, e.g. pluralist, ruling class, consociational, power elite, or corporatist models.

The survey approach in empirical elite research has to be distinguished from another use of elite interviewing in which elites serve as informants/experts about a specific field of investigation, e.g. Raab's study reported in Chapter 6. The two different uses of elite interviews imply differences in sampling and research design. While for expert interviews a qualitative approach seems most appropriate, quantitative methods are needed in order to gather reliable information on backgrounds, attitudes, and activities of elites. Critics have often maintained that it is impossible to use such a quantitative approach in elite research. They have argued that elites are reluctant to be interviewed by methods appropriate only for 'mass' surveys. The fact, however, that many quantitative surveys of national elites have been carried out successfully has proved them wrong.

The quantitative approach has a number of advantages as well as disadvantages. The use of a highly standardized questionnaire for a broad stratum of respondents working in rather different settings limits the depth of the information that can be collected about career patterns, role behaviour and decision-making activities. Similarly, the questions concerning perceptions of political problems and political ideologies have to be limited to a set of forced-choice questions.[1]

What is lost in detail, however, can be gained in broadness. The inclusion of different elite sectors each represented by a sufficient number of respondents, and the imposition of a common frame of reference by using forced-choice questions, allows study of the patterns of dissent and consensus among different elite and population subgroups, i.e. the structure of political cleavages in a country. Similarly, by asking respondents for their regular interaction partners, the overall structure of the elite network can be analysed, even when detailed information concerning the content, direction, and frequency of these interactions is lacking.

The West German elite study of 1981[2] was designed as a quantitative, cross-sectional national elite survey. Respondents were holders of elite positions in various sectors, i.e. political, civil service, business, trade union, mass media, academic, military, and cultural elites. The study is comparative in a threefold sense.

First, it allows the study of changes in the elites over time by comparing the results to those of two previous elite surveys in West Germany of 1968 and 1972 for which a similar design had been used (Hoffmann-Lange et al., 1980).

Secondly, an internationally comparative approach is ensured by the use of a number of questions on elite networks which had previously been asked in the United States and Australia (Barton, 1985; Higley et al., 1979).

Thirdly, some of the questions, mainly concerning value orientations and issue attitudes, have also been used in a general population survey in early 1982, thus allowing for comparisons between elites and the population at large.

2.2 The Sampling Procedure: Methods and Theoretical Approaches

Each sampling procedure presupposes a theoretical as well as an operational definition of the population about which assertions are to be made. On the other hand, most definitions of elites are rather imprecise and give only a little guidance as to the adequate sampling method to apply. Agreement among them is normally limited to a common focus on the macro level of societies, institutionalized power, and influence on collective decisions. But a definition of national elites as 'persons with power individually, regularly, and seriously to affect political outcomes at the macro level of organized societies' (Higley et al., 1979, p. 17), still leaves a wide range of choices to the discretion of the researcher in sampling an elite population. It allows for different forms of power wielding and different power resources: direct participation in decision-making within large-scale private and public organizations, influence on the definition of social problems and/or influence on public opinion. Each of them can be legitimately considered as qualifying a person as a member of the national elite.

In the reputational approach, experts are asked to indicate the most powerful persons in a social system. The usefulness of this approach is, however, limited to less complex social systems such as small or medium-sized communities where decision-making power is concentrated among a readily identifiable elite group. Decision-making on the national level of modern societies is instead much too complex to allow for the identification of all members of an elite by asking only a small number of experts. Reliable, though always subjective, knowledge about who the powerful are is usually limited to a few decision-making arenas and to elite members themselves since they are the ones with the most direct access to decision-making processes. The opinions of experts without such a direct access to the relevant processes are instead biased even more by subjective preconceptions about the power structure.

The decisional approach defines power as direct participation in political decisions. This approach has the advantage of using a behaviourally derived measure of power, but the necessarily small range of issues that can be studied empirically in order to identify decision-makers makes it difficult to generalize the findings to the entire power structure.

In determining national elite samples in complex, industrial societies, the positional approach has been the one most widely used. It is the easiest to apply in practice since it neither presupposes, judges nor requires lengthy decisional studies. Starting out from a list of elite sectors, the researcher then proceeds to select the most important organizations within each sector. In a third step, the top positions within each organization have to be determined. The current incumbents of these positions are then finally considered as members of the elite.

The three approaches of elite identification can be classified according to the degree to which they allow for two dimensions of power:

(1) formal vs informal power;
(2) direct participation in political decision-making vs indirect influence on political decisions.

The codified rules of political decision-making will be included in this classification, too. Figure 2.1 shows that these latter rules use the most restricted concept of power which the decisional as well as the positional approach each extend on one of the two dimensions but not on the other. Finally, the reputational approach measures power in the broadest sense, allowing for formal and informal power as well as for direct and indirect influence on political decisions.

Regardless of the approach used, each operational definition of elites has to solve an additional problem, namely to specify the boundaries of the elite universe, i.e. the size of the elite to be studied. Should it be limited to the very top stratum of powerful persons with broad influence over a relatively wide range of decision-making matters or should we go further down in the organizational hierarchy? In this latter case one would also include persons with a much more restricted range of decision-making power who, however, participate more intensively in individual decisions and thus may sometimes be even more important than those in the top stratum in shaping these decisions.

Figure 2.1 *Classification of the approaches of elite identification*

Power resources	Participation in political decision-making	
	Direct participation	Direct participation *and* indirect influence
Formal power	Codified rules of political decision-making	Positional approach
Formal *and* informal power	Decisional approach	Reputational approach

In the West German elite study, 1981, the positional approach was used to define the elite universe. The positional approach was, however, supplemented by the reputational approach: respondents were asked to name other persons who were important for decision-making in their own sphere of activity. The empirical relationships between these two approaches will be analysed in a later section.

Starting out from a rather broad definition of positional elites, altogether 3,580 positions in nine major elite sectors as well as a couple of minor sectors[3] were determined as belonging to the positional sample. The criteria used for the incorporation of positions into the sample depended on general assumptions about the national power structure and power within and among sectors. They were, therefore, inevitably somewhat arbitrary, and other scholars would have come up with a partly different sample.

Experience shows, however, that disagreement concerning the adequacy of such criteria is particularly pronounced with regard to the sector composition and the lower boundaries of the elite sample. The broad definition used in the West German elite ensures that at least no important positions have been omitted. Moreover, it allows the study of the effects of the inclusion of certain sectors and lower hierarchical levels on the survey results. Table 2.1 shows the sector composition of the sample of elite positions. Due to multiple position-holding and transitory vacancies, the number of position-holders ('target persons') was lower than that and amounted to a total of 3,164.

Table 2.1   Sector composition of the West German elite study, 1981

Sector[a]	Positions		Position-holders		Respondents	
	n	%	n	%	n	%
Politics	539	15.1	452	14.3	274	15.7
Civil Service	479	13.4	471	14.9	296	17.0
Business	837	23.4	688	21.7	285	16.3
Business Associations	394	11.0	295	9.3	174	10.0
Trade Unions	155	4.3	155	4.9	87	5.0
Mass Media	376	10.5	354	11.2	222	12.7
Academic	209	5.8	179	5.7	130	7.5
Military	172	4.8	172	5.4	43	2.5
Cultural	188	5.3	180	5.7	104	6.0
Other	231	6.4	218	6.9	129	7.4
Total	3580	100.0	3164	100.0	1744	100.1

Note: [a] See Appendix to this chapter for detailed list of organizations and positions

2.3 Field work: Organization, Access and Problems of Data Protection

Given the considerable size of the target population, the survey could only be carried out in co-operation with an opinion research institute. GETAS of Bremen, one of the major West German polling institutes with sufficient experience in social research, was entrusted with this task. It provided the technical infrastructure, i.e. its pool of qualified interviewers, printing services, the handling of interviewer payments, and the processing of the interviewer records.

The organization of the field work was divided between the research team and GETAS by a margin of one-third to two-thirds. The sample was, however, divided into two 'fields' or strata. Field I included the most senior position-holders for whom we expected greater difficulties of access, e.g. cabinet members, secretaries of state, presidents of business corporations, business associations and trade unions, editors-in-chief of the major newspapers, etc. Field II comprised the less senior position-holders in these areas.

The two fields were then organized separately in that we used two separate interviewer staffs: 85 interviewers in field II and 24 especially qualified interviewers in the top field. Members of the research team belonged to the latter staff. An intensive programme of interviewer training was also deemed necessary. This was supplemented by a written guide containing lengthy comments about the research goals and the intentions behind the individual questions.

At the beginning of March 1981, a personal and individually signed letter was sent to every position-holder in the sample, requesting an interview. The letters were posted in Mannheim in order to document that the study was university based and not a commercial survey. A reply postcard on which the respondents could indicate possible interview dates accompanied each letter. In April, a second letter (call back) was sent to those who had not responded to the first one.

The field organization did not differ substantially between the fields. All replies were registered by the field directors in charge. The dates offered were checked, and appointments were confirmed either by letter or by telephone. Refusals were mostly so definite that a second attempt seemed unwarranted. On the other hand, the frequent inquiries concerning the research goals and the sampling criteria were treated with special care in order to ensure the highest response rate possible.

Table 2.2   Response rates for successive waves of the field work

	Refusals		Completed interviews		Total	
	n	%	n	%	n	%
	%		%		%	
Reaction to	n 752	35.8	1350	64.2	2102	100.0
first letter	% 52.9		77.4		66.4	
First callback	n 178	60.5	116	39.5	294	100.0
	% 12.5		6.7		9.3	
Second callback	n 367	70.3	155	29.7	522	100.0
	% 25.8		8.9		16.5	
Position	n 123	50.0	123	50.0	246	100.0
reshuffle[a]	% 8.7		7.1		7.8	
Total	n 1420	44.9	1744	55.1	3164	100.0
	% 100.0		100.0		100.0	

Note: [a] Position reshuffles had to be treated separately because they invariably led to a peculiar contact pattern

By mid-May, the number of replies declined sharply. Since at that time about one-third of the selected position-holders had not yet reacted to either of the letters, a third wave to contact these persons was necessary. This was done by telephone. Table 2.2 contains the distribution of response rates for the three waves of the field work. It shows that the second and third waves were successful with regard to the absolute numbers of interviews they enabled us to conduct, even when the response rates were much lower than for the first wave.

All contacts with target persons and their personal staff were registered. The number of contacts required to obtain a result, either an interview appointment or a definite refusal, is a relevant indicator of the expenditures that are necessary to carry out a study like this. Only those contacts were counted, however, that occurred between the position-holders or their staff and the field directors until either a refusal or a first interview appointment was reached. Date and address were then handed over to the interviewer. The rather frequent postponements of appointments directly arranged among interviewer and respondents were not registered as separate contacts.

The minimum number of contacts necessary to establish a definite outcome was two for refusals and three for completed interviews. Table 2.3 shows that the number of contacts increased sharply for those persons who did not react to the letters of the first and second waves. Among this group (the 'second callback'), the expenditure for a refusal was nearly as high as that for a completed interview.

Table 2.3   Average number of contacts required to obtain a definite refusal or an interview

| | Average number of contacts | | |
	Total	Refusals	Completed interviews
Reaction to first letter	4.1	2.9	4.7
First callback	4.1	3.3	5.3
Second callback	4.9	4.7	5.5
Position reshuffle	4.1	3.1	5.2
Total	4.2	3.4	4.9

The field directors passed only those addresses to the interviewers for which they had obtained the consent of the respondent to be interviewed. The interviewers were asked to confirm appointment dates and also to check the correct interview address.

The interviewer reports on the interview situation (Table 2.4) reveal that most of the interviews were conducted under rather favourable circumstances. Only a few disturbances occurred during the interviews. The average interview length was 88 minutes and, hence, somewhat shorter than the length of 90 minutes we had announced in the letters. Differences between sectors can largely be attributed to the familiarity of the respondents with being interviewed and with the topics raised in the questionnaire which were mostly political questions.

Table 2.4 *Interviewer reports on interview situation*

	n	%
1.Evaluation of the interview situation		
Largely without interruptions	1404	80.5
Some interruptions which, however, had no influence on the interview situation	283	16.2
Frequent or prolonged interruptions with negative effects on the interview situation	40	2.3
Missing	17	1.0
2. Evaluation of co-operativeness of respondents		
Good	1459	83.7
Fairly good	157	9.0
Not good	36	2.1
At first good, then declining	23	1.3
At first bad, then improving	37	2.1
Missing	32	1.8
3. Number of interruptions		
None	975	55.9
One to three	663	38.0
More than three	84	4.8
Missing	22	1.3
4. Average length of interruptions		
No interruptions	975	55.9
1–5 minutes	456	26.1
6–10 minutes	150	8.6
11–20 minutes	93	5.3
More than 20 minutes	37	2.1
Missing	33	1.9

Politicians and journalists achieved the shortest averages whereas respondents in the business, voluntary associations, and academic sectors were less experienced and needed more time to answer the questions (see Table 2.5).

Due to legal regulations passed in recent years, the handling of data protection represented a specific problem. In general population surveys, anonymity of individual respondents in data files is usually accomplished by separate storage of the respondents' addresses and the survey data. Moreover, address files are normally erased immediately after the completion of the field work. The anonymity of the survey data is ensured by the rule that no variables are stored

Table 2.5   Response and average length of interviews

Sector	Respondents		Response rates	Average length of interviews
	n	% of sample total		
Politics	274	15.7	60.6	86.5
Civil Service	296	17.0	62.8	84.3
Business	285	16.3	41.4	90.4
Business associations	174	10.0	59.0	91.5
Trade unions	87	5.0	56.1	92.5
Mass media	222	12.7	62.7	83.5
Academic	130	7.5	72.6	90.9
Military	43	2.5	25.0	85.5
Cultural	104	6.0	57.8	84.5
Other	129	7.4	59.2	97.2
Total	1744	100.1	55.1	88.1

that allow for identification of individual respondents either alone or in combination with other variables, e.g. locus of residence, full address, employer, etc. In the case of elite respondents, however, such protection of the survey data is not possible because meaningful analyses of the survey data presuppose additional information about positional characteristics of the respondents.

The legal regulations of data protection permit the storage and analysis of personal data of this kind only under the condition that the respondents declare their explicit consent in written form. Respondents were therefore asked at the outset of the interview to sign a special form designed for this purpose. The form also contained information about the precautions taken to ensure confidential handling of the survey data at the University of Mannheim. This procedure which had been tested in the pretest of the study did not produce difficulties throughout the field period.

2.4   Response Rates and Implications of the Sampling Design for Analysis

The field period lasted from late March until the end of July, 1981. The overall response rate was nearly the same in both fields. At 55.1 per cent it is somewhat lower than the one obtained in the 1972 elite study and corresponds exactly to that of the 1968 elite study. However, the analysis problems which were created by extending the field period would have been greater than the advantages of a slightly higher response rate since the evaluation of political questions may be influenced by political events during the field period.

Table 2.5 contains the response rates for the different sectors. Compared to those of the two previous surveys they, too, show a remarkable continuity over time. Only the response rates in the sectors for military and trade unions have declined by more than 10 per cent since 1972. In the case of the trade unions, this is presumably due to the fact that a number of unions were involved in wage negotiations during the field work period. In the military sector, the main reason lay with the Federal Ministry of Defence which had been asked for a special permit for the military leaders to participate in the study long before the beginning of the field work. The permit was granted, however, only after more than one month of field work had already elapsed.

Altogether, 1,420 of the target persons could not be interviewed. Of the latter, 110 had expressed their general agreement to be interviewed but appointments could not be made due to the difficulties of finding a free date at which the interview could take place. Reference to an overcommitted time budget was the single most frequently mentioned reason. However, that claim could also have been legitimately used by any of the position-holders contacted. A tiny minority mentioned general reservations about survey research, and some expressed doubts concerning the confidentiality of the data.

Scholars have frequently suspected that the refusal rate in elite surveys increases as higher levels in the hierarchy are reached but that this fact is usually concealed because the relevant response rates are not reported. In order to test this assumption the elite sample was subdivided by seniority of position and separate response rates for these two elite strata were calculated. This was done by using similar classification criteria as in the assignment to the two interview fields. Table 2.6 indicates that the response rate shows no linear and simple relation to seniority of position. The suspected effect exists only in the sectors for politics and business associations. In the civil service, business, and trade union elites, response rates were instead somewhat higher in the top stratum.

The experience of the field work did not convey any testable suggestions concerning the factors determining individual reluctance or willingness to be interviewed for the study. A thorough analysis revealed no serious distortions of the sample of respondents as compared to the original sample. This means that the results can be viewed as giving a fairly true portrait of the entire West German elite sample with regard to the social characteristics of this group.

Table 2.6   *Response rate and seniority of position*

Sector[a]	Position-holders n	Completed interviews n	Response rate %
Politics I[b]	246	133	54.1
Politics II	206	141	68.4
Civil service I[c]	163	114	69.9
Civil service II	308	182	59.1
Business I	242	116	47.9
Business II	446	169	37.9
Business associations I	61	29	47.5
Business associations II	235	145	61.7
Trade unions I	33	19	57.6
Trade unions II	122	68	55.7
Mass media I	88	57	64.8
Mass media II	266	165	62.0

Notes:
[a] For the academic and cultural elites which do not display a comparably clear organizational hierarchy, no such subdivision was tested
[b] In this group, the especially low response rate among the members of the Federal Government is compensated by a rather satisfactory one among those of state governments
[c] Deviating from the classification for the field work, all Secretaries of State in Federal and State Ministries were counted as belonging to the top stratum

Moreover, given the predominantly conservative political preferences of the respondents, the danger that they represent only the more liberal part of the West German elite can be ruled out.

Elite sampling inevitably produces weighting problems due to power differences within an elite. Unlike voting where each vote counts the same, unequal influence has to be assumed in collective decision-making. The results of unweighted analyses are instead affected by the sample composition chosen by the researcher with regard to the inclusion of sectors, organizations, and positions. Predictions of decision-making outputs on the basis of an unweighted analysis of elite attitudes can thus be highly misleading, particularly when differences of opinion exist within an elite, e.g. between sectors or competing parties. It is necessary to keep different subgroups apart and to avoid unwarranted aggregations. Inferences about 'the elite' should be made with care and only after having analysed subgroups separately. Table 2.7 shows how much the results for a number of key variables differ between sectors. Furthermore, the subdivision of the main sectors according to positional subgroups shows to what extent the inclusion of second level position-holders affects the results for the selected variables. Though this effect is not very pronounced for many variables, it should nevertheless not be considered as negligible.

2.5 A New Approach for Locating National Elites

Sole reliance on the positional approach yields a sample of elite position-holders and allows the study of formal power. Although most scholars agree that formal competence derived from incumbency of leadership positions plays a much more crucial role in modern societies than in simpler systems, an identity in the structuring of formal and informal influence cannot be assumed. This means that power is never perfectly correlated with position (Putnam, 1976, p. 16; Scheuch, 1973, p. 1005 ff.). If we are interested in making inferences not only about the sample of position-holders but also about the group of persons actually most influential in national decision-making, a weight for the actual influence of different persons has to be found. This will solve two fundamental and interrelated problems of the positional approach simultaneously, namely differences in influence and the boundary problem.

Differences in influence can be caused by differences in formal competence as well as by the varying degrees to which formal competence is being transformed into actual influence by a person (cf. Mokken and Stokman, 1976, p. 52 f.). The boundary problem is likewise a twofold one: the positional approach does not provide a single criterion for determining the boundaries in different sectors and subgroups. The sector composition of a positionally defined elite sample reflects instead *a priori* resources, e.g. political decision-making authority, economic power, influence on public opinion, etc. In order to compare the influence or power of different persons or subgroups and to determine the overall boundaries of an elite population, an empirical measure of influence and a uniform boundary criterion are needed.

Since the late 1960s, various sociometric methods have been proposed that allow the empirical study of influence relations among elites (e.g. Kadushin, 1968; Laumann and Pappi, 1976; Moore, 1979; Higley and Moore, 1981). This is generally done by asking a positionally defined sample of elite respondents for interaction partners. Such an approach was also used in the West German elite study of 1981. The procedure chosen followed closely Kadushin's theoretical concept of social circles and its operationalization in two

Table 2.7 West German elite study, 1981: differences between subsectors for selected variables[a]

Sector[b]	Mean age	% Upper and upper middle class origin	% Academic degree	Mean years in position	% Party members	Party preference CDU/CSU	SPD	FDP	Left-right scale (mean)
Total (n = 1744)	52.7	35.7	68.5	6.4	52.3	51.3	28.9	17.8	5.5
Politics (n = 274)	49.4	24.7	64.9	4.2	100.0	47.5	41.9	10.2	5.0
A Cabinet members (Federal and State Governments) (n = 82)	50.5	33.8	76.5	3.9	100.0	48.1	44.4	7.4	5.2
B Other politicians (n = 192)	49.0	20.9	60.0	4.3	100.0	47.3	40.8	11.4	5.0
Civil Service (n = 296)	53.1	37.8	93.9	5.2	67.7	40.4	36.5	22.7	5.4
A Secretaries of State and Dept. Heads Federal Ministries (politically appointed) (n = 65)	53.7	44.3	92.2	4.7	64.6	26.2	49.2	24.6	5.2
B Secretaries of State Ministries (n = 100)	51.0	43.8	94.9	4.9	87.9	42.4	43.4	14.1	5.3
C Other (permanent subdept. heads in Fed. Ministries; heads of EC, Federal and State Agencies) (n = 131)	54.4	30.0	93.9	5.6	53.8	45.9	24.6	28.7	5.5
Business (n = 459)	54.8	43.8	72.3	7.4	31.8	74.4	7.2	17.7	6.5
A Chairmen of boards in business enterprises and business associations (n = 184)	55.7	48.0	75.0	7.2	32.4	74.0	6.8	19.2	6.5
B Other members of boards in business and business associations									

C Agricultural associations (n=37)	56.4	17.1	59.5	9.5	51.4	73.0	5.4	18.9	6.5
Trade Unions (n=87)	54.0	7.8	8.0	8.7	98.9	12.9	83.5	2.4	4.1
A Chairmen and vice-chairmen (n=27)	55.1	8.7	11.1	8.5	96.3	11.5	84.6	3.8	4.0
B Other members of boards, heads of districts (n=60)	53.4	7.4	6.7	8.8	100.0	13.6	83.1	1.7	4.2
Mass Media (n=222)	51.9	30.7	47.3	8.0	33.5	49.5	23.8	23.8	5.3
A Chief editors of major newspapers, directors of broadcasting stations (n=72)	54.6	43.8	59.7	9.1	29.2	55.9	19.1	25.0	5.6
B Other leading journalists in the press and in broadcasting (n=150)	50.6	24.6	41.3	7.5	35.6	46.6	26.0	23.3	5.2
Science (n=130)	51.3	39.1	96.2	5.9	18.6	50.0	23.7	25.4	5.5
Military (n=43)	55.0	53.7	32.6	2.1	14.6	74.4	7.7	15.4	6.7
Judiciary (n=38)	59.4	37.8	100.0	5.3	65.8	52.9	26.5	17.6	5.2
Cultural elite (n=104)	48.2	48.4	61.5	7.7	21.4	20.0	41.0	27.0	4.3
Other (n=91)	54.4	28.9	59.3	7.1	57.8	47.2	39.3	6.7	5.2

Notes:
[a] Results for subsectors deviating for a response category by more than 10 percentage points from the percentage of the whole sector (for percentage-based indicators), or by more than two units from the sector mean (for indicators expressed as means), are printed in italic.
[b] The assignment of respondents to the subgroups in the analysis deviates slightly from the classification used in previous tables.

previous studies of national elites in the United States (1971/72) and Australia (1975). Respondents were first asked to indicate the one national issue on which they had been most active during the last year. After having described the nature of this issue in some detail, they were further asked to name their most important interaction partners in the context of this issue.

This question can be regarded as measuring instrumental reputation for political influence. Since the focus was on issues of more than intra-organizational relevance, most respondents named political issues. The instrumental aspect was measured by asking for interaction partners, i.e. for persons who can be assumed to have tried to influence the respondent, or whom the respondent himself had tried to influence. Reputation was measured in so far as respondents were asked to name only the most important of their interaction partners. The number of designated persons was therefore presumably much smaller than the actual number of interaction partners.

With respect to the traditional approaches of elite identification, the nominations can be classified as a variety of the decisional approach based on reputational nominations. The instrumental as well as the reputational nature of these nominations ensures that they are not restricted solely to persons with formal power but that they also cover informal influence relations. The approach allows, in other words, supplementation of the original positional sample by persons with informal power. At the same time, persons holding only formal but no real decision-making power can be detected.

Network analytic procedures were then used to analyse these sociometric data.[4] They allow the specification of the boundaries of elite circles which are defined as aggregations of highly overlapping, 'face-to-face' cliques. Additionally, centrality measures can be calculated for each member of the elite sample that are based on the number and type of persons to which the sample member is linked. They can, in turn, be used as a weight for the political influence of a person.

The analysis revealed in all three countries the existence of a relatively broad central circle that included members as well as non-members of the positional elite sample from all sectors and active on different issues. Its sector composition differed considerably from that of the original positional sample.

Table 2.8 allows comparison of the sector composition of the West German positional elite sample with that of the elite network and the central circle. The network includes all respondents who nominated

Table 2.8 Sector composition of sample, network, and central circle

Sector	Sample		Network		Sample members in network		Other persons in network		Central circle		Sample members in central circle		Other persons in central circle	
	n	%	n	%	n	%	n	%	n	%	n	%	n	%
Politics SPD	199	6.3	172	14.0	143	14.6	29	11.6	90	16.1	83	16.8	7	10.9
CDU/CSU	208	6.6	168	13.7	137	14.0	31	12.4	84	15.0	73	14.7	11	17.2
FDP	45	1.4	59	4.8	43	4.4	16	6.4	34	6.1	29	5.9	5	7.8
Politics total[a]	452	14.3	403	32.8	323	33.0	80	31.9	209	37.4	185	37.4	24	37.5
Civil service	471	14.9	209	17.0	173	17.7	36	14.3	76	13.6	68	13.7	8	12.5
Business	688	21.7	138	11.2	126	12.9	12	4.8	66	11.8	64	12.9	2	3.1
Business associations	295	9.3	98	8.0	78	8.0	20	8.0	41	7.3	38	7.7	3	4.7
Trade unions	155	4.9	88	7.2	69	7.0	19	7.6	44	7.9	38	7.7	6	9.4
Mass media	354	11.2	107	8.7	80	8.2	27	10.8	46	8.2	39	7.9	7	10.9
Academic	179	5.7	96	7.8	64	6.5	32	12.7	46	8.2	37	7.5	9	14.1
Military	172	5.4	6	0.5	5	0.5	1	0.4	1	0.2	1	0.2	0	0.0
Culture	180	5.7	12	1.0	11	1.1	1	0.4	3	0.5	3	0.6	0	0.0
Other[b]	218	6.9	73	5.9	50	5.1	23	9.2	27	4.8	22	4.4	5	7.8
Total	3164	100.0	1230	100.1	979	100.0	251	100.1	559	99.9	495	100.0	64	100.0

Notes:
[a] Including non-sample politicians with other party affiliation or whose party affiliation could not be ascertained
[b] Including foreigners nominated

other persons and were themselves nominated by at least one other respondent. Non-respondents were included if they had received at least two nominations.

The results show that only about one-third of the members of the original positional elite sample belong to the network and only 15.6 per cent to the central circle. At the same time, however, only 251 persons who were not holders of elite positions entered the elite network, and even fewer of these, the central circle. Positional power and political influence as measured by the sociometric approach have therefore to be conceived as different though related concepts.

2.6 Conclusion

Compared to a general population survey, the collection of survey data on national elites poses a number of additional problems. The organization of the field work requires more effort with regard to getting interview appointments, adequate training of interviewers, and data protection. As a number of national elite surveys – not only in West Germany but also in other countries – have shown, the use of a highly structured questionnaire presents no obstacle and does not lead to insufficient response rates. The decision to use a structured interview guide has to depend solely on considerations of the research goal and not on imputed reservations of respondents to forced choice questions.

The validity of the results depends to a large extent on the sampling design. The positional approach is widely used for reasons of practicability. In most cases, however, the researcher does not just want to study a sample of position-holders in different sectors, but also wants to generalize the results to 'the elite', i.e. the group of the most influential persons in a society.

The positional approach precludes such inferences for several reasons. The first is that political influence and position are only imperfectly correlated. Secondly, due to the multidimensionality of power resources, power is not comparable across sectors. A uniform boundary criterion is needed in order to make cross-sectoral comparisons. The same is true for determining the overall size of an elite. Normally, the composition of the positional elite sample in terms of sectors, organizations, and positions, is used as a weight for the importance of the different subgroups. Varying degrees of power concentration and multiple position-holding, however, may preclude the realization of this intention and varying response rates may additionally distort the intended numerical relations. Finally, unequal power within the elite precludes inferences from distributions of attitudes within the sample of respondents to future decision-making outputs.

In order to identify the politically influential among the members of a positional elite sample as well as among persons not holding top positions, we need, therefore, an additional empirical indicator of political influence. This should allow the determination of the boundaries of an elite and should at the same time provide a quantitative measure that can be used as a weight for individual respondents.

The design used in the United States, Australian and West German elite studies tries to make up for the above-mentioned shortcomings of the positional approach. Starting out from a positional sample, respondents were asked to name other persons relevant to decision-making in their own field of activity. A network analysis of these nominations allows the detection of the network of interactions among elites and the central circle of this network. It also provides a measure of the centrality of persons in the network of relevant decision-makers, a measure that can be conceived as a weight of political influence. This approach, therefore, enlarges substantially the evidence that can be obtained from national elite surveys.

Appendix: The sample of the West German elite study, 1981: sectors, organizations, and positions

1 Politics
- Federal government: chancellor, ministers, and junior ministers;
- State governments: prime ministers, ministers, and junior ministers;
- Federal legislature ('Bundestag'): president, vice-presidents, chairmen and deputy chairmen of the standing committees; leaders of the parliamentary parties;
- State legislatures: leaders of the parliamentary parties;
- Political parties: members of the national committees; chairmen and deputy chairmen of the state committees.

2 Civil Service
- Federal ministries: secretaries of state, department heads (political civil servants)[a]; subdepartment heads (permanent civil servants);
- State ministries: secretaries of state (political civil servants);
- Federal and state agencies: directors, deputy directors.

3 Business
- Industrial, trade, and service corporations according to size of sales: chief executives, chairmen and deputy chairmen of the supervisory boards;
- Financial corporations (banks, insurances) according to size of sales:

chief executives, chairmen and deputy chairmen of the supervisory boards;
- Federal bank: members of the executive board ('Zentralbankrat').

4 Business Associations
- Peak associations of industry and employers: boards of directors, chief executives;
- Agricultural associations: presidents, vice-presidents, chief executives.

5 Trade Unions
- German trade union federation (Deutscher Gewerkschaftsbund, DGB) and its member unions: members of executive boards, district heads;
- Union of employees (Deutsche Angestelltengewerkschaft, DAG): members of executive board, department heads.

6 Mass Media
- Press (dailies, weeklies, and magazines) according to number of circulation: executive managers, chief editors, chief editorial staff of political and economic sections;
- Broadcasting networks: executive managers, program directors, chief editorial staff of political and economic sections.

7 Academic
- Universities: presidents;
- Non-commercial research institutes: presidents, department heads;
- Research departments of large industrial corporations: department heads;
- Public and private research foundations: presidents and chief executives;
- Economic advisory committee to the federal government: all members.

8 Military
- West German armed forces ('Bundeswehr'): all generals and admirals including those in the NATO staff.

9 Cultural
- Press and broadcasting networks: chief editorial staff of cultural and entertainment sections;
- Publishing companies: directors, chief executives, and editors.

10 Other
- Judiciary: presidents and chairmen ('Senatsvorsitzende') of all federal courts including the federal constitutional court;
- Local elites: mayors and administrative heads of the biggest cities;
- Churches: protestant and catholic bishops;
- Professional associations: presidents and managing directors of the associations of the medical, legal, and cultural professions as well as the civil servants' association (Deutscher Beamtenbund);
- Consumers' associations ('Arbeitsgemeinschaft der Verbraucher'): presidents, vice-presidents, managing directors.

Note:
[a] Political civil servants can be removed from their positions and sent into temporary retirement without further explanation.

Notes

1 We have tried to make up for this shortcoming by including some open-ended questions on the most important problems which the Federal Republic is facing today.

2 The study was carried out by a research team at the University of Mannheim. Principal investigators were Rudolf Wildenmann, Max Kaase and the author. It was supported by a grant of the Deutsche Forschungsgemeinschaft (DFG). The major part of the field work was organized by GETAS, Bremen. ZUMA, Mannheim, provided assistance during all stages of the project and particularly in the preparation of the data sets. The Zentralarchiv für empirische Sozialforschung, Cologne, produced a machine-readable code-book containing the marginal distributions of the answers for the different elite subgroups (sectors): authors were Rudolf Wildenmann, Max Kaase, Ursula Hoffmann-Lange, Albrecht Kutteroff, Gunter Wolf, *Führungsschicht in der Bundesrepublik Deutschland 1981*. Mannheim: Universität Mannheim, 1982.

3 See Appendix for a list of the sectors and positions included in the study.

4 The programs SOCK and COMPLT developed by Richard D. Alba were used for this purpose.

3

Studying Members of the United States Congress

BARBARA SINCLAIR
University of California, Riverside

DAVID BRADY
Rice University

3.1 Introduction

The United States Congress is fundamentally different from contemporary European legislatures; as a consequence, the questions political scientists have asked about it and the methods they have used to study it are also different. The governmental structure specified by the United States Constitution, particularly the separation of powers between legislature and executive, and the relatively weak party system have resulted in Congress maintaining for itself an important decision-making role in the policy process independent of the Executive. While the British Parliament, for example, participates in the policy process by scrutinizing and legitimating government proposals, it does not participate in decision-making. The executive, not Parliament, makes public policy (Norton, 1981, pp. 3–9). The United States Congress, in contrast, takes a real and independent part in decision-making on public policy. Furthermore, not only can the Congress kill or alter the president's policy proposals, it can and does initiate as well. Thus, the United States Congress is uniquely powerful and independent for a modern legislature.

A second characteristic that distinguishes the United States Congress from European legislatures is the unusual degree of autonomy enjoyed by its members as individuals. Because Congress has maintained its position as a key actor in the policy process, seats in the Congress are highly desirable. Because of the weakness of the party system, neither the president nor legislative party leaders control access to legislative positions. Consequently, neither house of Congress has for long been able to maintain a highly hierarchical form of organization (Cooper and Brady, 1981). Party leaders have seldom possessed the resources necessary to command. The most obvious indicator of member autonomy from party leaders is the lack of strict party-line voting. Few recorded votes pit united party groupings against each other. Both chambers have used seniority as the criterion for the distribution of certain valued positions – committee leadership and, to some extent, desirable committee assignments. This did create a number of parallel small hierarchies. But, even at their most powerful, committee chairmen had limited control over the behaviour of other members. Like party leaders, they could seldom affect significantly a member's chances of winning re-election. As the party system has weakened further in the last few decades, and in response to other factors as well, rank and file members have successfully asserted their claim to even greater autonomy. The 1960s and 1970s saw both chambers distribute influence more equally and afford the individual member still greater latitude.

These two interrelated characteristics, then, make the United States Congress unique. As a legislature it exercises power independent of the executive. Internally, its members exercise a very high degree of autonomy. The mainstreams of congressional research flow from these unique characteristics. On the one hand, congressional scholars have focused upon congressional decision-making. Such studies have taken a wide variety of forms and have had various foci: case studies of how a bill becomes a law; Stephen Bailey's (1950) study of the Employment Act of 1946 is the first and still one of the best; studies of congressional committees such as Richard Fenno's (1966) pathbreaking analysis of the Appropriations Committees, his very influential comparative committee study (Fenno, 1973), and more recent work attempting to assess how congressional reforms have affected committee decision-making (see Davidson, 1981 and Smith and Deering, 1984); studies of party leaders, their function, leadership styles and coalition building efforts (see Cooper and Brady, 1981; Ripley, 1967 and Sinclair, 1983a); studies of specific policy areas such as John Ferejohn's (1974) analysis of rivers and harbours legislation and Bruce Oppenheimer's (1974) *Oil and the Congressional Process*; studies of the relationship between and sometimes the relative influence of Congress and the president (see Chamberlain, 1946; Sundquist, 1981; Fisher, 1985);

and studies of the circumstances under which and the process through which the Congress passes clusters of non-incremental policy changes (see Brady with Stewart, 1982; Sinclair, 1982).

The second stream of research attempts to explain decision-making by individual members. Studies of roll-call voting behaviour make up the great bulk of work in this vein. (But, as we shall see, not all roll-call analyses have this as their object; many fall into the first category.) Because the Congress does make important decisions and because member voting behaviour is not simply predictable, members' voting decisions have been seen by political scientists as important and interesting phenomena to explain.

Their dependent variable – what they are trying to explain – differentiates these two streams of research. Approach and method do not. Because of the autonomy enjoyed by individual members of Congress, one cannot study congressional decision-making without studying the decision-making of individual members. And the internal democratization of the 1960s and 1970s has only accentuated that imperative. The necessity of basing explanations of institution-level phenomena upon an examination of member behaviour seems to account, at least in part, for the current popularity of the purposive behaviour approach (Sinclair, 1983b). Basic to that approach is the assumption that individuals rationally pursue specified goals, an assumption that fits the rampantly individualistic Congress of the 1970s well. The approach conceptualizes institution-level phenomena such as policy outputs as the result of members' behaviour, which is seen as a function of the interaction between members' goals and institutional constraints. This approach, however, only makes totally obvious the basic premise underlying the modern study of the United States Congress: to understand the Congress – how it works and its role in the policy process – one must understand the behaviour of congressmen, of junior as well as senior members, of rank-and-file members as well as officially designated leaders.

The modern study of Congress only dates to the late 1940s. Pre-Second World War work tended to have a heavily legal and historical cast; scholars relied primarily upon written records. The behavioural revolution very much affected the study of Congress and the 1950s and 1960s saw a flowering of behaviourally oriented studies of Congress (Peabody, 1969). Although similar in their focus on behaviour, these studies can be distinguished by their research strategy. The so-called insider studies were based upon participant observation. The American Political Science Association's

Congressional Fellowship Program, which began in the 1950s, facilitated such work by giving successive generations of congressional scholars the opportunity to work in the office of a member of Congress over an extended period of time. The outsider strategy, in contrast, involved the study of congressional behaviour via the analysis of publicly available quantitative data, most frequently roll-call data.

3.2 Roll-Call Analysis

Roll-call analysis is any analysis of recorded votes taken in a legislature. Since roll-call analysis is interesting only if alignments vary across votes it developed in the United States. Both because the United States Congress as the national legislature is intrinsically interesting to American political scientists and because of the easy availability of congressional roll-call data in machine-readable form from the Inter-University Consortium for Political and Social Research at the University of Michigan, the United States Congress has been the target of the majority of roll-call analyses.

The United States Constitution specifies that 'each House shall keep a Journal of its proceedings and from time to time publish the same . . . and the Yeas and Nays of the members of each House on any question shall, at the desire of one fifth of those present, be entered on the journal' (Article I, Section 5). Although this constitutional provision applies to both houses equally, procedures developed somewhat differently in House and Senate. Because of its larger size, the House of Representatives came to rely heavily upon the Committee of the Whole. It is in the Committee of the Whole that bills are amended and, until 1970, no recorded votes were possible in the Committee of the Whole. Often votes on amendments are the votes most critical to a bill's fate. Amendments can fundamentally alter the thrust of a piece of legislation; and amendment may have the intent and/or effect of killing a bill. Furthermore, a member's vote on a series of amendments of varying strength often provides the best gauge of the extent of his or her commitment on an issue. House rules specify that an amendment approved in the Committee of the Whole can be voted upon again in the House, in which case the vote is likely to be recorded. Frequently, however, such a second vote is not taken. Thus, until the early 1970s, roll-call votes in the House provided only a partial picture of floor decision-making on controversial issues. Because they took place in the House itself, votes on passage of a controversial measure would generally be recorded as would votes on various procedural motions, some of which can be very important and quite revealing. However, equally and sometimes more important decisions on amendments were not recorded and therefore cannot be analysed.

Consequently, the change in House procedure with the Legislative Reorganization Act of 1970 made important new data available. The Act provided for recorded votes in the Committee of the Whole; these are called recorded teller votes but, since the installation of an electronic voting system in 1973, that system has been used for all recorded votes, both those taken in Committee of the Whole and those in the House itself. (The exception is the vote on the speaker-ship of the House. This vote, which incidently is often the only strict party-line vote during a congress, is now the only true roll-call vote in which a clerk calls the roll of members and members vote orally.) The rules now specify that twenty-five members can demand a recorded vote in the Committee of the Whole.

The institution of the recorded teller vote resulted in an increase in the number of recorded votes in the House. During the 91st Congress (1969–70), the last before the recorded teller, the House took 443 recorded votes. The number jumped to 649 in the next congress and rose monotonically till the 95th Congress (1977–78) when it hit a high of 1540 (Ornstein *et al.*, 1984, pp. 148–9). It has since decreased but remains well above the pre-1970 level. Although the rules change was an important contributor to this increase, it by no means provides a total explanation. The number of roll calls was increasing before the rules change. Thus during the average congress of the 1950s only 170 recorded votes were taken. During the 1960s, the average was 357. Most congressional scholars trace the increase, at least in part, to the growing autonomy of individual members. Growth in the size and contentiousness of the work load was an important contributor, but so too was the increased willingness of members to force motions to a vote regardless of the wishes of party or committee leaders.

The Senate has never made much use of the Committee of the Whole device and now does not use it at all. Consequently, the constitutional provision requiring a recorded vote on request of one-fifth of those present governs. Yet, despite the constancy of the rules, the number of Senate roll calls has also increased. In the 1950s, the mean per congress was 312; this increased to 547 in the 1960s and then to 1114 in the 1970s. As in the House, the 1980s have seen some decline; the mean per congress for the 1981 through 1984 period was 797.

Because Senate rules allow the individual a great deal of latitude, the chamber has relied heavily upon norms or unwritten rules of behaviour to facilitate its functioning. During this period Senate norms with respect to recorded votes changed. Mike Mansfield, who became Senate Majority Leader in 1961, to a large extent supported any senator's desire for a recorded vote whether or not that senator could muster the one-fifth technically necessary. Senators quickly came to see this as their right. During the 1960s and 1970s, individual senators were offering increasing numbers of amendments to legislation on the Senate floor and increasingly were forcing these amendments to a recorded vote.

The United States Congress, then, makes a great many decisions by recorded floor vote. Furthermore, to a very large extent, the important decisions made at the floor stage are now made by recorded vote. To be sure, much that is important happens before the floor stage. Within both houses committees play the pre-eminent role in the shaping of legislation. If one's purpose is explaining legislative outcomes one cannot simply examine floor roll calls. Changes to rules during the 1970s required committees to record roll-call votes and these can be analysed by the same techniques applicable to floor votes. Many committees, however, make decisions without heavy reliance on formal votes. An understanding of committee decision-making processes requires data beyond roll calls.

A final point should be kept in mind when analysing roll-call votes. Voting is behaviour – public behaviour. The extent to which a member's behaviour can be taken as an indicator of the member's attitudes is an open question. One certainly cannot simply assume that a vote for a given policy position reflects the member's sincere belief in that position – or always even his support for that position. Because voting is behaviour and, in fact, official behaviour, it can have consequences in a way that an attitude expressed in an opinion survey will not. Consequently, we would expect, and there is a great deal of evidence to indicate, that members sometimes vote strategically. Members may vote for an amendment, the substance of which they disapprove, because they know adoption of the amendment is likely to kill the bill, which they oppose. A member may vote against the position of the party leadership or a president of his party when his vote will make no difference but support them when the outcome is in doubt.

Congressional roll-call analysis was initially dominated by one question: what is the role of political parties? Because members of the same party in the United States Congress frequently do not vote together against members of the other party, conceptualizing and measuring the extent of party voting have always been primary concerns for congressional scholars. In spite of almost one hundred years of research (Wilson, 1885; Lowell, 1902), assessing the effect of party on congressional voting is not an easy task, in part because party voting in Congress is a complex, multifaceted phenomenon, not a simple unidimensional one. As early as 1928, Stuart Rice developed an Index of Party Likeness to complement his Index of Party Cohesion because he recognized that the cohesion measure tapped only intra-party agreement and was therefore insensitive to inter-party conflict.

The four most commonly used measures of party voting in Congress are the Index of Party Cohesion, the Index of Party Likeness, the Party Vote Score and the Party Unity Score. The Index of Party Cohesion, as indicated above, is a measure of partisan unity on cohesion on roll-call votes. The Index ranges from 0 (the party is evenly split) to 100 (the party is unanimous) and is measured by the following formula:

Index of Cohesion = | Per cent of party for – per cent of party against |

For example: Democrats: Yeas = 32; Nays = 31
   Per cent for 32/63 × 100   = 50.8
   Per cent against 31/63 × 100   = 49.2
   Index of cohesion = 50.8 – 49.2 = 1.6
(See Anderson *et al.*, 1966, p. 33.)

The Index of Party Likeness focuses on the division or conflict between parties and measures the degree to which the parties differ from one another on roll-call votes. The Index ranges from 0 (high conflict) to 100 (identical party voting), and the formula for computing the Index is as follows:

Index of Likeness = 100 – | Per cent Democrats for – Per cent Republicans for |

For example: Democrats: Yeas = 14; Nays = 50
              Republicans: Yeas = 23; Nays = 13
   Per cent Democrats for   = 14/64 × 100 = 22
   Per cent Republicans for = 23/36 × 100 = 64
   Index of Likeness   = 100 – (64 – 22) = 58
(See Anderson *et al.*, 1966, p. 44.)

The Party Vote Score is also a measure of the degree to which the parties differ from one another on roll call votes. As initially formulated by Lowell (1902), it measures the percentage of times that 90 per cent or more of one party opposes 90 per cent or more of the other on roll-call votes. In recent decades, the standard has been shifted to a simple majority of one party voting against a majority of the other. Thus, as used by Turner and Schneider (1970) the Party Vote Score measures the percent of times 50 per cent of one party votes against 50 per cent of the other party on roll-call votes. The Party Unity Score measures unity or cohesion on party votes. As currently used, it measures the degree to which fellow partisans vote together on roll calls where 50 per cent of one party oppose 50 per cent of the other. The score is simply the actual percentage of members voting with a majority of their fellow partisans on party votes (Shannon, 1968).

These scores are usually aggregated over all roll calls in a Congress or a session and presented as averages for a Congress. Thus, for example, the 90th House of Representatives (1967–69) is characterized by the following scores:

Index of Party Likeness	= 74.2
Index of Party Cohesion	
Democrats	= 68.3
Republicans	= 67.9
Party Unity	
Democrats	= 75.3
Republicans	= 78.7
Party Vote Score	
90 per cent vs. 90 per cent	= 2.9
50 per cent vs. 50 per cent	= 35.8

These scores can be used to characterize the levels of partisan strength in the 90th House, or they can be used to compare the 90th House to other Congresses. Party unity scores can also be used to compare members to one another. Congressional Quarterly publishes these scores for all members of the House and Senate yearly.

Clearly, there are different dimensions or facets to the effect of party on voting. Not only are both the intra-party unity and inter-party conflict dimensions important, they are interrelated, and the pattern of interrelationships is critical for an understanding of voting in the United States Congress. Four archetypal patterns are evident:

(1) high unity-high conflict
(2) high unity-low conflict
(3) low unity-high conflict
(4) low unity-low conflict

Pattern 1, where both unity and conflict are high, represents a pattern in which party has a strong and comprehensive effect on roll-call voting. British and Irish parliamentary voting would fit this pattern. Pattern 2, where unity is high but conflict limited, represents a situation where party has a strong effect in some areas and little effect in others. If, for example, party voting was prominent in regard to social welfare and government control of the economy issues but bipartisanship dominated voting on agricultural assistance and foreign relations, we would have an example of 2. In pattern 3, where conflict is high but unity is restricted, party serves as a basis of division on issues generally but exhibits substantial weakness in internal cohesion. The so-called Conservative Coalition in the United States Congress provides an example. That is, across a wide range of issues, southern Democrats vote with Republicans against northern Democrats. Pattern 4, where both unity and conflict are limited, represents a pattern in which party is only of marginal importance as a determinant of vote. Here parties tend to disintegrate into factions and voting can be characterized by fluid and transitory factional combinations. Time series analyses of party strength in the United States Congress have shown all four of these patterns to be present at different points in time (see for example Brady *et al.*, 1979 and Clubb and Traugott, 1977).

In the first study of congressional voting, A. Lawrence Lowell (1902) compared party voting in the United States Congress and in the British House of Commons. Defining a party vote as one on which 90 per cent of one party opposed 90 per cent of the other as discussed above, Lowell found such votes to be much more prevalent in the Commons than in the Congress.

In the 1920s, Stuart A. Rice developed the aforementioned Indexes of Party Cohesion and Likeness. Although Rice did not have a specific substantive question in mind, he clearly distinguished the two dimensions of party voting – intra-party unity and inter-party conflict.

In the late 1940s and early 1950s, the question of responsible British style parties dominated much of the literature in United States politics. The work of E. E. Schattschneider (1942) was a prime motivating factor in the increased concern about the role of United

States political parties. Julius Turner (1951), in *Party and Constituency: Pressures on Congress*, argued that United States parties are more 'responsible' than the critics have suggested. Turner attempted to ascertain 'the relative effectiveness of pressures on Congress from certain sources' – specifically party and constituency (Turner, 1951, p. 11). Using Lowell's Party Vote Score and the Rice Index of Cohesion, Turner found that United States congressional parties were less cohesive and had less influence on roll-call voting than did either British parties or French parties in the Third Republic. Turner goes on to argue that United States parties nevertheless have a significant effect on voting. He used a Chi-square test to determine that party mattered on almost 90 per cent of votes. In fact he concludes, 'Party pressure seems to be more effective than any other pressure on congressional voting' (Turner, 1951, p. 25).

Turner's statistical techniques were primitive. The Chi-square test is a measure of statistical significance not a measure of strength of association and is inappropriate for his use. His measures of constituency characteristics were crude; he was forced to use demographic characteristics for the entire district such as proportion foreign born and urbanism. Nevertheless, and despite his own emphasis on the importance of party, Turner's work directed the attention of scholars away from the sole preoccupation with party and towards a more general search for the determinants of roll-call behaviour.

Duncan MacRae's *Dimensions of Congressional Voting* (1958) further changed the focus of roll-call studies by its utilization of cumulative Guttman scaling to classify roll calls and to place members of Congress on the policy dimensions revealed by the scales. Because Guttman scaling is still frequently used and because more complex techniques often require an understanding of Guttman scaling, a discussion of its basic properties is necessary.

Guttman scaling is a procedure designed to order both items (e.g. legislative motions on which roll calls occurred) and subjects (e.g. members of Congress) with respect to some underlying dimension. That hypothesized dimension may be as comprehensive as a general left-right dimension or as narrow as extent of support for wheat subsidies. A researcher may, for example, hypothesize that support for civil rights is a unidimensional phenomenon and that roll calls on four amendments offered to a civil rights bill are measures of that dimension. Assume for convenience that all the amendments would strengthen the bill, but to various degrees, with amendment A strengthening the bill most and D least. If the hypothesis is true, we would expect members to display only the vote patterns in Table 3.1. Members favoring a very strong bill would display pattern 5; they would vote for all strengthening amendments. Those favoring the weakest possible bill would display pattern 1; they would vote against all amendments. Those with intermediate policy preferences, however, provide the test of the model. If the assumptions are correct (and if legislators vote according to whether they prefer the passage of a motion to the status quo), no member should vote for a stronger amendment and against a weaker one (Weisberg, 1972). If, for example, a member is willing to strengthen the bill but only a little, he will vote for amendment D, the weakest of the strengthening amendments, but against the three stronger amendments, e.g. response pattern 2. If a member is willing to strengthen the bill to the extent represented by amendment B, he will also support amendments C and D which go less far.

Table 3.1   *A perfect Guttman scale*

Response pattern	Item				Scale score
	A	*B*	*C*	*D*	
1	No	No	No	No	0
2	No	No	No	Yes	1
3	No	No	Yes	Yes	2
4	No	Yes	Yes	Yes	3
5	Yes	Yes	Yes	Yes	4

Clearly, then, a Guttman scale orders items. Here we assumed for convenience of exposition that we knew that A was the strongest and D, the weakest amendment. From the discovery of a pattern such as that in Table 3.1 we can conclude that A is the strongest, etc. The scale also orders respondents in terms of the underlying continuum. That is, the scale scores, which are simply the number of yes votes, order members in terms of their support for civil rights. Note further that, with a perfect Guttman scale, knowledge of the number of items a member voted yes on allows one to reproduce exactly his or her response pattern.

Of course, one very seldom finds a perfect Guttman scale. Consequently criteria for deciding how much deviation from the perfect pattern is acceptable have been developed. To oversimplify and as a general rule, 10 per cent errors are usually considered tolerable so long as they are randomly distributed. Methods for assigning scale scores to members with non-scale response patterns have also been developed. Generally, assignment based upon the number of positive responses seems to work as well as more complicated procedures. See McIver and Carmines (1981) for an excellent discussion of these and other issues in Guttman scaling.

By his pioneering use of Guttman scaling in roll-call analysis, MacRae freed political scientists from either having to analyse roll calls one vote at a time or having to rely upon highly aggregated scores such as the party cohesion index. Scale scores provided meaningful multi-valued dependent variables that could be related to various hypothesized independent variables (see, for example, Shannon, 1968).

MacRae's work also raised important questions about the structure of roll-call voting in the United States Congress. United States political scientists like other politically attentive people have long tended to discuss United States politics generally and congressional politics specifically in liberal–conservative terms. Roll-call analyses, especially those using Guttman scaling, suggested that this was at best a gross oversimplification. Analyses produced multiple Guttman scales, not a single scale that could be seen as tapping a comprehensive left–right continuum.

Aage Clausen (1973), in a highly influential study, argued that policy content structures congressional voting:

> Legislators reduce the time and energy requirements of policy decision-making by (1) sorting specific policy proposals into a limited number of general policy content categories and by (2) establishing a policy position for each general category of policy content, one that can be used to make decisions on each of the specific proposals assigned to that category (Clausen, 1973, p. 14).

Clausen proceeds by subjectively classifying roll-call votes into five categories: social welfare, agricultural assistance, government management of the economy, civil liberties and international involvement. These pre-sorted roll calls are then analysed to determine whether or not they form a single policy dimension (see Clausen, 1967, for a description of the technique, which produces Guttman scales). Having ascertained the overtime stability of those policy dimensions, Clausen shows that on some of these issue dimensions – government management particularly – party structures roll-call voting, but that on others such as civil liberties and international involvement, party is relatively unimportant. He argues that where party is unimportant, members' constituency interests determine their voting (but see Fiorina, 1974, for a critique).

In short, Clausen argues that a pluralistic interpretation of voting in Congress best describes the real world, that different issues give rise to different coalitions of interests.

Recently, there has developed another school of thought which argues that in fact a single dimension underlies congressional voting (Schneider, 1979; Poole and Daniels, 1985; Poole and Rosenthal, 1984). The statistical techniques used, which are still in the process of development, are too complex to review in any detail (see Poole, 1983; Poole and Rosenthal, 1985). In their most recent work, Poole and Rosenthal use a general non-linear logit model. The model assumes probabilistic voting based on a spacial utility function. Guttman scaling is a degenerate case of their model. (That is, when there is no error in the data, their algorithm produces a perfect Guttman scale. This is a problem, however, because it precludes the estimation of certain parameters.) Testing their model on the 85th House (1957–58) and on the Senate for 1979–82, they found it correctly classified about 80 per cent of the individual votes cast by members over all contested roll calls. Their program produces scores for members that represent their positions on the liberal–conservative continuum.

Substantively, the finding that there is a single underlying liberal–conservative dimension in voting yields an interpretation of United States politics significantly different from Clausen's pluralistic interpretation. Which of these two basic models best describes congressional roll-call voting at a given point in time is still an open and unresolved question. What is clear is that both of the techniques are useful for particular sorts of analyses. When our interest centres upon the contours of policy and the determinants of policy stability and policy change, Clausen's procedure of sorting roll calls into policy categories before scaling is essential (Brady with Stewart, 1982; Sinclair, 1977; 1982). When one's interest is in broader trends, one may well be willing to sacrifice detail for simplicity (see Poole and Rosenthal, 1984), in which case the Poole–Rosenthal technique would be appropriate though, at this point, it is not generally available. In addition, the aggregate measures of party voting still have their uses. Cooper *et al.* (1977), Brady *et al.* (1979) and Clubb and Traugott (1977) have employed those measures to show how the impact of party on voting has varied over the course of United States history.

Roll-call analysis, then, provides a number of different and increasingly sophisticated ways of characterizing congressional voting behaviour. Our theorizing about the determinants of voting behaviour has also become more sophisticated, but the data needed for testing these more sophisticated formulations have not always been forthcoming. Party, constituency, and, to a lesser extent, the member's own personal policy preferences are the generic variables of concern.

Until the mid- to late-1970s, constituency was measured with census data. The normal procedure was that the researcher ascertained, for example, the percentage of blacks or of urban residents in each congressional district, and then correlated this measure with voting scores to determine constituency effects. However, as Fiorina (1974) and Fenno (1978) have shown, constituency is a far more complicated variable. Fenno distinguishes four levels of constituency: the geographic, the electoral, the primary, and the confidentials. These may be viewed as a series of concentric circles with the geographic containing the largest number and the confidentials containing the fewest. According to this view, representatives from heterogenous districts will not represent both urban and rural or labor and business interests; instead they will have an electoral constituency where one set dominates. Bullock and Brady (1983) have shown that United States senators from heterogeneous states do in fact have distinctly different electoral constituencies. A thorough test of constituency-influence hypotheses based upon Fenno's framework requires sample surveys within constituencies and thus far has proven prohibitively expensive. We do know that constituency is important and that the impact of constituency on voting behaviour varies with the saliency of the issue (Miller and Stokes, 1963; Kingdon, 1973). Yet there is much about this subtle and complex relationship that we do not yet understand.

Members' personal policy preferences cannot be inferred from their roll-call behaviour. Only interview data will provide an independent measure. Obtaining such data is by no means impossible (see Stokes and Miller, 1963; Kingdon, 1973; Schneider, 1979, and the discussion below). The time-consuming character of the enterprise has precluded studies that cover both large numbers of issues and large numbers of members. Consequently generalizations are at best tentative. When a member's personal policy preferences and constituency opinion conflict, apparently a relatively uncommon occurrence, the saliency of the issue appears to determine whether personal policy preference or constituency governs vote choice.

The ease of 'measuring' party seems to have inhibited careful conceptualization. Since at least Turner's time, roll-call analysts have been repeating that party membership is the single best predictor of vote, frequently without careful thought about what may be meant by that statement. If members of a party vote together, is it because they represent similar districts, or because they share policy views due perhaps to recruitment processes, or because congressional or extra-congressional party leaders possess rewards and sanctions with which to enforce party loyalty, or some combination of these? The extent of party voting over time appears to vary with the sanctions available to leaders and with the extent to which party members represent similar districts (Cooper et al., 1977; Cooper and Brady, 1981). Members who represent districts typical of their party tend to display higher party unity than those from atypical districts. A full answer, however, awaits progress on the constituency-influence hypotheses.

Although we have no definitive answers to questions about the determinants of congressional voting behaviour, we have made some progress and the routes towards further progress are fairly clear. Furthermore, roll-call analysis has been and will continue to be a useful tool in studies that focus upon dependent variables at the level of the institution. Scholars interested in the structure of conflict and the character of policy coalitions over time have made particularly extensive use of roll-call analysis.

3.3 Interviewing and Participant Observation

As valuable as roll-call analysis can be, there are many questions that it cannot answer. Pre-floor collective decision-making processes, specifically committee decision-making, can be only very partially studied via the analysis of committee roll calls. Often to understand floor voting alignments and floor outcomes we need data on various members' non-floor behaviour. If our interest is in the representational relationship between member and constituency, the members' voting behaviour may be the focus, but certainly other constituency-related behaviours should not be ignored. Whether the dependent variable of ultimate interest is at the level of the individual member or of the institution, we often need data on members' perceptions and attitudes, on their explanations of their own and others' behaviour and on member behaviour that is not on the public record. Interviewing and participant observation are the techniques available for obtaining such data.

Because the technique is better known, we will begin with a discussion of the interview. We will forego a general discussion and focus specifically on the congressional interview. After discussing the problem of access, we will cover questions of design and technique including questions about how structured a questionnaire is possible and desirable. We close with an assessment of the reliability of the data thus gathered.

In elite interviewing, questions of access always loom large. Obtaining access to members of Congress for interviews has become distinctly more difficult in the last ten or fifteen years. It is by no means so difficult as to make interview-based studies impossible for most political scientists, however. Access has become more difficult because the time demands on members have increased and because there are more scholars seeking interviews. There has been no increase and, in fact, there appears to have been a decrease in suspicion of academics. Membership replacement seems to have reduced to a very small number those who are actively hostile towards and suspicious of academics and consequently unwilling to talk to them. Most current members of Congress are quite well educated and, while they may not feel any sort of kinship with academics, they also do not feel insecure in their presence. The problem is not that members of Congress dislike talking with academics; the problem is time pressure.

This has direct implications for what it takes to gain access. First, being connected with a university, certainly as a professor but usually also as a graduate student, is sufficient to establish one's *bona fides*. Secondly, the greater the time pressure on a member the more difficult he is to see. This relationship results in problems of access being sufficiently different for House and Senate to warrant separate discussions.

Members of the House represent a smaller constituency, serve on fewer committees and are in less demand by the news media than senators. Consequently, although very busy, they are nevertheless much easier to gain access to than senators. There are, of course, exceptions. However, in our experience, only the Speaker of the House is as difficult to get an interview with as the typical senator. Thus, the primary prerequisites to interviewing House members are time and persistence. Most interviews will take place in Washington, DC and the researcher must be prepared to spend an extended period there – usually at least a week at a time. Arriving for an interview only to have it postponed is probably the norm rather than the exception. In such cases, the member's scheduler almost always seems to feel an obligation to reschedule the interview, but the researcher must be in Washington to take advantage of that. Having to wait well beyond the scheduled hour is definitely the norm. Consequently, one must leave considerable time between interviews. Two in the morning and two in the afternoon is the outside limit.

How is the initial interview obtained? Most scholars send a letter explaining who they are, what they are studying – very generally, details are neither necessary nor desirable – and asking for an interview. This is then followed up with a telephone call during which one attempts to actually set up the interview. In our experience, members' schedulers never simply say 'No, the congressman will never be able to see you.' They may, of course, say that the member has no time available during the period you will be in Washington. If this is a member you really want to interview and you will be in Washington for more than a few days, you say – politely – that, when you are in Washington, you will go by the member's office just to check if some time has become available. This you do, and you keep doing it. If nothing works out during that visit, you go through the same procedure the next time you are in Washington. Such persistence usually pays off. The staff interprets your willingness to invest your time as a sign of your serious intent, which it is, and they may come to feel they owe you something for it. Needless to say, it is critical that you remain pleasant and polite throughout such efforts. Staff are the gatekeepers; they can help or hinder the researcher's efforts to gain access immensely.

As an alternative or in addition to sheer doggedness, connections can help. The very best connection with a member of the House is to be a constituent; simply being from the same state helps. Obviously having an influential constituent or a respected House colleague speak for you can be very helpful. But by and large, while such connections, if you happen to have them, can make your life easier, they are not essential to obtaining an interview with most House members.

Gaining access to senators is a great deal more difficult. Unless one has excellent connections one can activate, a frequently lengthy cultivation of staff is often the only route. After one has got to know and has established a relationship of trust with senior staff, they may arrange an interview with the senator. This process is likely to take weeks or months, not days. Staff can, of course, be valuable sources of information in their own right. Appointment secretaries and even receptionists are usually knowledgeable and helpful in pinpointing which staffers perform various functions and which have been with the member for an extended period and thus are likely to be familiar with his thinking.

Once access has been gained, what can be expected of the interview? How frank are members likely to be? The Congress is a very open institution; most of its official business is conducted in open meetings. That which takes place behind closed doors seldom stays secret for long. Although individual members, of course, vary in their personal tendency towards openness, all must adjust to functioning in this open system and most learn that a reasonable level of frankness is, on balance, helpful. Our experience is that most members are quite frank in interviews, perhaps surprisingly so. Candidness does depend upon some factors that the interviewer can control. It is important that the member realizes you are a scholar and not a reporter and that his words will not appear in the newspaper the next morning. Most congressional scholars conduct interviews on a not-for-attribution basis; that is, the scholar may quote from an interview but will not reveal the speaker's identity. It is also important that the member realizes that you are not a political neophyte or a moralist, that you understand and do not condemn the political process. All members have a high school civics book lecture that they use with political amateurs. If, during an interview, a member answers a question in that vein it is essential politely to establish your expertise. Usually one or two comments illustrating that you understand how the process really works will be sufficient to get the member to shift gears and begin talking to you as a fellow professional. Because, to get beyond the civics book lecture one must establish one's expertise, using interviewers who are not social scientists is not recommended. Because they lack the specialized knowledge, even highly trained interviewers do not obtain the kind of depth and sophistication in their interviews that an experienced political scientist will (see Peabody, 1969, pp. 30–1).

Our experience is that, on the average, members tend to be more candid than staff and senior staff more candid than junior staff. Less secure and less experienced junior staffers may tend to be overly protective of the member (and of their own position). Consequently, they require more assurance that one has no incentive to 'kiss and tell'. Another but usually easily spotted problem is the junior staffer who does not want to admit his ignorance and reports his guesses as facts.

Related to the issue of frankness is the question of whether or not to use a tape recorder. Members of Congress are used to being tape recorded and will not be inhibited in an obvious way. Whether they are less candid when a recorder is used we simply do not know. Richard Fenno, almost certainly the most skilled interviewer among congressional scholars, refuses to use a recorder because it might reduce frankness (Fenno, 1978, pp. 279–87). Fenno has done extensive interviewing both with and without a recorder, and is nevertheless uncertain about a recorder's impact. Certainly when an interview covers a large number of different topics, a recording is invaluable; memory is most difficult in those cases. Being free from any note taking during the course of an interview aids the establishment of rapport and allows the interviewer to concentrate on appropriate follow-up questions. Use of a recorder also allows the scheduling of appointments somewhat more closely together. When a recorder is not used, it is essential for notes to be written up immediately after the interview. Nevertheless, even if use of a recorder is planned, one must be prepared to do without it. Although interviews are usually scheduled for the member's office, they may actually take place elsewhere. Often interviews with House members take place in the Rayburn Room, a large and usually noisy room off the floor of the House. Many interviews occur at least in part on the run as the member, questioning political scientist in tow, hurries from his office to the Capitol for a roll call. Probably the majority of congressional staffers work in surroundings noisy enough to make taping difficult. A final practical problem with using a recorder is the cost of transcription, which is very high. Thus, the question of whether or not to tape has no easy answer.

Whether to attempt a probability sample is another design question to which it is difficult to give a definitive answer. Of course, the research problem will be a primary determinant. If a subgroup of the Congress is being studied – a committee, an ideological grouping, a state delegation – it may be possible and desirable to interview all its members. If complete interviewing is not possible, should one attempt a true probability sample? Since a probability sample would always be scientifically preferable, the question is one of feasibility. Given problems of access, it is probably not worth trying in the Senate. The response rate is likely to be low; thus, substitutions will have to be made which call the sample's representativeness into question. Yet the costs of attempting to implement a sample are likely to be high. Probably the best one can do if interviews with the senator are necessary is to make sure various important types of senators are included in one's 'sample'. What the important types are depends upon the research question, but among the variables on which one is likely to want variation are partisanship, region (especially south/non-south within the Democratic party), ideology, and seniority. On the House side, in contrast, actually implementing a study based on a probability sample is much more feasible. John Kingdon (1973), for example, did so successfully in his study of how House members make up their minds on specific floor votes – a research problem that might be considered sensitive and, thus, one on which one might expect participation to be a problem. To ensure representativeness, Kingdon divided the House membership into strata on the basis of party regional membership (southern Democrats, northern Democrats and Republicans) and of three gradations of seniority and then sampled within strata.

How structured the interview should be depends upon the research question. Few congressional scholars have used the fully structured interview of the survey research type. The best known such study is the Miller–Stokes representation study. A sample of incumbent House members, their opponents and a sample of constituents were interviewed immediately after the 1958 congressional elections. A long (seventy-question) and highly structured interview schedule was used with members. The results indicate that it is possible to use such a questionnaire with members of Congress. Most of the interviews were completed; at least responses were obtained to all fixed-choice questions (Peabody, 1969, p. 30). However, according to Robert Peabody, a political scientist with extensive experience interviewing congressmen, 'only the top ten percent or so [of the Miller–Stokes interviews] would match the average quality of depth, content and sophistication that a close student of Congress can obtain using focused interviewing techniques' (Peabody, 1969, pp. 30–1). Whenever survey research is chosen over an alternative such as in-depth interviews, depth is sacrificed for breadth and representativeness. When the population of interest is an elite, the choice is often more difficult because there exists more depth to be sacrificed.

The semi-structured interview is most frequently used by congressional scholars. The interviewer has a core set of open-ended questions that he or she supplements liberally with probes and questions tailored to the specific member. The order in which the core questions are asked may vary if, for example, the member's answer to one question leads naturally to a subject other than that on the schedule. Uniformity will be sacrificed if the alternative is disrupting the flow of the interview. This sort of hybrid, flexible approach appears optimum for studies that require some quantifiable data but also a good deal of in-depth interpretative material. It is also consonant with the realities of the interview situation. If one knows that the interview may be cut short, one can ask the most important questions first. Information and insights gleaned from early interviews can be used to inform the questions asked in later interviews. If an event of interest occurs during the course of one's interviewing, new questions concerning it can be added.

The richness and flexibility characteristic of semi-structured interviews are bought at a price. The comparability across cases of data obtained from such unstandardized interviews can be questioned. In survey research, the interviewer is supposed to present the respondents with a uniform set of stimuli. The semi-structured interview which is tailored to the individual respondent obviously does not meet that criterion. On the other hand, one would expect the attitudes and perceptions of members of Congress to be well formed and stable; consequently, their expression should not be strongly influenced by extraneous factors such as question ordering.

There are always sufficient questions about the reliability of interview data, whether obtained with a fully or semi-structured schedule, to make independent checks highly desirable. Some sorts of information cannot be checked, but frequently other informants or even documents can provide at least partial verification. This is particularly possible and important when the interviewer is attempting to reconstruct events that occurred in the past. Because of the pace of life on Capitol Hill, memories seem to decay quickly; members and staffers easily confuse similar past events. Documents such as committee hearing transcripts and the Congressional Record, specialized publications such as *Congressional Quarterly Weekly Report* and *National Journal*, and even newspaper reports, will sometimes provide a check on information supplied in interviews.

An interview-based study requires that the researcher know enough about the problem at issue to be able to formulate an appropriate questionnaire. If the research problem is one on which little is yet known, participant observation may be a better research strategy. Participant observation is also an excellent choice when the research focuses on a process.

Participant observation, as the term implies, entails a situation in which the researcher participates in and observes over an extended period of time that which he or she is studying. For example, a congressional scholar interested in the decision-making process of a particular committee might serve for a time as a professional staff member for that committee.

Congress is now an extremely open institution and access for participant observations is remarkably easy. Political scientists have spent time in the offices of the House Majority Leader and the

Majority Whip, on the staff of the Senate Policy Committee and the House Steering and Policy Committee, both party committees, and on the staffs of many of the committees as well as in the offices of many individual members, House and Senate. Quite a lot of this participant observation has occurred under the auspices of the American Political Science Association's Congressional Fellowship Program and that program's good reputation certainly eases problems of access. Such sponsorship is not, however, essential.

Participant observation as a research strategy has some fairly obvious strengths. The researcher is often able actually to observe the phenomenon of interest and to do so repeatedly. The in-depth exposure enables the researcher to come to understand the perceptions of the various participants. Getting to know the participants obviously eases problems of access and increases rapport for interviews, which are always a component of such studies.

A primary disadvantage is the amount of time required. Most such studies require the researcher to devote a number of months to the project and all at one time. Gaining access usually depends upon the researcher agreeing to provide a service in return: usually to serve as a professional staff member.

A danger of this sort of research is that the researcher will 'go native'; that he or she will become so psychologically involved as a participant that scholarly observation is no longer possible. While there is no sure guard against that possibility, proper preparation for, and procedure during, the research make it less likely. Although research may be begun without clearly formulated hypotheses, one should have at least a preliminary list of variables or factors on which one intends to collect data. Periodic re-evaluation and revision of that list and, if possible, the formulation of preliminary hypotheses must be a part of the research plan, as must daily note taking. (By far the best discussion of participant observation as a strategy for congressional research is by Richard Fenno. See his Appendix in *Home Style*, 1978.)

3.4 Conclusion

Scholars who study the members of European legislatures sometimes have to justify their pursuit. What can be learned, they are asked, by studying the members of a body with little or no power independent of the executive, especially when those members have little or no autonomy of action? Congressional scholars do not confront any such challenge to justify their study. The United States political process, it is generally acknowledged, cannot be understood without understanding the Congress, and the Congress cannot be understood without understanding the behaviour of its members as individuals. Consequently an extremely broad range of questions at the level of the individual member as well as at the level of the institution are considered worthy of study prima facie.

The wealth of data sources available for studying the United States Congress are, in part, a result of its unique characteristics. The Constitution requires the recording of roll-call votes and the lack of strict party-line voting makes them interesting to analyse. Roll-call data are available in machine-readable form for the entire period of United States history.

In the course of legislating, the United States Congress produces a flood of documentary material. Committee hearing transcripts, committee reports and the 'Congressional Record' are the most useful to political scientists. The first provides information on the individuals and groups that testify on a given piece of legislation, their positions and the arguments they used; it may also reveal the positions and concerns of committee members. The second is the committee's justification of the bill it reports and may also contain dissenting views. If one is studying committee decision-making both are invaluable sources; they are not, however, sufficient in themselves because the process of negotiation and compromise so characteristic of congressional committee decision-making is seldom explicitly described. *The Congressional Record* purports to be a verbatim record of what occurs on the House and Senate floors and, in fact, is a serviceable record.

Because what the Congress does has an impact upon many groups in society, secondary materials about the Congress have proliferated. Congressional Quarterly, Inc. has published a weekly report on congressional activities since 1946. It also publishes a yearly summary *Almanac* and numerous special reports, on committee and subcommittee assignments and on congressional elections, for example. The *National Journal*, a newer publication and less exclusively focused upon Congress, also frequently provides useful in-depth coverage. The *Almanac of American Politics* and *Politics in America: Members of Congress in Washington and At Home*, the former now published by the *National Journal*, the latter published by Congressional Quarterly Press, are biennial volumes which provide biographical and political data on all members of Congress and demographic and political data on their districts. *Vital Statistics on Congress*, a recent addition to the growing body of reference works, is also biennial and collects together a large number of time series on the congressional membership, committees, staffing, workload and voting alignments.

The political scientist can also have direct access to the Congress and its members. Not only are virtually all floor sessions open to the public, most committee meetings are also. While access for interviews is perhaps more difficult to obtain than it used to be, it is certainly feasible to conduct interview-based research.

Compared with the other two branches of government, the Congress is incredibly open and easy to study. The result has been a very substantial body of excellent work. And, as a recent series of review articles in *Legislative Studies Quarterly* (1983–85) makes clear, congressional scholarship both in quantity and quality far exceeds the work on other legislatures.

Congressional scholars can perhaps be faulted for not always exploiting available resources as fully and imaginatively as possible, for allowing our relative wealth to sometimes make us lazy. It is difficult to argue that unavailability of data (except constituency data) or underdevelopment of analytic techniques are major barriers to progress in congressional research.

4

Interviewing party-political elites in Italy

GEOFFREY PRIDHAM
University of Bristol

4.1 Introduction: Elite Interviewing and Research on Political Parties

There are many possible advantages both practical and conceptual in using elite interviews as a research tool. Very broadly, they may be categorized as the 'objective' and 'subjective'. The former usually includes acquiring or confirming data or cross-checking information from other sources whether verbal or printed. For instance, the 'truth' about the inside story of a political event may be sought by questioning different participants involved in varying or conflicting roles. The 'subjective' advantages depend, of course, on the nature of the investigation, but they tend to mean revealing or probing attitudes as through in-depth interviews. Obviously, there is room for certain forms of overlap between these two advantages – such as in the element of subjectivity in the presentation of information, like tendentiousness or memory bias; while attitudes may have from the researcher's viewpoint an intrinsic 'objective' quality because they describe patterns of outlook which could be representative of the elite in question.

This overlap between the 'objective' and 'subjective' is most in evidence when focusing on the relationship between attitudes and behaviour, in any case a complex area since a variety of factors such as character traits and environmental determinants may impinge on this relationship – all of which may be highlighted more sharply by the interview technique. One extra side-effect of interviews may be to crystallize some interpretative slant on the research topic which may not necessarily originate directly in the interview; but which may have germinated already and be stimulated by the course of

ELITES IN ITALY 73

discussion – the welcome testing of hypotheses. Naturally, the actual value of elite interviews depends on whether they offer a central or secondary means of fulfilling a research project; and this depends first and foremost on the kind of problems being examined, but also on the availability and quality of alternative sources.

These general remarks apply particularly to political parties as an area of study, since one is dealing with a category of elite that, generally speaking in liberal democracies, is more open than most, or at least which is normally in business to be responsive to outside pressures, public opinion and the impact of events. The responsiveness of party elites may in part be determined by the subject of investigation, for some questions are clearly to be regarded as more confidential than others, when comparing such differing aspects as parties' political roles, policy-making, formulation or influence, party strategy, vertical structural relationships within parties and organizational matters. Equally, the specific subject of research may place a greater emphasis on 'subjective' over 'objective' responses or vice versa. Research on political parties in liberal democracies is all the more satisfying because of the common existence of alternative sources, that is, responses from interviewees can more readily than not be checked against printed sources, although the quality of these might vary. Since parties are relatively open institutions they are usually reported on in detail in the press, and their own documentation may be reasonably available to *bona fide* researchers. This is more likely to be the case than say with bureaucratic, business and certainly military elites. Nevertheless, dependence on these alternative sources compared with interviews turns on the kind of party development or behaviour being examined, while their quality, especially that of party material, reflects on the nature of the party in question such as its organizational state.

When interviewing the elites of political parties, there are other factors conditioning the nature of responses quite apart from the individual abilities and willingness of respondents. First, a party's ideological position may affect the reaction to a research programme. In my experience, respondents of the Left have generally been more willing to meet and provide more specific answers than those of the Right for several reasons: the association of political or social scientists and their critical investigative approach vaguely with left-wing sympathies; the fact that parties of the Left usually have a more developed sense of party life as in articulated structures or a tradition of policy debate; hence their activists more easily tune into the mental disposition of academic researchers. This generalization may, however, be qualified where parties of the Left are more 'closed' because of sectarian attitudes or a pronounced sense of party solidarity. Secondly, aspects of 'national culture' may colour the success of one's inquiries although this is a difficult question about which to generalize. For instance, Italy is a supreme case of where academic elites mix with political ones, not merely because a surprising number of active political leaders retain university posts but also as it is quite common for political scientists to engage in part-time journalism; just as political columnists frequently write books that are categorized loosely as 'political science'. I have been frequently mistaken for a 'journalist' even after presenting myself as a university teacher engaged in academic research. Furthermore, a great value seems to be placed among political elites in Italy on 'discussion' and 'talking to someone', in as much as political leaders there are generally ready to conceptualize about the political game in which they are involved. This readiness has been all the more evident because of a traditional interest in foreign opinion about Italy, its problems and its politics. This general accessibility can have different effects. On the one hand, political elites tend to recognize the value of academic research and are therefore potentially very responsive. On the other hand, this cross-fertilization between academic and political circles can create difficulties over political affiliation. However, this problem may well be neutralized or reduced by being a foreigner, for respondents may assume – rightly or wrongly – that a non-Italian background indicates a distance from the party battle in their own country.

My research on Italy has concentrated on change in the party system since the 1960s and more particularly on the dynamics of coalition behaviour or interparty relationships (Pridham, 1981; 1986). The latter project has involved various hypotheses or theoretical concerns: notably, that coalitional behaviour is, in Italy at least, intrinsically complex and therefore for analytical purposes should be treated as multidimensional; that there is an essential difference between party strategies as a general proposition and actual coalitional behaviour within Italy's multi-party setting, the relationship between the two determined by a series of intervening variables (institutional, political and situational); and, specifically, that political leaders are not necessarily free agents here, certainly less so than assumed by traditional coalition theories, for they are subject to different constraints. The inductive theoretical framework developed for this project on Italian coalitional behaviour has been constructed around seven dimensions (Pridham, 1987): historical, institutional, motivational, horizontal/vertical (involving sub-national levels of politics), internal party, sociopolitical and environmental/external (including, for example, international influences). These different dimensions essentially revolve around the ubiquitousness of Italy's *partitocrazia* or 'party democracy', as the most appropriate designation for that country's political system: the parties individually and together play the central part in formulating and deciding policy, in mobilizing support for their proposals and actions as well as in reflecting different sectoral or popular demands; they not only 'populate' the state, but also penetrate society. Put more broadly, the question of attitudes and behaviour and their interrelationship was indeed at the heart of this research programme. As comparative work on elites has shown, there is a strong diversity of motivation among political elites when viewed closely but this has been insufficiently studied systematically (Putnam, 1976, ch. 4). One way of broaching this basic question is to adopt the above-mentioned framework.

Given this multidimensional approach, the need for interviewing party-political elites is really self-evident. This is not merely because Italian coalitional behaviour is a remarkably unresearched field, nor is it generally because political elites in that country have cultivated their alliance politics as a fine art (there are many gradations of alliances ranging from the informal through the semi-formal to formal coalitions) with some aspects less public than others. It is obviously worth interviewing them to explain their role in coalition politics, for like politicians in other countries they rationalize their positions in public. It is primarily as the particular analytical approach adopted innately requires a strong reliance on elite inter-viewing. More specifically, with reference to the seven dimensions detailed above, discussion of the historical one may be largely based on secondary literature and to some extent this is also true of the institu-tional, but the others have to draw primarily on interview material.

4.2   Planning for Interviews

A strategic choice has as a general rule to be made – the sooner the better – about the exact potential interviews offer for satisfying the research objectives, since that determines basically both the selection and content of interviews. This entails thinking ahead and there are broadly three areas where preparatory planning is necessary: (1) the categorization and selection of respondents; (2) making contact with them; and (3) preparing for interviews.

(1)   Selection of respondents

Various theoretical considerations about elite identification arise in this the most taxing area of preparation, notably over the representativeness of the prospective sampling. For instance, Putnam has summarized much thinking on the problem of 'finding the powerful' among 'a number of functionally differentiated groupings' as following broadly three lines of inquiry: the positional, reputational and decisional strategies for identifying elites (Putnam, 1976, pp. 15–18). The main underlying difficulty concerns the interdependence of working hypotheses, research procedure and project results, for the answers to initial definitional problems are bound to influence the nature of the data which later emerge.

Seeing that political parties are the broad theme of this chapter, we are talking about such conceptual questions as the nature and location of power within them, the diversity of influences on their behaviour, variation between types of parties and not least their relationship with the state and with society. So far as Italy is concerned, there is considerable variation between the main parties which have dominated the scene and which tend to be highly structured (especially the Italian Communist Party (PCI)) and the range of different small parties which are not. In any case the paramount importance of person-to-person channels in Italy (which any researcher meets very soon) induces a certain scepticism about the formalities of political life there. All this might appear to confuse any conceptual design for the selection of respondents, or more constructively it points to combining the three strategies mentioned above. Nevertheless, as elite identification ultimately depends on the actual form of party behaviour being examined, we now turn to the research projects carried out in which elite interviews were employed.

The earlier work on Italy involved a regional case study of party developments in a period of, for post-war Italy, unprecedented change (e.g. Tuscany in the 1970s), and as such was more straightforward than the later project on coalitional behaviour in that country as a whole. The former project was geographically confined to thirty communes (selected according to economic structure, size of population and political tendency) in four provinces apart from the regional level of party activity, located in the capital city of Florence. Within that area, the decision was taken to concentrate on the main three parties (equally dominant in Tuscany as nationally, though with government/opposition roles reversed between the Christian Democrats (DC) and PCI for systematic interviewing, with respondents from small parties selected less rigorously. It was then a matter of identifying the relevant elites: at the regional level, party secretaries or key functionaries in the party offices were approached as well as leaders of the party groups in the regional council; at the local levels, the principal categories were mayors and party secretaries (or an equivalent influential functionary). It was found particularly in such a geographically and thematically demarcated area study that identifying the relevant elites could well profit from 'asking around' through informal contacts, whether journalistic or political. For instance, socialization patterns, or cross-party and mutual interests were such that rival party elites could prove useful sources for background on their opposite numbers. At the same time, *ad hoc* or individual considerations could impinge on the selection of respondents, e.g. time constraints, the absence or non-availability of intended contacts could settle one case over another within or sometimes outside the same category, not to mention that additional or unplanned contacts occasionally made themselves available and these were hardly ever refused. Altogether, this procedure of selection had sufficient method to it to help mitigate the general problem noted by Putnam 'that the hottest methodological debate has centred on studies of local communities, for the divergence between formal structures is likely to be greater in smaller, simpler social systems' (Putnam, 1976, p. 18).

This regional case study had promised an 'in-depth' treatment of party system change, so that its brief dictated a variety of thematic concerns which to a large extent determined the type of respondents, e.g. how party structures responded to new demands, the relationship between leaders and activists, and how alliance strategies were formulated and pursued. By comparison, the interplay between thematic concerns and possible respondents was much more complex for the later project on Italian coalitional behaviour, commenced in 1981, and accordingly the selection basis less easily definable. This was partly as the project was geographically far less limited for it encompassed the national level as well as selectively subnational levels (five regions and various major cities). Given the focus on Italy's *partitocrazia* as the broad point of departure, one could be guided by various hypotheses about this system: the elite identification should certainly not be exclusively institutional in its approach for, as commonly recognized by Italian specialists, the key operators are located in the central party organizations outside Parliament (although they are often also parliamentarians); and that, so far as possible constraints on elite behaviour were concerned, it was a question among other things of identifying internal party 'gatekeepers' who channelled influences or pressures vertically in addition to horizontal relationships (at the national level) between the party organizations and their representatives in government.

At first, some categories were obvious such as leading members of party secretariats as well as prime ministers and cabinet ministers; also, the heads of the national party departments covering regional and local politics as directly involved in vertical links. Again, more loosely, the fact that many regional and city party politicians were simultaneously members of national party executive organs, where strategic or coalition options are hammered out, meant they were useful both for vertical links and also as inside observers if not participants (apart from the practical advantage of their passing through Rome thus reducing the task of arranging interviews in different localities across the country). But, beyond these categories, the question of flexibility arose in the selection of respondents and this entailed one decision of principle: does one concentrate on a select number of key and/or well-informed interviewees, or how far should one push the systematic rather than random form of sampling in view of the problems of elite identification noted above and the practical or time constraints imposed on a researcher working abroad? Conceptually, such a decision must depend on whether the survey in question is seeking more to gather data, confirm evidence or probe attitudes, but it is equally not free from the interplay between thematic concerns and practical considerations.

(2) Making contact

Making contact with respondents in Italy is not by any means a straightforward application of a selected list of prospective personnel for interview. The first practical point that has to be made is that one needs a private telephone and a great deal of patience. I frequently encountered a mental block about fixing appointments more than a couple of days in advance. Arrangements might or might not work out at the last moment. In some cases, it was necessary to ring even the private numbers given me of contacts early in the morning to establish whether they would be free later that same morning or day. The alternative to a private telephone is to use the local bar where telephoning can be a frustrating activity as it is likely to be a noisy place at any time of the day (people regularly take coffee and talk loudly) and one has to keep finding sufficient telephone disks (*gettoni*), so that any long-distance calls can easily become farcical or infuriating depending on one's style or sense of humour. Sometimes long waits may be required, for as one close observer of the Italian scene has commented:

> Italians have a particularly close relationship with the telephone; not necessarily their own: in fact, the real virtuoso performances usually take place in public, on bar telephones, where the presence of other people acts as a stimulant even if the potential audience is not listening. (*The Times*, 7 December 1982)

As noted earlier, personal channels are the most magical way of opening doors. Writing letters of introduction was not regularly followed as it was felt this did not make a great deal of difference. Telephoning a party office, or preferably going along in person if not too inconvenient, might or might not work, depending on the willingness of the respondent or the efficiency of his secretary. A significant difference emerged, however, between the parties in this respect. PCI personnel were almost without exception responsive in a systematic sort of way, reflecting the organized nature of their party and distinguishing it markedly from the other parties. The Socialists could be similarly responsive, though usually in a less organized manner; while the smaller parties lacked the organizational facilities and mentality, so that contacts had to be made on a very individual basis. The greatest difficulty came with the Christian Democrats, and this derived from their internal structure of organized factions (*correnti*). The problem was not so much organizational as attitudinal in that experience in Tuscany and elsewhere in Italy, at both national and regional levels, strongly suggested that DC personnel from their party's left were much more available than those from other factions. In fact, it became difficult to locate right-wing Christian Democrats who were willing to talk. The apparent reasons were a basic view that politics was about power rather than ideas, making them much less interested than those on the DC left in discussing openly their role with a visiting academic; and the evident belief that social scientists were unlikely to be sympathetic to their political position, ideologically speaking. These assumed reasons seemed confirmed where such Christian Democrats did make themselves available, for they proved to be guarded in their responses to questions. In general, it could be said that practical and attitudinal considerations in pursuing contacts influenced the operation of the research design conspicuously, in addition to those problems already encountered in formulating it.

(3)   Preparing for interviews

There are usually two purposes in using a questionnaire: to translate the research objectives into specific questions, and to assist the interviewer in motivating the respondent to grant the required information (Cannell and Kahn, 1953). In this particular case, the questionnaires were constructed mainly with the first purpose in mind, while the second purpose was more often met by casual methods. The method therefore adopted could be broadly described as in-depth semi-structured elite interviews.

The main form of preparation for the interviews in Tuscany was to construct a questionnaire with three versions according to whether the respondent was active regionally, provincially or locally. These were subdivided similarly with sections explaining briefly the aim of the project, requesting personal-political background, information on the area concerned, party organizational matters, ideological and policy questions, inter-party relationships and miscellaneous questions. There were variations between these three versions in so far as some aspects could be pursued at one level and not others. The questionnaire constructed for the project on coalitional behaviour drew directly on the results of the Tuscany study on this aspect, especially with reference to different internal and external party determinants. These were incorporated into one section on constraints and determinants (supplemented by a diagram explaining my hypothesis here, and shown to respondents for comment), the idea being to evaluate among other things the role of ideology in inter-party alliances not in isolation but against other party factors of a political, structural or electoral kind. Other sections of this questionnaire were: an introduction about general party strategy and relations with other parties; the internal party process of alliance formation (internal divisions over, who instrumentalizes this process and at what level); external or environmental determinants; and the subnational level of alliance formation and its significance for national politics compared with the impact of region-specific factors. The less systematic preparations for interviews included acquiring information from printed or verbal sources on both the prospective interviewee and the area in which he was active, which was brought into the interviews as they progressed to draw out interviewees by showing a knowledge of national or local conditions.

4.3 The Conducting of Interviews

The main methodological conclusion to be drawn from the experience of elite interviewing in Italy is that, whereas the questionnaire was essential for providing a general direction and a specific reference framework, the actual handling of the interviews usually depended on various unpredictables of which the most salient was personal rapport. The general literature on elite interviewing has strongly emphasized the importance of the relationship struck between interviewer and respondent as necessary for drawing out the latter's responses more openly and fully, especially on attitudes (Oppenheim, 1966; Dexter, 1970). Working with Italian party elites has borne out this lesson all too definitely. Building on the common interest in this topic between interviewer as theoretician and respondent as practitioner, the preliminary questions about the purpose of the project (preferably stated succinctly and briefly so as not to bore the interviewee) and his background were important as 'rapport builders'.

This, however, leads us to a number of general problems commonly recognized in the early literature on elite interviewing, for instance, that of controlling the 'interview situation'. It was important that the respondent was clearly aware of the level of political and intellectual sophistication being aimed at. In a few cases, the respondent began by assuming an elementary grasp of Italian politics on the part of the interviewer. Occasionally, a respondent might be such a keen talker that he would grab the microphone from the start, metaphorically if not literally. I recall one instance when the interviewee in question, having just heard my brief exposition of my subject, proceeded to give an extremely lengthy version of his ideas on it and resented interruption. So long as such a response fell within the scope and direction of the questionnaire it did not matter too much, and there are even advantages in seeing how a respondent links analytically the different aspects of the subject; but, it was otherwise preferable to steer him back to the right path, interposing a relevant question where necessary. Another response that had to be watched was a set speech 'explaining' the party line in a rather stereotyped fashion. This may reflect on patterns of party solidarity – it happened in a few cases with Communist party functionaries, though by no means all – but invariably personal rapport could help to overcome this problem.

A principal concern in the interview experience is the actual use made of the questionnaire. Should this provide a strict or systematic framework, or merely a point of reference with elite interviews? The answer must plainly reside with the nature of the inquiry, that is, how much it is seeking to gather data or to probe attitudes. The Italian projects aimed to do both though with more emphasis on attitudes, partly as much relevant data on the party composition of local and regional administrations as well as national governments was available from printed sources. Accordingly, the so-called 'funnel' method was usually favoured in that general questions of party strategy were placed at the beginning before embarking on the more specific aspects of alliance behaviour. These specific aspects include internal party divisions, and questions relating to this should preferably be asked when some degree of confidence has been established in the interview – although there is the risk that this introductory phase might only produce very generalized and non-informative responses. Subsequently, the interview could become geared to the particular experience of the respondent, i.e. those areas about which he or she was most knowledgeable and reliable as an informant. The questionnaire had to be applied flexibly, it was found, in view of the different levels of knowledge, insight and experience of the selected members of the party elites.

In addition to such universal problems of elite interviewing, research experience in Italy has pinpointed a variety of practical or technical matters of possible cross-national relevance. In particular, there is the question of language and with it the use of terminology. This arises at once when contemplating research on a foreign country's politics, particularly in Western Europe where there is a multiplicity of languages with some countries being bilingual or trilingual. One criterion would be whether the political elites in a given country are fluent in English or perhaps French (though not in Italy, where party elites have a low linguistic knowledge). This applies particularly when one is including a given country in a cross-national research project and when its language is difficult or not much spoken abroad. But as a general principle it was regarded as essential to interview elites in their own language, since then they speak much more freely and fully, and the nuances of their responses are more detectable. Another related problem is the use of terminology or conceptual language even when one knows the native language fluently. This is sometimes simply a matter of defining basic terms in reference to party tradition and behaviour, but difficulties could surface involving cross-national cultural differentiation. Indeed, there are also differences of conceptual language used by the various political parties – notably between the Communists with their dialectical style of discussion on the one hand and the Christian Democrats and the centrist parties on the other with their partiality for more 'pragmatic' diction. Italian is, in any case, a language which uses a high degree of conceptual terminology so it is advisable to be aware of differences from English, even with words which have the same linguistic root and look the same.

In generalizing about conducting interviews, it is difficult to escape the conclusion that the problems identified here are very country-specific in the form and the extent to which they arise in practice. Furthermore, party-political variation was salient in the style and organization of interviews (e.g. it was not unusual with the PCI for several functionaries to join in the interview for what turned into a virtual round-table discussion, an occurrence that was rare with the other parties). It was also true for the nature of responses which could vary considerably: Communist interviewees were frequently more explicit and more readily understood the kind of political science questions asked than representatives from the other parties, with the exception of some Socialist respondents.

4.4 The Utilization of Interviews

The main problem here is one of scientific method or what has been called 'transforming the highly subjective process of "getting insights" into a systematic method for the collection of social data' (Cannell and Kahn, 1953). We are therefore faced once more with the relationship between the 'subjective' and the 'objective', but precisely how much this creates difficulties for the utilization of interview material does, of course, depend much on the nature of the inquiry. 'Subjective' or 'biased' responses might be what one is actually looking for as they are revealing of attitudes and possibly motivation, and this was to a valuable degree true of the field work carried out in Italy.

It was found in collating and systematizing this material that mixed impressions soon emerged. One became only too aware of the deficiencies of one's interview approach, particularly in those interviews conducted earlier on since then the broad analytical framework of the project was not so strictly formulated. With the benefit of hindsight, some of these interviews could have been more methodical in pursuing a particular issue – although, in a number of cases, it was possible to re-interview at a later stage. On the other hand, the research theme as a whole began to crystallize in a way and at a pace that was not possible during the research programme in

Italy itself, not least because of time pressures. There are also deficiencies that relate to the interview method as such rather than to circumstances involving respondents, like the problem that responses are always time-bound, the differential style and content of responses between the various parties and those connected with the personal qualities of respondents (intelligence, state of inside knowledge of party affairs, openness, etc.). The first of these, while inevitable, is usually recognizable to the informed researcher and can be taken into account. However much responses may be time-bound, they may well reveal longer time patterns. Putnam noted in the light of his own experience in elite interviewing in Italy that although politicians 'live in a world of foreshortened time perspective . . . it is doubtful that the style of their thought or the pattern of their ideals change markedly from day to day, but the events to which they apply their thought and ideals do' (Putnam, 1973, p. 12).

These various deficiencies do altogether seem to underline the limitations of the 'scientific' potential of the elite interviewing method. But apart from the intrinsic quality or richness of the material, including the extent to which (as in this case) political actors were prepared to lift the curtain on the more confidential side of coalition politics and the informal thoughts or latent assumptions that surface when working on material, what is essential is the means of classifying material. This is all the more important as it may be labour-saving in the business of transcribing material from extensive tape-recordings: in this case, some hundred interviews were carried out in Tuscany, each lasting on average between one and a half and two and a half hours; while for the second project, there have been the same number of interviews of roughly the same length.

The general scheme of categorizing material was as follows:

(1) *Summary notes:* passages which could be listened to for interest, were not worth quoting and demanded only the occasional note-taking, e.g. repetition of a well-known viewpoint, details on a town's political background or on the state of party organization; also included are those sections where respondents were especially verbose or where control of the interview collapsed temporarily.

(2) *Intermittent quotes:* sections that have to be listened to with greater attention, because the occasional sentence or phrase may be worth taking down; also, it is useful to note any revealing features of the nature of the responses that might facilitate interpretation of the subject, e.g. tone of voice, hesitation in

responding to a searching question or some remark of possible significance one may have missed during the interview itself.

(3) *Extensive quotes:* these may be of paragraph length or even longer, and are selected primarily because they encapsulate much insight into, or provide a powerful description of, an aspect of the research subject.

It is important to emphasis with respect to (3) that translating from the Italian was done at the final stage when direct quotation was incorporated into writing, when this was really necessary, because translation is invariably time-consuming. During the preparation for writing up the research results, the method used was to compile reference charts for each prospective chapter section. These would be themselves subdivided according to the key aspects of the theme of the chapter section, and such subdivisions would then be used to classify material thematically. This was done by brief telegram style summaries of the main point of each reference with an indication of the page in the notes of transcriptions. Quite often there were several page references together referring to the same point, whether in interview material or printed sources. Ultimately, reliance on memory proved an important complement to this approach, but it was found that the very exercise of working out the reference charts helped greatly in crystallizing the interpretation of the interview material and pointed to many a conclusion. The main practical purpose of this technique was to facilitate the use of material during the writing process with a clear and easy means of reference via the charts to the sources and the detailed notes on them.

4.5   Elite Interviewing and Other Forms of Research Material

Bearing in mind the point in the introduction about the common existence of alternative sources in work on political parties, some brief comment on these and their relationship to interview material is worthwhile.

Clearly, this relationship basically depends on whether elite interview material is the central or the auxiliary source which may also vary within a project according to the aspect in question.

Broadly speaking, elite interviews provided the principal means of fulfilling both research projects, although other sources were still helpful or even indispensable as background or confirmatory evidence. These could be identified as six types:

(1) *Party documentation:* this usually existed in some form or other, though again variation between parties was the salient feature: this was most abundant in the case of the PCI, reflecting its elaborate organization, and was often detailed and statistical in nature. More often than not, accessible DC material typified the party's style of bland policy statements and one usually needed to be well-versed in party matters to interpret them (e.g. quite often it might emanate from one particular DC faction). Documentation from the smaller parties was sparse and usually consisted of speeches or policy positions. As a general comment, party documentation had a limited value as it amounted to expositions of party strategy rather than providing clues to coalitional behaviour in the wider sense.

(2) *Official statistics:* most useful were those detailing all coalitions whether national, regional or local, and here the researcher in Italy is lucky. The PCI's own electoral studies office provided several compilations of these, while the electoral office of the Ministry of the Interior in Rome had statistical collections although not so well organized. For Tuscany, the regional administration was exceptional among the Italian regions for its statistical publications such as on the party-political composition of all 287 local councils and administrations. All this saved having to rely on interview respondents for hard evidence.

(3) *The press:* this is heavily party-political or interest-affiliated in Italy, but nevertheless if perused carefully can yield some useful information and offer clues, as on the everyday side of coalitional manoeuvres.

(4) *Quantitative surveys:* these were not seriously employed, largely out of a scepticism about their potential value for my particular approach to coalitional behaviour. In the case of the Tuscan study, I made one attempt at a written questionnaire of the members of the regional council, but the response rate was poor and the results were not that fruitful. On the subject of professional surveys, poll institutes have done occasional surveys of attitudes among party members on alliance preferences, which were quotable but, again, subsidiary to more direct evidence on how coalition politics operated.

(5) *Books and articles:* given the neglect of this subject, these proved auxiliary rather than central for researching coalitional behaviour. These are either historical and/or journalistic and as such informative rather than elucidating; while academic monographs or even articles have been few and far between.

Italian archives and libraries are notoriously disorganized and inefficient, but fortunately the contemporary slant of the projects and the lack of secondary literature made reliance on them minimal.

(6) Current research by other academics, especially in Italy: this existed, though almost entirely on local politics, and opportunities for contact were taken during visits to Italy.

4.6 Conclusion

Referring back to the opening theme of this chapter, it is not always easy and is sometimes impossible to disengage the 'objective' and 'subjective' responses in elite interviews from each other. But this may well be less of a problem than appears at first sight, for so much depends on the subject of investigation and the demands of its research goals and design. Furthermore, all the way through a perpetual interplay between theoretical concerns and practical and human considerations is encountered. Elite interviewing like other methods of research involves a continuous learning process.

There is evidently much room for variation in this experience associated with cross-national differences as well as the general theme of study. However, what about general lessons on the methods and discipline of elite interviewing? One reaction has to be a certain dissatisfaction with the strictly 'scientific' quality of this form of research, quite apart from its intrinsic interest value, its stimulating effects and the richness of feedback. The main problem derives from the fact that material from in-depth elite interviews, notably when probing attitudes, is not readily systematized, or for that matter computable. While a well-ordered questionnaire is crucial in providing a general direction and a specific reference framework for conducting interviews as well as a basis on which to evaluate the results, it has to be applied flexibly if only because of varying personal abilities and information levels on the part of respondents. Other factors inhibiting the 'scientific' nature of this form of investigation would be the period-boundness to interview responses and, mentioned in various contexts, the differential reactions from different party elites. These deficiencies may in part be overcome by methodical techniques of arranging interview material, but ultimately the researcher has also to depend on his or her own developed grasp of the research subject. This reliance on individual judgement in addition to or in place of quantitative methods of organizing the results is perhaps inescapable in view of the likely overlap between 'objective' and 'subjective' evidence noted before.

Nevertheless, to summarize the whole experience, one should not be too sceptical about its academic value for there are a variety of benefits. Elite interviewing is essentially more a qualitative than a quantitative exercise, its role particularly that of providing hard information and illuminating insights as well as testing hypotheses even if not always in a rigorous manner. Its importance in research is all the more crucial when there is a dearth of other appropriate sources, as in the projects outlined in this chapter.

5

Studying a religious elite: the case of the Anglican episcopate

KENNETH MEDHURST
University of Stirling

GEORGE MOYSER
University of Manchester

5.1 Introduction

This chapter arises from an investigation which sought to interpret the Established Church of England's role in the nation's social and, particularly, political life (Medhurst and Moyser, 1982; 1985). We have investigated the Church's internal distributions of authority in order to see how these affect links with the national polity. Within this context it must be recalled that the Church now enjoys a significant amount of self-government. Though still ultimately subject to Parliament, the latter has devolved its powers in ecclesiastical matters to a tri-cameral and largely elected Synod representing laity, clergy and bishops. The last are now constrained to share their authority with others. Since 1976 they have also been the subject of a revised appointments system involving greater consultation among churchmen. The monarch still appoints on Prime Ministerial advice but only after expressions of largely binding ecclesiastical opinion. Our general concern has been to understand the factors underlying these developments and their implications for the Church's contribution to public debate. We have also examined how its leadership has reacted and contributed to the changes under review.

We initially endeavoured to set this agenda in an historical context

We wish to acknowledge the financial assistance of the British Economic and Social Research Council for the project on which this chapter is based.

by consulting standard historical works and relevant sociological materials (Gilbert, 1980; Welsby, 1984). This meant becoming sensitive to developments over very long periods. It became apparent that many of the Church of England's prevailing assumptions were so deeply embedded in long-established social frameworks, that some account had to be taken of pre-mediaeval, mediaeval and post-Reformation history. Our criteria of relevance became greatly extended as a direct consequence of our initial work. In doing so, we were aware that successful biographies of English episcopal leaders have often been written by those whose training or background makes them very conscious of the historical dimension. In approaching our contemporary materials, we were made aware that the significance of many phenomena could not adequately be grasped without at least implicit understandings of historically conditioned assumptions or structures.

In considering the role of the contemporary Anglican leadership we embarked with a broadly positivistic approach. Notwithstanding our own personal commitment to ecclesiastical institutions, we were concerned to isolate general trends, patterns or relationships between otherwise apparently discrete phenomena with a view to identifying the extent to which the behaviour of those concerned was the product, respectively, of social, economic, political or ideological/ theological factors. The aim was to step well back from the institution and its environment so as to generate hypotheses likely to elude those enmeshed in its daily operations. Thus, when we came to evaluate the elected (non-episcopal) Houses of the Synod, we employed relatively standard survey techniques of a sort conventionally associated with this general style of research. Three mailed questionnaires implemented over a six-year period not only enabled us to assemble a unique body of evidence concerning ecclesiastical activities, values and opinions, but also made possible some charting of processes of change within the Church.

Even here, however, some empathy with those concerned was appropriate. Such empathy is arguably necessary if all the appropriate questions are to be asked. For example, we identified strikingly systematic correlations or affinities between particular sets of political attitudes and particular theological positions. These correlations were obviously no accident and raise major questions about the way belief systems among such individuals come to be formed. But they could not have been uncovered if theological niceties, not generally of concern to social scientists, had been ignored (Gill, 1975; 1977). Similarly, even when it was a matter of handling a relatively straightforward questionnaire, understanding would sometimes have been impossible without knowledge of the specialized and even coded language of theological and ecclesiastical discourse. Obviously enough, there is the danger that respondents of specialized questionnaires (and still more respondents in face-to-face encounters) would be alienated by inappropriate use of specialized jargon. Such mistakes would undermine the credentials of the investigator. The respect of those concerned has, at least in some measure, to be earned by careful preparation.

The questionnaire material provided an indispensable background to the next major phase of our enquiry which was to study the backgrounds, attitudes and behaviour of episcopal and related Church leaders. In this instance, the structured questionnaire method was rejected. An earlier experience had indicated that bishops were unlikely to reply in appropriate numbers.[1] Our main objection, however, was scholarly. Use of the structured questionnaire method, albeit in postal rather than face-to-face form, had exposed its limitations. There was a tendency to impose our own presuppositions and so to limit the options open to respondents. Similarly, this method necessarily tends to filter out a sense of the uniqueness of individual contributions, to treat them solely in terms of statistical aggregates. In short, with an elite of this kind, there seemed a need to balance the search for positivist patterns and uniformities with a phenomenological concern for the personal or individual. Not least, relatively open-ended and unstructured interviews made some opportunity for entering the mind of those concerned and of seeing the world as they might see it.

In a sense, interviews play some part in confronting the perennial problem of biographers. This is partly to amass relevant factual detail of a 'scientific' kind but is also to create out of this information a rounded picture which conveys the main-springs of conduct, what there is of coherence in the individual's life and a sense of his or her overall impact on the world around. It would be pretentious to assume that a series of even lengthy interviews with a group like the English bishops could accomplish such a large task but it may be a useful tool to this general end. This is not least true given that, within the elite in question, there are major differences in the roles or impact of individuals, partly stemming from occupancy of specific posts (the two archbishops and bishops of such sees as London, Durham and Winchester are in a distinct category from others) and partly from spiritual or intellectual qualities.

5.2   Setting Up Interviews

The obvious problem is that of gaining access to those concerned. In our case, this generally proved relatively straightforward because of certain advantages of which we were possessed. First, work already done and published in Church journals had a certain legitimizing effect. Indeed, resistance initially encountered in attempting our postal surveys gave way to later requests for help in the execution of a similar quasi-official enterprise. Such a status can entail dangers that we will later discuss but it undoubtedly helped to open doors of heavily committed people who might otherwise have been on their guard against academic inquirers. Secondly, our initial interviews were facilitated by personal recommendations from eminent academic theologians themselves 'linked with' ecclesiastical networks. Our own involvement in academic 'dialogue' between theology and the social sciences was obviously helpful in this respect. Accreditation from our financial backers, the British Economic and Social Research Council, provided help of another kind in establishing *bona fides*.

Thirdly, it should perhaps be observed that both investigators could truthfully represent themselves not only as academic observers but also as active members of orthodox Christian communities and, in one case, of the Anglican Church itself. This undoubtedly helped to neutralize any idea that we could be in the business of mischief-making or debunking. It may also have demonstrated our willingness or capacity to empathize with the values and aims of those concerned. We argued that social science methods could be used sympathetically to increase the Church's own self-awareness. Indeed, some interviewees responded in like manner. They claimed to see our encounters as not merely a personal favour but perhaps as a means of illuminating the institution they served. We acknowledge possible dangers in such complicity but here simply wish to underline what might make for relatively easy access. Finally, the comparative novelty of our particular enterprise gave us the bargaining power of a kind less readily available to those working in already well-researched fields.

However, some of these apparent assets were potentially two-edged weapons. First, support from academic theologians might, in the case of some conservative bishops of High Church or Evangelical background, give rise to some 'consumer resistance'. The interviewer might be held guilty, by association, of holding heterodox 'liberal' positions. Secondly, whereas some respondents positively evaluated social science credentials as a possible guarantee of cool detachment, others apparently feared sociological reductionism and a trespassing on 'sacred' ground.

This is partly explicable in terms of the academic background of those concerned. None was trained in the social sciences and only a handful had active social scientific interests.[2] Nevertheless, similar experiences gained by one of us in studying a highly traditional South American Roman Catholic hierarchy suggests that this particular problem is probably much less acute in the case of Anglican leaders than in the case of some other religious elites. The Anglican Church is traditionally quite tolerant of ideological diversity and is sufficiently well integrated into the surrounding society and with the academic community to leave open doors that, in the case of more enclosed or sectarian communities, might be shut (Wallis, 1976a and b). It is striking that, out of a total of forty-four diocesan bishops interviewed by us, only two offered initial resistance and only a further one admitted to hesitations. If anything, our problems were not so much those of gaining access but the severely practical issues of criss-crossing the country to sometimes inaccessible residences and fitting in with the schedules of already over-burdened figures.

5.3 The Interview Situation

The conduct of the interviews themselves raised a number of methodological issues. Questions had to be devised which simultaneously satisfied the demands of a tight schedule and of academic illumination. Deliberate reliance on open-ended questions that afforded respondents ample opportunity to think aloud and possibly to volunteer otherwise unavailable information made this particularly difficult. Some structure or sense of direction had to be inserted by us in order to elicit materials of a more or less comparable kind. Otherwise, something approximating to a 'stream of conscious-ness' approach seemed appropriate. This had the advantage of shedding light in dark corners or opening up lines of inquiry that the uninitiated might fail to anticipate. Such methods avoid the limitations or distortions entailed in imposing a carefully pre-arranged agenda – an agenda which implicitly assumes that the inquirer is already aware of all the relevant dimensions of a given issue. It enables the observer, in ways otherwise more difficult to achieve, to enter into the minds of interviewees and to tap their distinctive expertise.

There are, however, associated disadvantages. Not least, it means generating hypotheses that may not always be testable with reference to all the individuals concerned. In that sense, the methodological purist might see some loss of academic rigor. But this seems a small price to pay for the richness, diversity and even intimacy of the evidence thus accumulated. In any case, such evidence, when taken together with written sources, may well provide the basis for significant if provisional generalizations.

This general approach also raises problems of a more severely practical kind, albeit with possible methodological implications. Thus, in a relatively fleeting encounter involving perhaps complex flows of ideas there is none of that time for reflection which encounters with the printed page make possible. Negotiating the cross-currents while simultaneously pressing in an ultimately appropriate direction is a skilled business. By the same token, there is a danger of losing the initiative and so wasting precious opportunities. There is always the possibility of interviewees accidentally or deliberately holding the enquirer at bay with streams of possibly irrelevant or purely anecdotal material.

In our particular case, the enterprise was rendered more complex but also more potentially rewarding by operating as a team. Ill-coordinated teamwork could muddy the waters and alienate interviewees. However, a basic sympathy between the two partners makes for a division of labour which enables one fruitfully to complement the other.

Such considerations point to factors of a more obviously methodological kind that need to be given attention in the research process. Obviously, an interview is quite unlike any other method of acquiring insights for it inevitably involves complex flows of sympathy or traffics in personal influence. Whereas the researcher responds to the printed page in the light of previous knowledge or prejudices, an interview involves a two-sided effort to exercise influence and a certain striking of implicit or even explicit bargains (see Bogdan and Taylor, 1975). Equally, it is a matter of actively seeking to establish a general climate within which transactions may be most productively pursued. One elementary but important point concerns mechanical aids. While having self-evident advantages, the recording of conversations can present practical and even ethical difficulties. On the practical level, there is the possibly inhibiting effect of tape-recorders. We, however, rarely found this to be the case. For the vast majority there was already sufficient trust to overcome opposition to recording. Equally, we have no reason to believe that the flow of conversation was unduly affected. It is true that, on occasions, we were asked to switch our machine off so that the interviewee could make a delicate point about an episcopal colleague or some as yet unfinalized ecclesiastical decision. Most, however, quickly adapted to the taping process and behaved as if engaged in normal conversation.[3] Indeed, being freed ourselves from lengthy and conspicuous note-taking, we could play our part in sustaining a friendly relationship which might not otherwise have been possible.

At the same time, we noticed that useful background information often came from informal asides made before or after recording. In principle, these too formed part of that general set of impressions out of which a more carefully designed pattern could be finally woven. Such asides can easily be neglected. To do so, however, is dangerous for they may convey crucial messages concerning the substance of recorded exchanges and the weight to be attached to them.

The question of quality of information raises the fundamental issue of the particular attitude or stance to be adopted in interviews. In principle, this might range from the inquisitorial or adversarial posture to the deferential. In practice, it seems that interviews are likely to be a blend of differing approaches with the mixture varying somewhat according to the individuals or issues concerned. In our particular case, the general tendency was to veer in the direction of the more deferential or polite approach. This was partly a matter of personal inclination but more importantly it was because of the particular elite involved. Virtually from the outset, it was apparent that they normally operated within a consensual and eirenic frame of reference. Even when sincerely complaining of exaggerated deference being shown to them it was evident that they were not accustomed to that type of tough questioning which politicians might regard as an acceptable occupational hazard. Occasionally, when faced with vacillation or particularly controversial assertions, we invoked less gentle tactics. But if these proved successful it was because they occurred in the context of otherwise courteous conversations in which considerable trust and rapport had already been established. The obvious and general expectation of our interviewees, based on the mores of the institution with which they identify, was that we would respond amiably to the courteous tone they themselves set.

There are potential pitfalls in this strategy or style. There is the possibility of being drawn into complicity with the interviewee and even of being co-opted into the service of his particular purpose. Equally, delicate issues may be evaded and assumptions or assertions too easily left unquestioned. Such risks, however, have to be weighed against the potential gains of establishing relationships based on significant degrees of sympathy and trust. For our particular exercise, the gains seemed clearly to outweigh the losses. Our approach enabled us to break down the resistance of those initially suspicious of our methods and purposes. Not least, it established for ourselves an apparently positive reputation among the bishops. Within this relatively small and close-knit group, word seems to have been passed down the line which helped to smooth our path in later encounters. Feedback from bishops or their associates also indicated that earlier interviews had been perceived as productive encounters or, at worst, less traumatic and without purpose than first supposed.[4]

The question of purpose raised another important issue, namely, the usefulness of the exercise and the question of what the investigator might conceivably have to offer to the investigated. Such considerations give rise to tacit or even explicit bargains. These form part of that trafficking in influence to which reference has been made. Interviewees are obviously more likely to give fully and frankly of themselves if they perceive a worthwhile objective. Meditation upon our experience suggested that this particular elite saw as many as five types of benefit accruing from participation in the exercise.

First, most of those concerned claimed to see some disinterested academic gains to be made. As a largely university-trained elite containing high numbers of former academics, they seem to have had a general disposition to place some value on a scholarly inquiry.

Secondly, a substantial proportion of our group recognized that our results could help to sharpen ecclesiastical awareness of factors conditioning or constraining the Church's involvement in social or political affairs.

Thirdly, some interviewees clearly perceived an opportunity to provide themselves with a platform from which to perform a teaching function or to clear away what they saw as misunderstandings about their theological positions. Obviously, all interviewers have to be on their guard against attempts, however well intentioned, to shift the ground rules of the encounter in this fashion.

Fourthly, and on a rather different tack, a number of respondents fed back to us their view of the interview as an unusual opportunity for self-expression, self-examination and the critical analysis of official tasks. Some even suggested that our questions had prompted fresh thoughts about occupational problems and had drawn to the surface some previously implicit assumptions. In the case of political matters, deemed to lie within our sphere of competence, bishops were known to ask our views or to acknowledge the need for some reallocation of their own priorities. To this extent, we were caught up, in a very small way, in the business of perhaps affecting the subject matter of our research. It was particularly interesting to find how busy and, in some senses, isolated figures seized an exceptional opportunity to unburden themselves or to air professional doubts and difficulties.

Finally, we have to acknowledge the possibility that, as in all interviews of this kind, the opportunity may be used to edit the historical record, to enhance personal reputations or even to downgrade colleagues. Obviously, there is a problem here of weighing in the balance evidence of this sort by setting it against the oral evidence of other relevant individuals as well as available documentary materials. This raises the whole question of evaluating interviews and the allied question of parallel source materials. It is, therefore, to these questions that we now turn.

5.4 The Evaluation of Oral Evidence

The possibility of interviewing contemporary protagonists obviously opens up advantages not given to the historian (unless it be the historian of very recent periods). From personal encounters one may acquire a general feel concerning the attitudes and dilemmas of those under review. A general sense can be acquired of those personal and social factors that mark the group as an identifiable 'elite' as well as those factors which tend to mark off groups and individuals from each other. There is a certain degree of involvement with those concerned which may help to create a picture of how the group thinks, feels and functions. Elements of their experiences can be brought to light that would not readily emerge in other ways. For example, it is fairly clear from tackling bishops one by one that subtle yet potentially important shifts have occurred in the way they as a group approach their corporate responsibilities and decision-making roles.

Some of this may surface in the public arena in the form of speeches, sermons, letters to the press, diocesan pronouncements and press comment. But much of the detail may be generally hidden from view if only because those concerned see such matters as 'in house' questions which are of little public interest. Equally, views and personalities may be involved which make it difficult for protagonists openly to debate the issues at stake even though such issues may ultimately have considerable significance for the evolution of the institution. By privately and separately tackling virtually all those immediately concerned we were not only able to capture and pin down shifts of attitude, we were even able to chart shifts as they occurred. The net result is a relatively rich and sophisticated account of otherwise elusive phenomena – phenomena that even future historians with access to documentary materials currently denied to us could not at all points capture with quite the same sense of immediacy.

Direct access to a given group may open up otherwise unlikely possibilities of getting behind their public persona and of sensitively presenting unfolding events. But allowance has also to be made for associated difficulties. First, there is the paradox that direct access to participants may on occasion blur reality more than would be the case if they were kept at a distance or mediated through the historical record. Reasons for this have already been hinted at. Even the most open and cordial of interviews may, if only in an unconscious fashion, become a performance designed to impress the researcher or to give a partial account. Not least, protagonists may be more concerned to conform to general public expectations of their office than to reveal private convictions or preoccupations. It may be that interviewers as well as interviewees can be the prisoners of particular images or pre-conceptions and these may stand in the way of effective communication. For example, there may be those whose particular theological presumptions make it difficult for them to admit, even to themselves, the existence of doubts concerning Christian commitment or episcopal responsibility. Equally, the Church's consensual norms and prevailing conceptions of the bishop as an ecclesiastical unifying force may make it difficult accurately to evaluate the extent of conflict in the Church.

There may even be difficulties arising out of ambiguities built into the very structure of the interview situation. Thus, though such encounters are private affairs, normally accompanied by guarantees of confidentiality, there may in practice be some confusion as to whether the meeting is private or has some elements of a performance given for the ultimate benefit of a wider audience. Indeed, it could be that interviews fluctuate back and forth between these two poles. On the positive side of this account, the way may be open to calculated and revealing indiscretions communicated on the assumption that there is only the remotest possibility of causing personal upsets or professional damage. But much care and sensitivity has to be exercised in determining the precise importance or validity that can be attached to information imparted in such conditions.

These are problems which can, in the first instance, only be tackled with reference to one's overall reaction to particular informants and, a little more objectively, to careful comparisons with the responses of other interviewees. In such a process of cross-checking, one must always allow for the possibility that particular individuals may be so idiosyncratic as to provide an unreliable basis for comparison. For example, the position of the Archbishop of Canterbury is in many respects necessarily *sui generis*.

Whether idiosyncratic or not, all interviews obviously contain within themselves the possibility of offering as hard objective fact what may be the product of subjective opinion or faulty memory. Equally, there is always the possibility of overstatement and the kind of selectivity that tends to present necessarily hazy and confused developments in overly coherent ways. This may be a matter of the interviewees giving random impressions or thoughts a degree of order they do not in reality possess. On the other hand, the social scientific preoccupations of the interviewer may lead him so to search after causal connections that links or patterns may seem to be established where the reality may in fact be much more confused. At worst, interviewers can unwittingly impose over-orderly schema on their interlocutors or put words into their mouths.

Such difficulties are hard to avoid and can only be dealt with through sensitivity to the nuances of the situations under discussion and of the specialized language being employed. One of us encountered these kinds of problems in especially pronounced form when endeavouring to undertake some elite interviewing in Spain and Latin America where the special problems of an alien culture were also involved. In the work being discussed here, we are obviously 'insiders' *vis-à-vis* the national culture and even the Church itself. Hence, obstacles of this nature have not in this instance been met to any significant degree. Nevertheless, qualities of empathy and imagination were still necessary to the enterprise.

We also perceived a need to sustain a subtle blend of detachment and involvement. Fruitful results could only be obtained by getting alongside interviewees and communicating with them at an ordinary human level about matters on their mind. Yet simultaneously we had to stand back in order to keep in our minds broader, more academic or analytical frames of reference. For example, we had constantly to remember that though, as political scientists, politics is for us a major consideration, it was for our interviewees a perhaps significant but secondary preoccupation. We had simultaneously to bear in mind the imperatives of the political domain as well as the theological or ecclesiastical imperatives to which the Church leaders in question saw themselves principally responding.

5.5   The Role of Documentary Evidence

One obvious point to emerge from the above discussion is that, for the most part, the modes of analysis employed have been of a qualitative rather than quantitative kind. Certainly, the whole interviewing process does not generally lend itself to the latter type of approach. The open-ended nature of much of the questioning and the unequal or even non-comparable nature of some responses must preclude the ostensibly rigorous statistical analyses commonly associated with mass survey data and deemed by some to be especially characteristic of the social sciences. Certainly, our experience of results produced by our mailed surveys (to the bulk of elected General Synod members) contrast with the products of our interviewing activities. Orthodox questionnaires by definition presuppose a uniformity of framework that can only be imposed at the risk of filtering out much relevant material. To give one example, personal encounters enable one to set particular individuals against the background of specific locations and in the context of dealings with such third parties as secretaries, wives and even chauffeurs. To converse with a bishop from the back of his chauffeur-driven limousine or to wait in his private lounge does positively contribute to the building up of a subtly nuanced and detailed picture – a picture offering pointers that might otherwise be missed.[5]

It is, of course, true that more statistical or quantitative methods can be brought to bear upon the study of a group of the kind with which we have been concerned. Thus, with reference to this country and elsewhere, standard statistical surveys have been done which isolate the numbers of churchmen of differing kinds coming from particular social classes, regions or educational backgrounds. Equally, standard career patterns can be isolated through such methods as changes in backgrounds or the general types of recruitment that may have taken place over a particular period of time. This sort of exercise has certainly been conducted in connection with the nineteenth- and twentieth-century English episcopate (Morgan, 1969). Similarly, one might cite the example of work on the Colombian hierarchy showing its very clear small-town, regional and other forms of bias (Medhurst, 1984). Such work, however, only acquires its full and proper significance when set against the background of a total social, cultural, economic and political context. The meaning of the statistical evidence can only be extracted and exhausted in the light of background generally not lending itself to this same form of analysis. Only other forms of evidence will begin adequately to indicate precisely to what extent, through what mechanisms and to what ends the background impinges upon or constrains the thinking and activity of a particular institution and its leaders (Edinger and Searing, 1967; Crewe, 1974; Whiteley, 1978).

This is not to say that appropriate statistical work does not remain to be done. In the English context there are modes of statistical analysis that might be used to yield additional understanding. For example, content analysis could be employed to elicit fresh insight into underlying trends or patterns of thought and activity (Holsti, 1969). This might certainly be one way forward for those generally concerned with the relationships of politics and religion. Interesting insights could be derived concerning shifts in the use of language and symbolism. Such shifts, however, can only be properly interpreted in the light of prior theological, historical and other forms of understanding not readily susceptible to statistical reductionism.

This raises the question of other sources of evidence available for the purposes that we have indicated. We have so far focused particularly on the process of interviewing because one of our own possibly distinctive contributions has been systematically to seek out and share views with a whole generation of national Church leaders. So far as we are aware, this has not previously been done in Britain. Nevertheless, we have obviously used a whole range of written sources that, for the historian at least, are everyday tools. In fact, our enterprise has in significant measure been a constantly sustained dialogue between oral and written evidence. We prepared for initial encounters with Church leaders by drawing on historical and sociological materials. The encounters themselves pointed to new sources as well as raising a whole range of fresh questions that could be addressed in the course of consulting the written word. Interviews illuminated the written word in ways otherwise hard to imagine; they went forward against the background of an already accumulated corpus of evidence. It remains briefly to indicate the range, characteristics and possible limitations of such sources so far as our religious elites are concerned.

The documentary evidence in question can be divided into primary and secondary sources. The former can be subdivided in turn into private sources perhaps not available until well after the death of those concerned (and perhaps not even then) and matters of public record available both to present observers and to future historical commentators (Plummer, 1983).

First, there is the personal and professional correspondence sustained by prominent churchmen and those close to them.

Contemporary diocesan bishops preside over extensive bureaucratic enterprises, which generate significant amounts of work (Medhurst and Moyser, 1982, 1985; Thompson, 1970). Certainly the future commentator might have an embarrassment of riches on this front. Even in the past, in less bureaucratized days, some of the more senior clerics generated very considerable collections of papers which served sometimes as the basis of important biographies. George Bell's huge biography of Archbishop Randall Davidson would fall into this category. Letters and other private papers can sometimes obscure as much as they disclose. Underlying motives may even be hidden from the writer himself and certainly committal to paper may sometimes be a means of disguising real thoughts or intentions. On occasion, the spontaneity of the interview could get behind such masks in a manner perhaps otherwise unavailable. Nevertheless, the very fact that papers are private and generally not formally addressed to posterity does mean that, consciously or not, additional information and novel insight is made available.

The potential that episcopal letters may represent is illustrated by those of Hensley Henson, inter-war Bishop of Durham (Braley, 1950). An advertisement in *The Times*, so the editor of the volume recalls, elicited 'no fewer than 1,450 letters from all parts of the world'. They 'provide the material', he suggests,

> for an authoritative judgement of his character – which must form an important contribution to the religious history of the Twentieth Century . . . [Henson's] comments on persons throw not a little light on the man himself. The freshness of their first-hand and unreflecting character gives most of them their interest. (Braley, 1950, p. XIV)

Despite the genuine substance of such claims, letters are not without their problems. As indicated above, they are scattered among a host of recipients, not all of whom would willingly offer them for publication. Some might not even have retained them. Furthermore, the nature of these individuals (or organizations) would have affected the message conveyed in ways that may be hard to discern. In any event, as Plummer notes, letter writing is 'a dying art' (Plummer, 1983, p. 23) to be replaced gradually but inexorably by the telephone – a medium of communication that does not (except in very rare cases) leave any permanent record for social scientists, biographers or historians to work with. Finally, as noted in Henson's case, the publication of private letters does pose certain ethical dilemmas, at least for those written in the last decade or so. As Braley put it:

the publishing of some of these letters is a delicate matter. On the one hand, it may hurt the susceptibilities of, and even be thought to cast some reflection upon, certain persons; but, on the other hand, the withholding of it may deny some understanding of the character of the writer. This is particularly the case in regard to Hensley Henson for even in his published writings and public utterances he revealed an incisive and accurate mind, a tremendous sense of humour and a devastatingly sharp tongue and was fearlessly outspoken. It must therefore be expected that in his private letters he would be even less restrained. (Braley, 1983, p. XV)

Such issues are not, of course, confined solely to private letters. They can affect all documentary (and oral) evidence produced in the expectation that they would enjoy a degree of confidentiality.

Given the quasi-bureaucratized nature of the episcopal job, access to 'business logs' or engagement diaries would also make for interesting reading when it comes to evaluating the pressures, priorities and preoccupations prompting those concerned. (If such were made available, they could lend themselves to statistical as well as other forms of analysis.) The only substitute for this would be to 'tail' protagonists for indefinite periods but that is a luxury few can afford, and in any event could only be done for a very limited period. Margaret Duggan's recently published biography of Archbishop Robert Runcie illustrates what use can be made of such sources (Duggan, 1983).

Finally in the category of private documentation might come personal diaries. In recent times, of course, prominent politicians have kept and published such diaries and they are already proving invaluable sources for scholars. Their chief advantage is that they provide blow-by-blow accounts of events as they seemed to protagonists at the time. Recall at a greater distance gives more scope for forgetfulness or even, albeit unconsciously, for editing the record. There is a greater chance of imposing an artificial orderliness on events when hindsight is involved. Equally, the emotional impact of particular turning points can evaporate with the passage of time. Of course, there are instances of diaries being deliberately composed for posterity's benefit and this must always be taken into account. Nevertheless, they can have a unique value. That makes it all the more disappointing that in the case of the particular group we have studied only one such diary, as far as we know, is accessible (Henson, 1942–50). This, however, may in itself be a significant pointer to the nature of the group. It is not merely that they have heavy schedules but more importantly that the norms of their profession tend to dictate a certain personal reticence. After all, they do regard themselves as having pastoral responsibilities for others often in situations of delicacy or distress.

Under the headings of published primary sources, generally available for inspection, we might single out (leaving aside such things as general newspaper reporting and other media coverage) three items. First, there is the written work of the major protagonists themselves. For instance, the famous Bishop Barnes of Birmingham wrote three significant books of a partly scholarly and partly controversial kind, mainly on the relationships of science and religion. He wrote a whole range of articles on similar subjects (Barnes, 1979). Bishop Jenkins of Durham is only one of a number of more contemporary bishops with major and sometimes scholarly publishing records. The importance of such works in evaluating individual contributions and long-term institutional preoccupations is obvious enough. Other contributions may be of a much more occasional but nevertheless instructive kind. We think particularly of the regular flow of information and opinion contained in the episcopate's diocesan newsletters as well as of speeches and published letters that have been left on the record. They are all pieces that may help to make up the general jig-saw.

Reference to speeches points to a second major primary source, namely the proceedings of deliberative assemblies in which the episcopate is caught up. The General Synod most obviously comes under this heading but so does the House of Lords. Hansard and the General Synod Proceedings, therefore, become grist to the mill. These obviously constitute verbatim reports of public and at times official postures and so must be weighed in the balance. But, as our own interview evidence intimates, this is only one part of the picture. Speeches may well be the tip of an iceberg, and submerged from view is a considerable amount of activity of a private, informal kind entailing interaction between different portions of the Church itself as well as churchmen and politicians.

In similar vein, there is much to be gained from the records and publications of central Church committees and other bureaucratic agencies which might in principle be made available in the Church's headquarters at Church House, Westminster. There again, acquaintance with implicit understandings, nuances of language and private or informal networks is necessary for the richest possible interpretation of the written word. For example, conflicts embodied in official reports may be the public expression of hidden tensions which can only be readily known to those acquainted with the personnel and modes of theological discourse involved. The other obvious factor to bear in mind is that the greater part of the Church's life and episcopal responsibilities proceed at a local level and that an undue focus on the centre necessarily produces a lop-sided or distorted view of society's impact upon the Church and vice versa.

We must now turn to the more widely known matter of secondary sources. Leaving aside general works of Church history to which we have referred earlier, we would focus particularly on autobiographies and biographies. The arts involved here are a major subject in themselves (see Gittings, 1978), the problems of which we have already fleetingly mentioned. On the subject of autobiography, we would simply say that examples are relatively rare. We think of Bishop Wand of London and Bishop Mervyn Stockwood of Southwark. The famous Bishop Bell of Chichester is an example of a writer who failed to finish an autobiography because of death. What is more, those writing such works are, by definition, of a self-selecting group who may in important respects be atypical. Much of the work of the institution in question may be carried forward by lesser known figures unlikely to see autobiography as an appropriate form of self-expression.

The matter of self-expression also raises problems for clearly autobiography may, albeit in undeliberate fashion, too readily become an exercise in self-justification or even obfuscation. The biographer of Hensley Henson is convinced that the autobiography hid much of the real man from view (Chadwick, 1983). The autobiography may be an important source of raw data and tell us something about the subject's self-image but it is the biographer who may, at least on occasion, present a more truly rounded picture. Students of the Anglican Church are perhaps fortunate in having good biographies of some of the more important leaders. We think, for example, of biographies of Archbishops Cosmo Lang, William Temple, Geoffrey Fisher, Archbishop Garbett of York, Bishop Mervyn Haigh, the two Bishops Chavasse, Bishop Kenneth Kirk, and Bishop Henry de Candale (an unusual example of a biography of a suffragan).

Of course, in evaluating such works one has to bear in mind the assumptions, backgrounds and intentions of the writers. There is nearly always a sense in which a biography is a celebratory exercise that could get out of hand to the point of becoming hagiography. But it is fair to suggest that, whatever their inevitable imperfections, modern biographies of Church leaders, even when written by other churchmen, do not for the most part fall into these traps. This may contrast with Victorian biographies which were much more overtly laudatory (Gittings, 1978). For example, Iremonger's biography of William Temple frankly acknowledges errors of political judgement (Iremonger, 1948). Ecclesiastical biography, in company with biography as a whole, is a literary and historical form that has matured considerably in recent times to the benefit of all serious students.

5.6 Concluding Reflections

As this chapter has perhaps implied, the study of religious elites poses many of the methodological and ethical issues raised in the empirical investigation of 'top people' in other walks of life. One must, for example, consider with care whether or not the particular individuals identified for scrutiny are indeed appropriate for the research task in hand. In our study, the answer seems to be a qualified yes. Our materials do indeed confirm that the Church of England's episcopate exercises an especially significant mediating role in relationships within the Church and between the Church and its general environ-ment. As our ultimate interest was in the behaviour of the organization as a whole, attention to the leadership supplied by its episcopate was, to that extent, justified. On the other hand, a number of bishops in the course of our conversations conceded that important policy initiatives derive from advisors, bureaucratic agencies or more informal groups or factions within the Church. To that extent, our image of the directing and managerial stratum of the Church has been modified and clarified. Of course, in other religious institutions, leadership may be exercised in a very different way: who the 'religious elites' are will vary enormously. However, such questions of comparability and elite status are not unique to the religious domain.

Similar general issues arise in the methodological field. There are diverse strategies available for studying elites – social background analysis, the examination of public and private documentary materials typically thrown up by elite individuals, personal interviewing and yet other methods. Though our present research has been largely confined to one, albeit major, religious elite in one country, our general impression is that study of such leaders has been, in terms of the techniques used, rather traditional and therefore limited. But, as Crewe has noted, this seems also to be true on a wider front (Crewe, 1974). He called for bolder methods and new theoretical initiatives in the study of elites. We certainly share that opinion. Indeed, our seemingly innovatory set of interviews with one entire religious elite is, in our view at least, a step in this general direction. Not that personal interviews of a relatively systematic and social scientific variety are a complete answer. On the contrary, we believe that, as with any elite group, interviews should be undertaken, if at all, in conjunction with other strategies. Only by such a multi-method approach will the study of religious elites, as with others, establish relatively firm empirical patterns through which theoretical breakthroughs may then come.

In the ethical sphere, too, issues arise in connection with religious elites that can be found elsewhere. Questions concerning censorship and preservation of confidentiality certainly were present. For example, at forty-three, the group in our case was relatively small and its members so well known to one another that it might be possible for ecclesiastical *cognoscenti* to identify respondents from evidence internal to non-attributed quotations or from the context in which they were set, thereby breaching our guarantees of confidentiality. In the case of some of the group's well-known national figures, even the informed general reader might be able correctly to identify our sources. Another, possibly not unique, ethical issue involved the 'partisan' potential that elite data can sometimes represent (Van Schendelen, 1982). We were ourselves asked for privileged access to our materials on a current and potentially controversial ecclesiastical issue so that support for one view of that issue among senior members could be gauged and appropriate strategies devised for its handling in the Church's national deliberative assembly. Here there is something of a dilemma between pressure to help an institution which has helped the investigator and pressure to respect the canons of social scientific neutrality.

To the extent that definitional, methodological and ethical questions arise that are common to the study of religious and other elite groups, the general field acquires a flavour which marks it off from examinations of 'ordinary' citizens. However, too much should not be made of this. Religious elites pose their own particular problems and problems which vary widely according to context. Thus, the need, for example, to reconcile the 'worldly' and the 'other worldly', the language of social science and of theology, is one unique to the understanding of religious phenomena and perhaps the most pronounced among religious elites. On the other hand, the way in which such a reconciliation or empathetic understanding may be achieved will vary according to circumstance. The leaderships of dissident Baptists in the Soviet Union, or of the Roman Catholic Church in the Vatican, and the Islamic authorities in Iran, all require this general capacity on the part of the investigator but in very different particular ways. The same may equally be said of many other aspects of research involving religious elites. To that extent, our experiences and reflections are necessarily partial and limited, but hopefully they may also stimulate a greater concern for questions of substance and method in one of the major spheres of human existence.

Notes

1   However, it is a tribute to the versatility of the postal survey method that, despite a schedule (in 1975) some twenty pages in length with several 'open-ended' items taking thirty minutes to one hour to complete, the response rate was some 79 per cent. It should also be noted that among those who replied were figures arguably themselves elite persons in secular as well as religious terms.

2   Among these we might mention David Sheppard, Bishop of Liverpool (1983) and John Habgood, Archbishop of York (1983).

3   We might note that our tape recorder was selected precisely because it was physically unobtrusive. We sacrificed some quality in the recording by dispensing with an external microphone but hopefully gained in rapport and the general quality of the responses.

4   The operation of a 'grape-vine' depends upon how 'connected' the individuals are who comprise the particular elite in question and the nature of that connection. In so far as, by their nature, elites do form relatively integrated networks, the effect will tend to be encountered in most studies involving elite interviewing. By contrast, it would be very unusual for it to arise in interviews with members of the mass public. Issues of response 'contamination' also arise.

5   A vivid illustration is our casual discovery, while waiting in a senior bishop's dining room for his arrival, of that evening's list of guests for a private dinner party. This indicated, better than perhaps any other evidence how well connected he was to Britain's social and political 'establishment'.

6

Oral history as an instrument of research into Scottish educational policy-making

CHARLES RAAB
University of Edinburgh

6.1 Introduction

The aim of this chapter is to consider some substantive and methodological issues arising in a study of the making of Scottish educational policy especially from the 1940s to the present (McPherson and Raab, forthcoming). That study attempts to cast light upon the changing interrelationships between the way the Scottish education system is governed – the policy process and the organizations, roles and persons involved in it – and the policies and educational provision that are among its outputs. It makes extensive use of tape-recorded and transcribed material from lengthy interviews conducted with sixteen of the leading figures in this field in the post-war period. These interviews, together with supplementary material drawn from documents and from secondary sources, and including our analytical commentary, form the basis of an account of policies and policy-making with particular reference to secondary education. We have not attempted to write a definitive history, but to use interview material to initiate several lines of investigation into policies and into the processes through which they were formed and implemented, and to gain an overview of the changing system of Scottish educational governance through to the 1980s.

This chapter first briefly describes the empirical focus of the study.

I wish to acknowledge the financial assistance of the Moray Fund of the University of Edinburgh in this research; and to thank Andrew McPherson for his comments on an earlier draft of this chapter. I am also grateful to Anthony Seldon for his helpful remarks on the research discussed in this chapter.

Some conceptual and theoretical issues are raised in order to point up their connections to a research strategy which brings to the fore first-hand accounts by persons who were closely involved in the governance of Scottish education. The methods and interview procedure employed in the research are next discussed, followed by a commentary upon some of the methodological and ethical issues involved in gathering and using interview material in writing a book which is intended as a contribution to historically-based policy studies. The chapter concludes with a brief discussion of oral archives (see McPherson and Raab, forthcoming, for a fuller discussion of methodological dilemmas).

6.2   The Nature of the Research Project and its Setting

Much has changed in the forty years since the passage of the 1945 Education (Scotland) Act. The school-leaving age was raised twice, secondary education was reorganized along comprehensive lines, the O-grade was introduced in the early 1960s as a fourth-year examination, and there was a trend towards staying on after the leaving age. Major reforms of the curriculum and certification were undertaken. The expansion and contraction of the size of the population served by the system have involved heavy expenditure on resources such as school buildings and the supply of teachers, and have exacerbated problems in their planning and distribution.

In the same period the array of organizations and roles through which policies were made, implemented and evaluated were transformed at the central and local levels of the system, and between them (Raab, 1980, 1982b). Structural relocations of advisory and executive functions gave rise to a kaleidoscopic succession of patterns. These were produced in various ways: by hivings-off to non-departmental bodies, by the abolition of other such bodies and the reassumption of their activities by the Scottish Education Department (SED), and by the devolution of decision-making to educational establishments and local education authorities. Shifts in the balance of political, bureaucratic and professional influence occurred as elected politicians in local and central government found new and often more strident voices, and as teachers discovered their collective strength in pursuit of trade-union goals and in search of greater participation in the making of policies. Inside government, policy and administrative developments affected, and were affected by, relationships between educational inspectors and administrators within the SED, between the SED and the Scottish Office of which it is a component, and between the Scottish Office and other parts of central government in the United Kingdom.

The main purpose of our research into these changes was to explore the effects that the education and policy-making/ administrative systems have had upon each other. We sought to understand the interweaving of substantive aspects of educational provision, such as certification and the curriculum, with the procedural and structural aspects of government through which advice was given, decisions were made and carried out, and resources were provided. The strength and direction of the relationship between these two broad strands, the changes that took place in that relationship, and the way in which professionals, administrators and politicians thought about and made policies are among the central foci of the study.

Academic writing on policy-making in Scotland has been sparse, perhaps stimulated more by the currency of political issues like devolution than by a concern to cumulate a tradition of systematic research. Allen (1979) notes that policy problems have been plentifully discussed in the literature; not so the processes of policy-making, concerning which the small body of work has been pre-occupied with administration and with descriptions of institutions. He explains this, in part, by reference to the main features he sees in the Scottish political system. These severely constrain the style and content of what is written: centralization, administrative primacy, exclusiveness, secrecy, corporatism and authoritarianism:

> The exclusiveness of the system lies in the restriction of influence over decision-making to a small body of fairly senior Civil Servants and MPs, and a large but still modest group of persons regularly consulted or involved in the various boards, committees and commissions established by the Scottish departments and their appointed bodies. While the latter group include a small proportion who owe their selection to having been elected to these or other bodies, or who regard themselves as representing a general interest, the bulk of the membership consists of persons with a professional or sectional interest, accountable only to those who appointed them. (Allen, 1979, pp. 27–8)

The supposition that government in Scotland is centralized, bureaucratic and exclusive has implications for research strategies and methods. If power lies within a 'black box' constituted by these persons and organizations, then explanations of its exercise, and evaluations of the resulting policy outputs, can only come from attempts to look inside the box at the dynamics of the policy process. Concentrating attention on small bodies of participants who control decisions enables one to see how these coteries are constituted and what distinguishes those who are recruited to them. Research that brings to light the way in which policy agendas have been constructed through the actions of these participants, through the machinery they created and operated, and through the understandings that they brought to the performance of roles in the policy process, is essential to an account, whether appreciative or critical, of Scottish society and government. Studies of the State which do not develop empirical knowledge about those who are thought to run it cannot adequately test propositions about central control, and can have little to say about how that control has been developed and maintained.

The concept of a 'policy community' is part of a descriptive theory of British government in which policies in substantive fields are seen as being made and implemented through the direct involvement of a network of persons and groups in central and local government and elsewhere, denying the conventional distinction between the government machine and outside pressure groups. Theoretical work and empirical applications of the concept are still at a formative stage in the literature of policy studies, and much remains to be done in relating the concept to the existing analytical frameworks in which pluralist, corporatist, and elite theories predominate (Richardson and Jordan, 1979; Rhodes, 1985). The educationists and others whom we have interviewed were key members of a policy community whose values, beliefs, relationships and actions (or inactions) were crucial determinants of educational policy and its implementation (Raab, 1982a). Research on Scottish educational policy-making might shed some light on what Dunleavy has termed 'ideological corporatism' and the large part played by policy-community professionals in

the effective integration of different organizations or institutions at the level of substantive policy making by the acceptance or dominance of an effectively unified view of the world ... an ideological cohesion which may exist on substantive policy questions. (Dunleavy, 1981, p. 7)

McPherson has described how, in the first half of this century,

elite educationists' and others' experience of Scottish education ...

was selectively structured so as to confirm for them the validity of an inherited, traditional and egalitarian, view of Scottish culture and institutions. (McPherson, 1983, p. 217)

The research deals with a more recent period, but the continuities are very strong. Most of the persons interviewed were raised and schooled in that tradition before the Second World War and their public careers continued into the post-war years, finishing in most cases in the 1960s or 1970s. The educationists who came to dominate decision-making in Scottish education had in their youth been among the successful, selected products of a schooling system which prided itself on its egalitarianism and democracy. They simultaneously exemplified this 'Scottish myth' and perpetuated it in the administrative, advisory, and other organizations which they – mostly teachers and former teachers – were chosen to run and through which, in turn, they recruited others like them to participatory roles. McPherson's study of the content of the national cultural and educational tradition shows how leading educational and literary figures acted as transmitters and as living 'proofs' of those parts of the tradition which were positively valued as representing the 'real' Scotland. These values were carried into the machinery of governance and of policy advice through processes of appointment which underrepresented those who came from career backgrounds in the more social class-differentiated school environments of the big cities (principally the Glasgow conurbation), and which reflected instead the small-town, pre-industrial 'historic heartland' of the Scottish myth.

Referring back to Allen's assertion, the controlling features of Scottish public affairs in education, but probably also in other fields, seemed to owe more to selection than to election. At least until the 1960s, local councillors and Members of Parliament exercised relatively little influence over policies. The main axis of control consisted of central and local officials and members of the teaching profession serving in the classroom, in committee rooms, and in administrative posts in educational institutions. Officials tended to be recruited from the educational world itself. This characteristic marked the SED off from the normal civil service pattern in which administrative generalists achieve the highest posts. The 'dominie' became the nominee or the public servant in a relatively closed world of educational governance whose definitions of problems, goals, criteria of evaluation, and evaluations themselves prevailed, although it was sometimes successfully challenged.

There is some tension here, on the theoretical plane, between the openness and permeability of processes of policy-formation as postulated in pluralist theories, and the gatekeeping or controlling functions exercised by key participants through organizational and ideological means. In line with the latter is Schattschneider's well-known thesis:

> All forms of political organization have a bias in favor of the exploitation of some kinds of conflict and the suppression of others because *organization is the mobilization of bias*. Some issues are organized into politics while others are organized out. (Schattschneider, 1960, p. 71; emphasis in original)

Lukes' 'three-dimensional' view takes this argument further in stating that power is exercised even where there is no overt conflict present or decision-making taking place. For him, bias might be sustained 'by the socially structured and culturally patterned behaviour of groups, and practices of institutions' (Lukes, 1974, p. 22).

Although our investigations were not initially framed precisely in this terminology, we sought to gain a purchase on the processes through which 'bias' could be said to have been 'mobilized' historically and up to the present. For this, it was necessary to understand the factors affecting persistence and change in the way education was thought about and organized, and the way in which entrenched conceptions and problem definitions were reinforced by decision-making machinery and by patterns of recruitment to roles within it. We hoped to understand these matters better by inter-viewing prominent figures, all retired, in the world of educational policy in Scotland. They were able to interpret the educational system over some forty years or more. We were also interested in the parts they themselves had played and the circumstances in which they had played them. By engaging them in extended conversations about their careers and the states of the system in which they functioned, we might also be able to see how and to what extent the 'Scottish myth' figured in the 'assumptive worlds' in which their actions were framed.

Young has used the term 'assumptive world' to refer to 'policy-makers' subjective understanding of the environment in which they operate', incorporating 'several intermingled elements of belief, perception, evaluation, and intention as responses to the reality "out there" ' (Young, 1977, pp. 2–3). To what extent, however, is the assumptive world or, in the present discussion, the myth, open to reformulation as a result of policy-makers' experience in trying to enact it? Is the policy community a learning system? Young and Mills' argument might be taken to suggest that it is:

> The assumptive world is created for the individual by cultural transmission, and constantly reconstructed as an adaptive response to the exigencies of the everyday world. The world as experienced rarely corresponds to the world as imagined, and this leads to both marginal adaptation of the imagined world and to manipulative behaviour in the experienced world. The tensions between image and experience serve to develop additional models of the world *as it might be*, and such models provide the incentive for action. In the case of policy-makers, it is just such action that forms the subject for policy analysis. (Young and Mills, 1978, p. 8; emphasis in original)

On the other hand, another story might be told about how assumptive worlds relate to policy-making: one in which '[a] convincing body of alternative experience cannot be accumulated about ideas or forms . . . whose practice has been forgotten owing to the selective operation of myth on the past' (McPherson, 1983, p. 236).

Or indeed, operating on the present through the workings of patronage in the appointed policy-making and advisory machinery. It might be difficult to bring to bear in policy-making those tension-creating experiences which would result in strong calls to action to change the world. Rather than looking through clear glass to see such discrepant patterns, elite educationists seemed more often to look into the mirror and to like what they saw. In places where the silvering had worn off, the incentive was stronger to re-apply it than to look through the holes and to change what was viewed.

In other words, a learning model need not form part of the foundations of research about how beliefs and actions relate to each other. That model presupposes that policy actors are open to experiences and that they adopt a 'scientific' stance in the mutual adjustment of image and reality. This in turn presupposes that neither the organizational arrangements nor the ideological features of a policy community substantially inhibits the search for, or the apprehension of, new knowledge which might question the basis upon which the policy community exerts control over its field. Indeed, Young and Mills recognize that this may be a questionable assumption in personal construct theory, which they think is useful in looking at assumptive worlds. They refer to Festinger, saying: 'as the theory of cognitive dissonance suggests ... information contradictory to existing constructs may be ignored, and, as a person's behaviour tends to be habitual, constructs may become self-fulfilling prophesies [sic] with little scope for change' (Young and Mills, 1978, p. 14).

Learning is problematic. Any theory of policy-making is simultaneously and necessarily a theory about how information flows through a system, though, of course, it is also more than this. That flow depends upon the channels, transmitters, receptors, and interpreters that structure it. Power inheres partly in the ability to shape these elements of structure, to use them, and to control access to them. Whether or not such communication systems enable policy communities to learn depends in part on the extent to which the policy-making process is accountable. And to be accountable, it must take place sufficiently in public political forums in which questions can be asked effectively about performances and the answers can be scrutinized and evaluated adequately by those whose experienced worlds might differ from those in control of policy (Gray, McPherson and Raffe, 1983, ch. 17). Scottish policy-making has not been accustomed to encourage such public interrogations; nor have public systems, like education, in which professionals' assumptions have historically held sway. Interviewing elite participants in Scottish educational policy-making is a way of gaining insights into these matters of substance and process by means of creating new source material for their investigation.

6.3   Methods and Issues

The use to which we wanted to put interview texts strongly influenced many of the procedures that were used in collecting them. We did not intend to produce a conventional history or a policy-making 'case study' in which interviews would play a background part or provide occasional quotations to enliven a discussion or to illustrate a point. Instead, in any envisaged book the interviews were to be proportionately large, and to play a major part, in relation to primary and secondary written sources and to our analytical commentary. In many chapters, interview material would provide the main substance of the discussion with relatively little supplementary writing.

Books in this manner have added immeasurably to knowledge

about English education. Kogan and his associates have used interviews extensively in their exploration of educational policy. In one of them, long interviews with former Ministers of Education, Edward Boyle and Anthony Crosland, were presented consecutively to make up the main body of a book, following a long introduction. In the others, the same format was used to present interviews with several local authority Chief Education Officers, again preceded by an introductory essay in which comparisons and contrasts among the separate accounts are discussed (Kogan, 1971; Kogan and van der Eyken, 1973; Bush and Kogan, 1982).

This was not a model that we wished to follow in all respects, although it too was based on taped interviews with important figures who had retired from their education posts, or whose careers in public life had since moved on. Each of these books deals with the performance of a particular role by different persons in the system of educational governance (Secretary of State for Education; Chief Education Officer), and works outward from the role to its inter-connections sideways, upwards or downwards in order to reveal the wider structure of processes and events. In our study of Scottish education, we too were interested in roles and relationships in the making of policy. But perhaps to a greater extent than in those books, we were additionally concerned with how thought and action had developed within a policy community, with changes in governmental machinery, and with the mutual impingement of substantive policy and governmental structure. This difference might to some extent simply be one concerning the starting point. However, it reflects a more fundamental one involving the nature of the Scottish educational policy community and our ability to map its dimensions and historical development in our interviews.

We were particularly concerned with personalities and with interactions among our interviewees in order to understand the extent to which they were part of a network that stretched across different institutions and levels. We also wanted to collect accounts of the same events, processes and policy developments from the variety of viewpoints represented by their different roles. These accounts were intended to be used not consecutively but spliced, interwoven and juxtaposed in order to create a sense of cross-talk via ourselves as the interviewers. Differences and similarities could be useful for gaining insights into the structure and ideology of a policy community as well as for understanding history and policy.

Cross-talk is not necessarily an artificial effect to create in Scottish circumstances. If Whitehall is a 'small village', filled with people who grew up together (Heclo and Wildavsky, 1974), the 'village' of elite Scottish educationists went beyond the corridors of the Scottish Office (which, on the education side, recruited from the educational world) and embraced a remarkably close-textured policy community. Among the generation that came to occupy influential positions after the Second World War, and into which the interviews tap, many had known one another from university days between the wars. Many had later seen each other at close range and continuously, in their jobs or on various public bodies and committees. In a small country with a small policy and administrative stratum, each could, as his career progressed through its stages, move across to occupy positions in different but interrelated institutional or geographical parts of the educational system.

Years later, in retirement or after having left positions of importance in the education system or in its governance, members of this elite had the time available and, in the event, were willing to reflect upon their experiences for research purposes. They were able to augment the public record of events by bringing additional information to bear upon it: in particular, information about motives, understandings and outlooks which helps to explain actions and constraints. They were able to provide insights into the way educational and governmental assumptions were, or were not, intertwined in the minds of those who could translate either or both of these sets of ideas into authoritative action. Moreover, they were able to talk about their social and academic backgrounds, formative influences, careers and observations on the state of the educational system as far back as the 1920s. This was particularly important, given the absence of an earlier generation of 'elite interviewers', in helping us to learn more about some of the leading and legendary figures who had been our subjects' colleagues, teachers, or patrons.

The sixteen persons with whom we tape-recorded interviews between 1976 and 1980 had occupied, among them, a large number of positions in the education system in the course of their careers. Their salaried posts are too numerous to list here, but they included the following: Scottish Office junior Minister, Secretary of State for Scotland, Senior Chief Inspector of Schools, Secretary and Under Secretary of the SED, Permanent Secretary of the Scottish Office, local authority Director and Deputy Director of Education, Principal of a College of Education, Headmaster, and top official in the Educational Institute of Scotland, the General Teaching Council, and the Scottish Council for Research in Education.

Their unpaid positions included roles in the Consultative

Committee on the Curriculum, the Scottish Examination Board, the Advisory Council for Education in Scotland, the Scottish Council for the Training of Teachers, the General Teaching Council, a local authority education committee, various departmental committees and working parties, and several liaison, consultative or negotiating bodies consequent upon their jobs. Three had knighthoods and most of the rest had received lesser honours. Except for the two politicians and two of the civil servants, all had spent part of their careers in school-teaching. None had had experience in Roman Catholic schools, and none was a woman; we were unable to secure an interview with a woman who had been a junior Minister. More recently, we also held, but did not tape-record, conversations with a few other persons including a Chief Inspector, two prominent head teachers (one chaired the Consultative Committee on the Curriculum, the other the Scottish Examination Board), a junior Minister, a local education committee chairman and a university Professor of Education, but we lacked interview material which dealt with the universities' influence on secondary schooling.

A few of the interviewees were acquainted with one of us and were among the earliest subjects. One offered to help secure the co-operation of another to whom we wished to speak. But personal connections apart, each person was also approached by a letter explaining the nature of the research, describing the methods, and mentioning the names of those whom we had already interviewed. We requested a preliminary meeting to discuss his participation and to explore in general terms the areas that might be covered in an actual interview. At this stage we made no official approach to the Scottish Office.

Except for two former Ministers, every person to whom we wrote readily agreed to a preliminary conversation. One ex-Minister pleaded the pressure of other business, and the other failed to make a substantive reply to several letters. The exploratory meetings were brief. An hour or so was spent in amplifying what had been written in the letter and in gaining information about the range and depth of the person's experience with a view to learning how a subsequent interview might be most fruitfully conducted. We gained an impression of the value of each subject as a potential source of information about particular policy initiatives or processes, and most of them began to talk substantively about some of these topics. Handwritten notes were taken in order to help prepare for the next occasion, but we expected to go over some of this ground again when it came to the actual interview. It was made clear to each person, in writing, that the transcript of the tape-recorded interview would remain his property until a final version was agreed and approved, whereupon the approved transcript would be at our disposal for use in future publications. We agreed to send a memorandum of the topics to be dealt with and, in a few cases, a somewhat more detailed outline was furnished as well. Most subjects were asked to send us biographical information to supplement what we knew from *Who's Who?* and from other public sources. Some volunteered to send us copies of their publications and other documents in their possession which would be relevant to the conduct of the interview. A date was chosen for the tape-recorded session.

Before the second meeting we also prepared, for our own use, an outline of the questions and areas we intended to cover. For the later interviews, these briefs were considerably more detailed. By that time we knew a great deal and were able to bring into play material from earlier interviews in a search for comparisons of points of view and information on specific points, and in eliciting reactions to the interpretations we had provisionally made. Our preparations involved intensive re-reading of previous transcripts, secondary sources, publications of governmental and other bodies, and, if any, the subject's own writings. This preparation contributed greatly to our ability to move the discussions forward and to follow some unexpected trails that appeared in the course of the actual interview. We had some knowledge of the public record as contained in official files released under the thirty-years' rule, although much of our exploration of it came at a later stage in the research when it was useful in checking interview accounts. In writing the book, however, it has only been quoted sparingly. There is no doubt that public records are a necessary adjunct for research of this kind and that their embargo creates difficulties; these, however, are not always insuperable.

The interviews varied considerably in length, from about two hours to fifteen hours, and produced final transcripts ranging from about forty double-spaced pages to about 320. In most cases, each was conducted in one day, several interviews being started in the morning and continuing after lunch. Most of the interviews took place in university rooms; two were held in the subjects' homes. In all cases, we aimed to make the physical conditions as near to those of drawing-room conversations as possible, with comfortable chairs arranged casually around a table on which the microphone was placed, although in a few cases the interviewee wore a lapel microphone instead. The recording machine was placed as unobtrusively as possible on the floor near the table, so that tape-changes and technical adjustments could be made without much interruption of the flow of conversation. The break for lunch, or for tea and coffee, was a convenient way of taking stock, together with the interviewee, of what had already been discussed and of considering where to go next. It also enabled the interviewee to say things, if he wished, off the record, which we noted in longhand for background use only.

Most of the people we interviewed found the sessions reasonably relaxed and comfortable. The microphone was a familiar device to many of them, and the atmosphere was informal. They had met us before and some of them had been able to reassure themselves by talking to somebody whom we had previously interviewed. The fact that they had had prior sight of, and had contributed to, the outline of topics also contributed to this positive mood. We were not using a cut-and-dried questionnaire, but conducted the interview as a conversation for which those round the table had prepared. They realized that we already knew a fair amount about the topics, and each knew that we had spoken and were intending to speak to others besides himself. Where it was relevant, we sometimes told the person what a previous interviewee had said on a particular matter, and invited him to comment on the other's opinion or account. This was a valuable way of 'triangulating' on certain points and of clarifying them.

Once the interview was completed, the tapes were transcribed verbatim by an audio-typist. Except for a few interviews at the end of the series, we did not use sophisticated or high-quality recording equipment. In retrospect it would have been better had we done so throughout; the sound quality of a few of the tapes made transcribing more laborious than necessary. We ourselves then listened to the tapes and checked the typescript against them, filling in gaps and correcting errors and mis-hearings, and making other small changes of a purely cosmetic kind. The transcript was then re-typed to produce a presentable copy for our subject to consider. Although we asked some of them to clarify a few passages and to supply additional information, they were invited to make any other changes they saw fit. Some took the opportunity to insert new material at considerable length, but most made changes that were substantively minor or merely stylistic. When an amended transcript was returned to us, we incorporated the changes in a re-typed version which was then sent to the interviewee for his final approval. However, in a few instances where the subject had altered or deleted valuable passages which we wished to preserve, we put forward a reasoned request for reinstating the material in question, perhaps in a blander form.

In nearly all cases there was no difficulty in mutually agreeing a version that could be released to us. One person, however, wanted to wait to see what portions of his interview we wished to use, rather than approving the entire transcript. Another, who had spoken very freely and frankly in the interview about other named persons, found it impossible to modify the transcript satisfactorily without losing the point of the accounts he had given. While we cannot quote this unapproved material, it has been important as background information in our thinking on a number of topics. So, too, has been an interview with another subject which produced a discursive text from which quotations could not usefully be extracted; we therefore did not proceed to a final version.

This description of method leads to a consideration, briefly, of a few problems inherent in our approach and in the use of oral evidence. Some of them give rise to questions for which there are no ready answers. One of the important issues that arose in the course of this research was the question of confidentiality, in which ethics and method are intertwined. Among the persons interviewed were several former senior civil servants and a Minister who had to bear in mind their obligation under Section 2 of the Official Secrets Act 1911 not to divulge without authorization what they had learned in the course of their work. This is not the place to discuss the question of official secrecy at length. However, not only statutory provisions but also the ethos of officials and Ministers have often inhibited the dissemination of certain kinds of official information for research and other uses. On the other hand, Heclo and Wildavsky, Kogan, and more recently Young and Sloman (Young and Sloman, 1982; 1984) are among those who have conveyed a great deal about the folk ways of Whitehall within these constraints. The latter authors, in fact, published lengthy quotations from broadcast interviews with named civil servants.

We eschewed a crusading approach in negotiating our research. In no sense were interviewees, whether or not they were formerly officials (and the Official Secrets Act does not only apply to them), being invited to be indiscreet, nor would they have wished to be so. We needed their co-operation and some of them, in addition, had helped us secure interviews with others. In a sense we were tapping, for research purposes, the trust which functionally and morally binds the policy community together. Even in retirement, most of our interviewees remained part of the educational policy community or were active in public affairs. In addition, as researchers we had to ensure that lines of access to the policy community would remain open beyond the life of this study for ourselves and for present and future colleagues in the research community.

The assurance that our subjects would retain control of their transcripts until they released them for our use was an essential part in reinforcing our *bona fides*. With one exception, the former civil servants on their own initiative submitted their transcripts to the Scottish Office before approving them, and this appeared to be little more than a formality. The one exception was a person who had approved his transcript and given it to us, but then died before the Scottish Office saw it. At that point, we reached an understanding with the SED that they might see and comment upon our final book manuscript.

A further problem is how the validity of the material we received is to be assessed. Are the points from which we purport to 'triangulate' truly independent, given the interconnections of the people to whom we spoke and the assistance they gave in identifying other key members of the policy community? We have made considerable use of official sources, public records and the specialist press. But how far can oral evidence be checked against documents, given the closure of official files for the most recent decades, the 'trans-event' nature of many aspects of educational policy that are of interest to us, and the contestability of written sources themselves as 'truth'?

There are no sure answers to these questions. However, while oral testimony strengthens the evidence about the extent to which leading members of the policy community shared a set of educational beliefs and values, it also brings to light important areas of disagreement over policies and over the way power and influence should be distributed and exercised. Dissent gave us useful information and alternative explanations.

Our interviews helped to clarify matters of consensus and conflict, posing for us, however, the further dilemma of how to read the evidence in terms of continuity or change in values, policies and organizational relationships. But the rehearsals of arguments which fill many pages in a number of interviews suggest that the opportunity to tell one's own story, perhaps to justify one's position, or even to get one's own back, was attractive for some. Then, too, the interview could become an educationist's testament, one which he had never had, and probably would never have, the occasion or the inclination to commit to paper otherwise. Through the interview a story, both synthetic and analytical, could be created for others to comprehend or to challenge. Without it, there would only be public records of official reports, statistics, Acts of Parliament, government circulars, minutes, and examination results to testify to a lifetime's dedication to the service of education in Scotland.

What happens to such testaments? Although there is an active oral history archival industry in Scotland, little of its attention has been given to recording, in word or print, the recollections of persons who have been close to the arenas of decision-making in governmental, professional and industrial life. *Scotland's Record* is an oral archive which was begun in the late 1970s as a means of preserving on tape and in transcribed form accounts of public affairs by leading Scottish public figures (Seldon and Pappworth, 1983, p. 100). This is a rich source of material on a variety of governmental and economic topics, but it consists of narrative accounts and lacks the dialogue and inter-action that occur when an interviewer's knowledge and critical questioning transforms the story into an exploration of the topic with the person interviewed.

Something of the latter is found in the British Oral Archive of Political and Social History at the London School of Economics and Political Science. This contains the tapes and transcripts of inter-views with several dozen retired Permanent Secretaries and Ministers, the first wave of a projected large-scale oral history enterprise. In compiling this, Seldon has contributed greatly to the sources for British elite oral history, the underdevelopment of which he has described in a survey and guide which discusses the use of oral evidence in many fields (Seldon and Pappworth, 1983). Copies of archive interviews with important Scottish figures are lodged with *Scotland's Record* in the National Library of Scotland, and they as well as other oral archive material have been useful adjuncts to our immediate focus on Scottish educational policy.

But while these accounts illuminate the assumptive worlds of important figures and shed light on the making and administration of policy through first-hand descriptions elicited in interviews, each of them is a self-contained record of the public life and times of its subject. While cumulatively they enable a broad picture of a govern-mental and administrative elite to emerge, they are less well suited, in themselves, to research into particular policy fields or into specialized policy communities. Interviews were conducted for archival purposes rather than to be used for a specific piece of research. For us, therefore, interviews with elite subjects served a different function, although their usefulness was not exhausted with the completion of one piece of analysis. The transcripts are important as public documents for verifying the use to which selected portions have been put in a written study, just as are secondary and primary sources of the usual kind, and like them, the transcripts can be made available to others who may have need of them in their own research.

II

Economic Elites

7

The fly on the wall of the inner sanctum: observing company directors at work

JOHN T. WINKLER

King's Fund Institute, London

7.1 Introduction

The first task of science, any science, social as well as physical, is to observe and describe the phenomena under study. Accurate observation and detailed description are prerequisites for establishing regularities in behaviour, associations with other variables, and causal relationships. Equally, they are prerequisites for any phenomenological understanding of action.

In elite studies, this first fundamental step of research has often not been undertaken. We have detailed ethnographies of vagrants and criminals, of ordinary conformist folk, indeed of whole communities, but few of our social elites. Researchers measure with stop-watches the activities of manual workers, but have only rare audiences with their bosses.

The reasons for this omission are not neglect or purposeful avoidance. But elites control entry to their world even more rigorously than most people and are frequently disinclined to allow outsiders to watch them. At least, social scientists often assume they are so disinclined, and hence forbear to knock on the doors in the corridors of power. As a result, we commonly do not know what elites actually do.

Of course, we have much testimony from elites asserting what they do. Society's leaders are more able than most to publish memoirs, diaries and autobiographies, which researchers may subject to content analysis. Occasionally, social scientists interview them. But these approaches produce accounts of action, not the observation and description of action. Like all accounts they are vulnerable to fallible memory and selective recall, but perhaps more than most accounts, elite renderings are vulnerable to self-justification, the impulse to rationalize and to tidy, to conceal the illicit, to ascribe decent motives for action, to present behaviour as the outcome of intention logically implemented, to interpret failure as the result of recalcitrant outside forces rather than personal incompetence. Such laundering of reality does not imply more-than-normal duplicity on the part of elites, merely that the social expectations of those in leadership roles are more-than-normally demanding, the losses consequent on a fall from status are larger, and hence the risks of candour correspondingly greater.

Thus, with elites, it is more-than-normally important not to rely solely on their own accounts of their lives. Social research on elites requires direct, systematic, replicable observation of their activities, conducted by outside, non-elite observers.

7.2   Some Limitations of Dynamic Observational Research

Of course, the limitations of observational methods are themselves obvious and well analysed: the selective perception and partial recording, the restricted ability to probe for motive and meaning, so that the researcher documents 'behaviour' not 'action'.

These problems become particularly acute when the observation is conducted dynamically, as most elite observation is likely to be, without recording on film or tape. Compared with the repeated post-event analyses of recorded action common in kinesics or ethno-methodology, compared even with the multiple observer records of small group studies conducted in laboratory conditions, dynamic observation in real life contexts is a crude instrument.

Observational methods are also vulnerable, in extreme form, to a problem latent in all elite studies, namely the relationship between the researcher and the elite. The heightened social significance of the elite means that the interpretation of data, implicitly if not explicitly, intentionally or otherwise, commonly has an evaluative character. It confirms or denies the social status of the subjects; at the extreme, it reveres or exposes them.

The study of elites by observation facilitates and increases the tendency toward exposé. The researcher observes the elite in normal contexts of work or leisure. The researcher sees, in some degree, the private self behind the public presentation of the elite self. A selective attention to discrediting evidence may develop. Discovering the 'reality' behind the 'facade' may come to seem the principal or the only research task.

Sometimes the exposures are relatively harmless, showing merely the common humanity of the celebrated, that they are venal and vulgar, that they belch and fart like the rest of us. Sometimes the exposures may be malignly tendentious, purposefully setting out to demonstrate that the powerful are timorous, the moralists are concupiscient, and so on. Elite studies in general and observational studies in particular are vulnerable to degeneration into an intellectually respectable form of muck-raking.

These then are a few of the more serious difficulties in using observational methods in the study of elites. But if we look at the broad pattern of elite studies, there is a noticeable shortage of basic descriptive material. What do elites do, with whom, in what locations, at what hours, in what manner? If omissions can be obvious, then these are among the most visible things that are not there. In consequence, speculation about elites both precedes and exceeds information about them. If we go back to the square one of science, this deficiency in our knowledge must be filled, however imperfect the methods by which we make the attempt.

Investigating what elites do is not ethnographic empiricism for its own sake. The focus is not on the cultural anthropology of Mount Olympus, on the peculiar rules of etiquette which apply in the directors' dining room, or such like. Researchers are interested in elites because they are, in various ways, important people in society. The precise content of any investigation into what elites do should be determined in the context of their particular significance in political, economic and social life. The aim is to provide the evidential base for inducing or testing theories about structural regularities in society.

7.3   The Company Director Study

The foregoing rationale for observational studies of elites has been composed in reflection, after rather many years of introspection on the subject, but the fundamental point about the need to observe and describe elites in action became apparent to Ray Pahl and myself very early on in a study of company directors.

The research was commissioned by the Institute of Directors as a background study in a larger research programme on the physical and psychological health of its members.

Like many researchers venturing into a new field, we began by reading the relevant literature. While there is a vast amount written about capitalism and management in general, there is relatively little about company directors in particular. Most of what there was at that time fell into four categories.

The most common form of academic research on business elites has been the social background study. This investigates the social status of elites' families and their own education. A subcategory of this research is the network study, which traces the social connections among business elites.

Beyond this, there are remuneration studies, often conducted periodically by management consultants, detailing the salaries of directors of various types in different industries and companies of different size. There are a substantial number of how-to-do-it books, which seek to prescribe good boardroom practice in a rather formalistic manner. Finally, there is the literature of tycoonery, autobiographies of the successful describing 'how I made my pile', 'clawed my way to the top', or 'ran my empire'.

Thus, at the time we began our study, we searched in vain for any serious description of company directors' activity, at work or at play. This void was so conspicuous, fundamental and significant that it determined the entire future course of the research.

The design of the project involved two cardinal decisions. The first was to frame the research question as: What do directors do? The context in which that question was investigated was the political economy of an advanced, but embattled capitalist society: What is the role of the company director in that changing environment? The second decision was the methodological choice to answer that question by observing directors in action. We did employ other methods – informal interviews, discussion groups and a diary study – but the principal research technique was observation.

The remainder of this paper is a description of the practicalities and problems of doing research in this manner at this level. (For results, see Pahl and Winkler, 1974a and b, and Winkler, 1975a and b.) It concentrates on methodological issues which will face anyone considering similar research themselves, grouped under two headings, gaining access and what to observe.

One final, perhaps fatal, preambulatory qualification is morally as well as scientifically essential. The subject of the research was company directors, not elites *per se*. The operational definition of the economic elite conventionally adopted for research purposes is a company directorship. This is a crude notion, much criticized in the literature. Our project confirmed those doubts about positional definitions of elites (Pahl and Winkler, 1974a).

Many of the men in our research were genuine elites under any conception of the word. And most economic elites will, under present arrangements, be company directors. But the vast majority of company directors are most certainly not economic elites. Thus, in a rigorous sense, ours is not a study of elites. But then, for the same reason, neither are most of the other researches which purport to deal with the economic elite. What follows is for the undaunted.

7.4   Issues in Access

Biblical authority notwithstanding, knocking is no guarantee that anything will be opened unto researchers. Access is commonly a major practical problem in observational research, often the issue on which the fate of the entire project hinges.

Observation research in its classic form of participant observation, that is, where the researchers are legitimate actors in the setting in some other naturally occurring role and their identity as researchers is not known to the other participants, is usually impossible with elites. Social scientists are, alas, unjustly seldom societal elites. 'Access' therefore means obtaining elites' consent to watch them (and any with whom they interact) in the course of their normal lives, openly identified to all as a researcher. Observational methods demand a great deal from subjects, in terms of trust as well as practical co-operation. Understandably, many refuse, even when they do not have elite reputations to nurture.

The first step in gaining access, therefore, involves clarifying what one wants access to. Thereafter, the access process falls into a number of intellectually separable but practically overlapping stages: sampling, approach, sponsorship, negotiation and withdrawals.

The logical, orderly progression of action presented here was consciously designed as a rational researcher's guide. It derives partly from a retrospective analysis and reconstruction of what we did in our project, partly from a consideration of the decision points and options that apply in elite observation generally. The actual doing of our work at the time was, I am compelled to add by the super ego who observes me over my shoulder constantly (without ever even requesting access), much less tidy, planned or even conscious.

In the directors project, we made a number of background decisions to define, limit and make manageable our observations. We decided to follow individual company directors through one complete working day each, going with them wherever they went, one researcher to one director. We initiated no formal questioning, but we responded to conversations begun by the directors themselves. We restricted the study to executive directors, and because we were interested in the internal dynamics of a board, we sought to observe the complete set of executive directors in any company. Thus, in practice, we had a double access problem; first, to gain entry to a company, then to obtain the co-operation of the individual directors.

These choices suited our purposes, but there is nothing intrinsic to the observational method which made them inevitable. Alternative techniques in observation will be appropriate in other elite projects: more extended following of fewer subjects, static observation of selected important settings through which elites pass, triangulation through multiple observers, combining observation with other research methods, recording with tape or video.

Different types of elites vary in the extent to which they are covered by adequate sampling frames. If one is willing to accept a positional definition of elites for, say, Ministers, bishops, generals or Central Committee members, the category is clearly defined, the numbers are relatively small and comprehensive lists exist. If one is concerned with leaders in taste, criminal bosses or company directors, however, then the world is not conveniently organized for rigorous sampling.

But the real sampling problem in observational research concerns not the frame, but the refusal rate. We anticipated, correctly, many rejections. In the end we studied nineteen companies. To get into these we had personal negotiations (one or more face-to-face meetings or extended telephone conversations) with over 130 firms, and more distant contact with many more. At a rough estimate, I spent one-third of the research time – approximately one year of a three-year project – simply negotiating access. By the most generous interpretation, we had a refusal rate of over 85 per cent.

There are no norms for what constitutes an acceptable response rate for overt observational research. We are unable to say whether 15 per cent represents good or bad practice. At the time, it felt like a massive achievement. But undoubtedly the acceptances could have been increased and the time required to get them reduced if we had known as much at the beginning as we knew at the end about the techniques of negotiating access.

Because we expected an outcome something like this, we opted for a crude quota sample of companies. We constructed a simple 3 × 3 matrix of the economy (large, medium and small companies in the primary, secondary and tertiary sectors) then set out to fill the boxes. We succeeded in studying at least one company of each type we sought, except for a large, metal-based engineering firm.

We spent complete days observing 82 executive directors, but more than 100 days within the companies because the men regularly invited us to attend extra events which they knew would interest us, like annual general meetings, loan negotiations, or visits to installations.

Obtaining subjects' co-operation in overt observational research, of the type we were doing, almost always requires extended face-to-face negotiation. Because the commitment demanded from subjects is so great, they naturally have questions, about the nature and value of the research and what is expected from them. Because of the method's intimacy, they require more than the conventional guarantees of confidentiality. One of the unspoken purposes of the face-to-face meeting with prospective subjects is to give them the opportunity to assess the legitimacy, seriousness, competence and trustworthiness of the researchers.

In sum, obtaining subjects for overt observational research is a time-consuming and labour intensive process whose outcome is uncertain. Researchers are liable to underestimate the time, effort and risk involved. Certainly we underestimated them badly. Therefore, it is important that the initial approach to prospective subjects be prepared carefully. We used three techniques, with very different results.

First, we organized a 'group discussion' on the role of the director for an invited group of company chairmen and managing directors. It was held over drinks in a meeting room at the Institute of Directors, then in Belgravia, just after the close of the normal business day. It was extremely successful, in terms of the percentage of invitees who came, the number of attenders who agreed to participate in the observational research, and even in the quality of the discussion on the nominal subject of the meeting.

This was a successful recruitment device for two reasons which became much clearer in the subsequent research. First, many elite individuals feel anxious about their status, and hence seek to confirm it by participating in elite gatherings and comparing themselves with other elites. Secondly, there is a norm among business elites which makes it acceptable to extend invitations to, and accept invitations from, other business elites whom one has never met. Effectively, therefore, our discussion group was an elite meeting ground, packaged in acceptable social paraphernalia. So they came. With hindsight, I am astounded and ashamed we did not use this approach technique more often.

More frequently but less successfully, we wrote short, ambiguous letters to the chairmen and managing directors of our sampled companies, briefly describing the project and requesting meetings to explain it more fully. Effectively, we were relying on the Institute of Directors' sponsorship to gain us entry.

The letters gained us enough meetings to encourage us with this technique, but most of the long negotiations that ensued came to nothing. It became clear that the 'institutional' sponsorship of the research by an organization sympathetic to the subjects was a necessary condition for access, but was not sufficient. We only won the co-operation we needed when we supplemented this with 'personal' sponsorship.

Researchers on elites will vary in the extent of their pre-existing personal contacts in the group they are studying. Our networks in the upper reaches of business were limited. But we did try to gain direct entry to selected companies through individual directors whom we knew. This was successful a few times where the individual was the effective boss of the firm. But we never negotiated access where our initial contact was a director other than the chairman or managing director. This was a forewarning of the boardroom power structures which the research subsequently documented.

Most effective was the indirect sponsorship of a senior business-man who personally introduced us to his friends. Three types of individual were particularly useful in this role: leading management consultants with a large range of corporate contacts, what are known in the trade as 'professional directors', that is, men with large numbers of non-executive directorships, and business philosophers, successful men who have proved themselves in the competitive struggle, who now like to reflect on broader economic issues and hence welcome occasional abstract conversation with researchers. Our discussions with them were always surrounded with conventional alcoholic and gastronomic bribery. Gaining access to elites can be expensive as well as arduous, but not without its diversions.

Having won the co-operation of the critical chairman/managing director of a company, we usually made a presentation about the research to all the executive directors on the board to gain their individual consent. But we were not always successful in this. Autocratic chairmen sometimes simply ordered subordinates to submit to our observation. This always created problems later because the other directors, non-elites certainly, were understand-ably suspicious of our purposes.

The access process does not end with entry to the institution. Some who agree in the collective meeting change their minds later and seek to withdraw. Unavoidable engagements, real or invented, sometimes intervene and one must renegotiate consent. More complex are partial withdrawals, when subjects seek to prevent observation of selected events. The two most common scenes where exclusion became an issue were when the subject had to deliver bad news or a reprimand to subordinates, and when elite members of other organizations became involved. Effectively we were re-negotiating access to specific parts of the subjects' days.

The most dramatic example was when we were blocked at the last moment from attending a meeting of the industry's cartel. Feeling guilty, the director explained in great detail how the group fixed prices. His strategy for this meeting was to agree in the cabal, then cheat on the agreement immediately afterwards to gain market share. In this instance, candour compensated for censorship.

Given the inconvenience, potential risks and inadequate reciprocity, why do so many elite subjects agree to be observed? On reflection afterwards, it seems several reasons played a part. First is the flattery implicit in any research, that someone else is seriously interested in your life. Some were simply paying off obligations to our personal sponsors. A few chairmen saw the research as a different, intellectual kind of stimulus to the board. Some were sympathetic to research in general or our project in particular. Central for many, however, was the psychology of elite status. Any researcher who has observed a substantial number of elites in their private work settings, behind the front presented to the world, knows more about certain aspects of elite behaviour than the elites themselves. The researcher has data on which to make comparisons. Many of our subjects wanted to know what it was like for the others and how they rated alongside the famous.

Why then do social scientists not do more observational research on elites? Certainly the time, effort and expense of negotiating access makes it prohibitive for many projects. So too does the risk: the directors project almost collapsed on the access problem. Further, some researchers have methodological preferences which make them suspicious of qualitative techniques in general, and observation particularly.

But there is a psychology of the elite researcher as well. Some are apprehensive of the access process. They convince themselves that rejection is inevitable and so shrink from asking. Differences in social status of several kinds may underlie these inhibitions. Elites are usually of higher social class than those who research them. Elites are frequently older men, researchers usually younger and, in the social sciences, often women. A conventional sense of age gradings may intimidate. So too, particularly in business, may well-institutionalized sexism.

More consciously, political differences may intrude. Elites are commonly leaders of established social institutions. Social scientists are often, in varying degrees, social critics. Certainly many of the research reports on British economic elites, particularly the social background studies, are explicitly or implicitly critical of their subjects, seeing their privileged origins and lack of technical training as a manifestation of systemic social injustice and a cause of national economic mismanagement. Many who hold such a view anticipate that they would not be acceptable to their subjects for any form of fieldwork involving face-to-face contact, so their elite research gets done at arm's length or in a library.

More intensely, one conception of socialism views research on elites as *prima facie* stigmatizing. Some researchers who have a strong political commitment to the working class and the exploited in society, professionally take the view that established institutions have more than enough research resources and hence that they should commit their own efforts to the disadvantaged. By extension, what one does research on and who one does research with become indicators of the researcher's values. Elite research is interpreted as colluding with, not just learning about, the enemy. Therefore, research on economic elites implies a commitment to capitalism. While such an interpretation is by no means general, it prevails in some sections of British social science and acts to inhibit research on elites.

Though not often openly acknowledged, conventional normative barriers may repress approaches to elites. Observational research creates a very unusual social situation. The researcher watches in what is normally the private space of the individual. It is not just subjects who sometimes find this intrusive, but also researchers themselves. Requesting access for observational research involves breaking social conventions. Thus, Wolfe commented,

> The initial problem is always to approach total strangers, move in on their lives in some fashion, ask questions you have no natural right to expect answers to, ask to see things you weren't meant to see, and so on. Many . . . find it so ungentlemanly, so embarrassing, so terrifying even that they are never able to master this essential first move. (Wolfe and Johnson, 1975, pp. 50–1)

Whatever the complex reasons for researchers' reticence, the consequence is that we have very little basic descriptive material about the behaviour of elites. We have failed in the first task of science.

7.5 Issues in Observation

Most of the methodological literature on what is conventionally, if often inaccurately, called 'participant observation' concerns how to become a participant rather than what to observe. The central problem with dynamic observation, the basis for doubts about both its validity and reliability as a research method, is its inevitable selectivity. It is a fantasy to suppose that the researcher can observe everything or even be open to the full range of behaviour enacted in any setting.

After a long development, scientists working on body-motion communication were able to reduce the time for analysis of filmed episodes of individual behaviour from one hundred hours to a single hour per second of film (see, for example, Birdwhistell's *Kinesics and Content*, 1971). The analysis of taped conversations is similarly extended. Measured against these standards, observing the interaction of groups as it takes place in natural settings is bound to be incomplete.

The first step of observational research is to acknowledge that fact. The next is to articulate abstractly what one is looking for in order to specify what one is going to look at. Doing this with sufficient precision to make dynamic observational research truly replicable is a methodological Holy Grail, but one must try, at least, to define the selectivity.

Dynamic observational projects themselves vary in the rigour of their methods. They range from informed impressions to studies which count and time-selected behaviours specified in advance on observational schedules.

Structurally, the directors project was a difficult one in which to focus the observation in advance. We were not interested in the mechanics of directors' behaviour (how many letters answered, meetings attended, or calories consumed at lunchtime) but their role in a capitalist economy. So the scope of the project was large, the settings varied and unpredictable, our familiarity with what was likely to happen within them relatively low – all characteristics which make pre-structured observation difficult.

We also intentionally wanted to be as open as possible to this, for us, new subculture. Of course, we always noted the basics – who was present, where, when and for how long – but beyond this our observation was purposely unstructured, and therefore technically unreplicable.

We frequently debriefed one another, however, comparing and analysing not only what we had observed, but why we had observed what we had observed. Out of these extended exchanges evolved a shared understanding of what we were attending to and how we interpreted it. We may exemplify the method with five of the more important categories: patterns, transitions, transgressions, omissions and the volunteered.

By 'patterns' are meant regularities in behaviour generally and variations around recurrent events specifically. Take two examples, one clearly in the heartland of the research, board meetings, and the other apparently trivial, approach rituals.

Most board meetings we observed were formalistic affairs, with meagre debate, few probing questions, little serious discussion even. They were certainly not the forum in which the critical decisions of capitalism were made (Winkler, 1975a). Effectively, the board was a legitimating institution for decisions taken earlier and elsewhere.

But in following directors around prior to these meetings, we observed the intense political manoeuvring to obtain a negotiated agreement among the executive directors and to so structure their presentations that assent of the non-executive directors became inevitable, a striving to ensure that everything did indeed go through without challenge in the board meeting itself.

This manipulation of the board was itself part of a larger pattern. In the bigger companies, the monthly board meeting was only the culmination of a series of preparatory gatherings, among executive committees, subsidiary boards, senior management groups, functional specialists, etc. Here too, in only slightly diluted form, the common practice was to pre-negotiate the outcome on significant issues.

In time, the relationship became apparent: the more important the meeting was in formal organizational terms, the greater was the effort expended to control its results in advance, and hence the fewer were the substantive decisions made in the gathering itself. By the time it came to the annual general meeting, the executive directors created a ceremony of acclamation, a pure ritual.

'Transitions' between two settings are moments when patterns often become most clearly visible, as actors adjust their behaviour to changing contexts. As Goffman, one of the greatest practitioners, indelibly documents, doorways are excellent sites for observational research, since they define the boundary between settings (Goffman, 1972). Sitting inside directors' offices we were in a good place to watch how others, including especially other directors, approached them.

Variations on the common act of entering an office became apparent, effectively behavioural options for the entrants. The basic alternatives were knocking on the door and waiting to be called in; knocking and opening the door without waiting for permission but then only sticking one's head through the aperture or partially entering the room; knocking and entering but then waiting for the incumbent to initiate the conversation; knocking, entering and initiating the conversation oneself; or entering without knocking.

The point of noting all this is that, even between two directors on the same board, the approach format chosen invariably manifested the status relationship between the two men. Nothing unusual here, of course. Status rituals on encounter are standard in all cultures. But these finely modulated manifestations of status were important in our study because they conflicted with the prevailing late twentieth-century ideology of the board of directors. In the many normative statements of good boardroom practice, the board is presented as a collegial body in which directors set aside individual responsibilities to consider the firm as a whole. The board is explicitly the cabinet government of business. An astounding number of directors believe this is how boards should operate, indeed how they do operate in companies other than their own. They interpret their own board as atypically hierarchical and the deference rituals which they must go through as indicating that they are not 'real' directors.

Sometimes in the flow of routine action, it is not immediately apparent to outside observers what is really taking place. The rules of the game often only become apparent when they are broken. 'Transgressions' of norms thus become important moments in observational research. Sometimes, conveniently for observers, the reaction of others is aggressively articulated in censure, complaint, challenge or conflict, indicating a norm that will not only be espoused but actively enforced.

At other times what had been broken is less clear because the reaction takes the form of irritation, frustration, surprise, disappointment or even mute displaced attention. Sometimes transgressors themselves display guilt, embarrassment or surreptitiousness. Occasionally all parties collude to define the event as an 'accident', a 'misunderstanding' or an 'interruption'.

One of those exhilarating moments in research, when many separate bits of evidence coalesce into an argument, was triggered by another manifestation of transgression, some apparently insignificant apologies. I was spending the day with the managing director of a company. He began by apologising that he had to spend the next few hours reading papers. Repeatedly during the morning he broke off his reading to explain that this was not a typical day for him, to express sorrow that so little was happening for me to observe, to assure me that normally he was much busier, etc. I kept asking myself, 'Why is this managing director apologising to me for reading?'

Later, the fountain pen with which he was taking notes ran out of ink. He then began a long explanation of how his pens were normally filled each morning by his secretary, but she was ill and her temporary replacement did not know what to do, etc. I asked myself, 'Why is this man apologising to me because his pen went dry?' Clearly, because such a thing should not happen to a managing director. Other incidents with other managing directors came back to me when unanticipated disruptions to the planned flow of events had caused similar annoyance, violating their conception of themselves as the men in control.

In some cases, it is not what subjects do, but what they do not do which is important in observational research. Logically, of course, these 'omissions' are potentially infinite. But, in common sense terms, researchers may anticipate what they might find in their subjects' lives, who would be present and what taking place. Then, against that rough standard of *prima facie* plausibility they may be attentive to what does not appear.

In our study, workers and shareholders were equally conspicuous by their absence, and non-executive directors appeared little more than legal obligations required. Having noted what is 'missing', researchers may analyse the rest of their evidence for both the causes and consequences of this absence and for any surrogate mechanisms which replace face-to-face contact with those who are not there.

This kind of analysis was carried out in detail for the absent workers in our study (Winkler, 1974). Among its conclusions for example were: that non-contact was a purposeful, if not always conscious strategy for the management of industrial relations. One consequence was large gaps in directors' knowledge of what was going on in their own companies and as a result, vulnerability to manipulation by the information control strategies of their subordinates. In one extreme example, a transport director discovered during my day with him that a series of strikes had occurred during the previous year in one of his depots and that the senior manager in charge was not only keeping them secret, but blaming 'board policy' for the actions which provoked the strikes.

One of our methodological background decisions, noted above, was that the directors study should be strictly observational. We did not wish to interrupt the flow of events with interviewing. Many of our subjects were incredulous. They frequently initiated conversations. We later analysed the content of the remarks which they 'volunteered'.

Several types of spontaneous remarks were significant. First, they probed our bona fides with varying degrees of directness: How did we obtain the research commission? How did we meet the chairman? What was our relationship with the sponsor? A few times there was a straightforward trial by interrogation: What were we really after? Whose side were we on?

Second, they tried to structure our perceptions of what we were observing, anticipatorily or retrospectively. Sometimes they would explain the 'background' or 'history' of the event we were about to witness, or give us 'biographies' of the principal actors. Afterwards they might explain the 'complexity' or 'significance' of what we had just seen in a way that rationalized their role in it.

The most important conversations, however, took place 'after hours'. At some point our subject would indicate that his directorial day had finished. We reciprocated by putting away our pen and notebook. This is the equivalent in observational research to turning off the tape recorder in interviewing. We went back over the events of the day and they asked how we interpreted what we had seen. But often, under various layers of camouflage, they asked about what we had observed in other companies. A few asked the question nakedly, 'How do I compare with other directors?'

Beyond conversation, what our subjects sometimes offered to us was opportunities for further observation at unusual events. They were volunteering to be observed again, often in contexts which would test their competence as businessmen. This behaviour is a suitable introduction to one of the major issues of observational research: how representative of subjects' lives are the occasions which the researchers observe?

Doubts exist on two scores: first, that the very act of observation distorts normal behaviour; second, that subjects may structure events to create an impression, in effect, put on a show for the observer.

Being closely and continuously watched for long periods is a very unusual experience and even fully co-operating subjects may behave abnormally. It would be absurd to deny that observational methods may have what is conventionally known as an 'observer effect'. Researchers can do much to put subjects at their ease. But, the best guarantees of normality are the other actors who enter the setting. They bring with them their usual expectations of the subject who is under observation and either extract normal behaviour or in some way react to the difference.

More importantly, subjects may control what is observed. They may exclude the researchers from some types of event altogether. This is relatively easy. In most overt observational research, the subjects actually specify when the observation will take place. And what subjects do allow researchers to observe may be carefully constructed to deceive. The potential for creating unrepresentative episodes is great.

But researchers are prone to err on the side of methodological pessimism. We need to ask: (i) do subjects try to stage such performances? (ii) if they try, do they succeed? (iii) if they succeed, does it destroy the observation?

One indicator of normality is the presence during observation of elements that would not be there if the subjects were wilfully putting on a show – the illicit, the discrediting, or simply the uncontrollable. We were twice admitted to companies while strikes were in progress, three times we witnessed chairmen dictating spurious minutes for board meetings that never took place, a punishable offence. One director was sacked and another went to sleep in our presence. On three occasions we sat in on price-fixing negotiations. In one company the chairman and the finance director raised the annual profit figure 11 per cent over night because the earlier sum had not quite fulfilled their prediction. In another the junior directors discussed at length in our presence what they should do about a senior manager they had discovered defrauding a public authority. They decided to do nothing.

Was all this part of the charade? The simple fact must be acknowledged, however insulting it may be to researchers, that some subjects are not sufficiently concerned about the opinion of such people to bother putting on a show.

Some of our subjects, of course, did try to put on a show for us. We know they did because it collapsed before our eyes. Usually it was others, superiors, outsiders, subordinates even, who were not part of the plot, who gave the game away by their reactions. Sometimes uncontrollable events intruded. In one company a strike broke out while we were there, in another a large shareholder threatened to disrupt the annual general meeting.

Not all performances end in shambles, of course. But even when they succeed the researcher may ask, what kind of show was being put on? What messages were the performers trying to convey? The answer depends, in part, on what kind of spectator the players thought the observer represented.

We tried to be alert to the identities which our subjects projected on to us. One mentioned earlier was that we were the boss's spies. Not far from that, we were seen as management consultants sent to assess their competence. For some, encouraged perhaps by our German-sounding surnames, we were psychologists ('Austrian shrinks') who could fathom their unconscious propensities, particularly in matters sexual. For others we were reflective academics with whom one could discourse about higher things. To a few we were irrelevant academics, contemptible for our inexperience of the 'real', 'hard' world of business. To most, however, we were simply men like themselves, to whom they transferred their own values. The man who apologised for reading, for example, did not see me, academic though I be, as a bookish scholar. Rather, he assumed I shared his conception that reading was not a proper thing for a managing director to be doing. The performances enacted by those who tried to put on a show were mostly plays at being a good director. In so doing, they displayed for us the conventions of the sub-culture in which they lived.

7.6 Conclusions

This paper has concerned itself with method not findings, with the techniques of observing elites, not with the substance of what was observed. But illustrating the arguments have been indications of our results: the anxiety of elites about their relative social standing, the organized vacuity of board meetings, the dissolution of normative collegiality into hierarchy and manipulation, and ultimately that directorship for executives is not a role at all, but an honorific social status with only minimal attached behavioural obligations, a kind of corporate knighthood.

None of this apparent iconoclasm is really very unusual if we compare it with what we know about human behaviour in other institutions, in other contexts. But it certainly does contrast with the ideology of the board, with public assertions directors sometimes make about their work, with the accounts outsiders have sometimes given of the directorial role, with the social significance that is commonly attached to a company directorship. Observing directors yielded a different description of their life than that available from other sources, and that produced by other research methods. The intent here has been to demonstrate that the observation of elites in action is both technically feasible and substantially valuable.

8

The study of a business elite and corporate philanthropy in a United States metropolitan area

JOSEPH GALASKIEWICZ
University of Minnesota

8.1 Project Overview and the Role of Elites in the Study

This paper draws on a study of business elites and corporate philanthropy in Minneapolis–St Paul (USA) (see Galaskiewicz, 1985). The purpose of this article is twofold: to describe a fairly complex research methodology that might be useful for studying elites in other systems and to suggest ways to improve upon our efforts. After a brief overview of the study and its main findings, we will discuss how we identified the corporate philanthropic elite, interviewed them, and operationalized variables measuring their impact on an urban grants economy. This will be followed by discussions of ways to improve the methodology and ethical issues that arose both during and after the study.

The research is a study of corporate contributions to nonprofit organizations in the Minneapolis–St Paul (Twin Cities) metropolitan area. The Twin Cities are located in the upper midwest and had a population of 1,982,000 in 1980 (United States Bureau of the Census, 1984). For the most part the Cities were settled in the latter half of the nineteenth century. Lumber and flour milling were key industries in this period, and some of the most prominent companies in the cities today can trace their roots to this era (e.g. Pillsbury, General Mills, International Multifoods, Peavey, and Cargill; see Larson, 1979). While many of the successful entrepreneurs of that era had 'Yankee'

Funds for this research were provided by grants from the National Science Foundation (SES 800–8570) and the Program on Nonprofit Organizations, Yale University.

origins, most of the working class was Scandinavian or Slavic. Today the Twin Cities are as equally well-known for their 'hi-tech' industries such as Control Data Corporation, Honeywell, Inc., and 3M, and for retailing (e.g. Dayton–Hudson and SuperValu). The Twin Cities have a national reputation for their firms' generosity to charitable causes (Galaskiewicz, 1985, pp. 1–3).

The purpose of the research was to describe how corporate philanthropy functioned in the Twin Cities. The period studied was from 1979 to 1981. The case study approach made it impossible for us to explain why company contributions were greater in the Twin Cities than elsewhere, but it did allow us to examine the social dynamics of this one case. Hopefully our findings will lay the groundwork for further research that will be able to ascertain why company giving varies across community settings.

Looking at the contributions budget of 69 large publicly-owned companies (all with over 200 employees) headquartered in the Twin Cities area, we found that firms whose chief executive officer (CEO) was more tightly integrated into the networks of a corporate philanthropic elite tended to give more money to charity, even controlling for the size and market position of the firm. Also, those firms which gave more money to charity were viewed by more members of this elite as 'very generous' to non-profits and as 'more successful business ventures'. The latter effect held even controlling for firms' actual performance. Effectively we found a pattern of serial reciprocity where companies gave more money to non-profits if their executive was in elite social circles and the more they gave, the more they received recognition from this elite as generous and successful businesses.

Looking at a stratified sample of 229 public charities in the community, we found that corporate contributions tended to go to non-profit organizations which were recognized and evaluated positively by professional staff members who were responsible for administering grants for their company. However, the ones they viewed positively were non-profit organisations which were used and supported by more members of the corporate philanthropic elite. In other words, the charitable organizations which were used or supported by more members of the corporate philanthropic elite tended to be recognized and evaluated positively by more professionals which, in turn, resulted in their receiving more corporate contributions.

In a related but slightly different analysis, we found that the size of the contribution, from a specific corporation to a specific non-profit organization, tended to be larger if more members of the corporate philanthropic elite were associated personally with both the corporation and non-profit. Apparently the corporate philanthropic elite acted as a conduit through which corporate contributions were channeled. Thus, the elite not only prompted greater contributions from firms but channeled the flow of funds to their favourite charities.

The prominence of the elite in this corporate grants economy prompted us to examine more closely their backgrounds. Comparing them to the CEOs of all 98 publicly-held firms that had more than 200 employees and were headquartered locally, we found that the elite tended to be better represented in local exclusive clubs and on cultural boards, to be heads of Fortune 50 or 500 firms, and to have an Ivy League undergraduate education. The corporate philanthropic elite also tended to be local: 60.0 per cent were born in Minnesota and 76.7 per cent were born in the upper midwest (Minnesota, Iowa, or the Dakotas). Finally, the elite were much more likely than other CEOs to rationalize contributions as enlightened self-interest. At first we thought this tendency to rationalize contributions in terms of the collective interests of business and elite involvement in philanthropic affairs could be due solely to upper-class socialization and local roots. However, we must remember that at the same time corporate money was being funneled indirectly to the elite's favourite charities. Thus, while home and hearth could have been important in prompting the elite's civic involvement, so could the fact that the non-profits which they used personally and supported were benefiting in the process.

8.2 Identifying the Corporate Philanthropic Elite

Obviously the corporate elite was central to this urban grants economy. In this section we will describe how we came to know that an elite existed and how we identified the members of the elite. To help us make our way through the following somewhat complex discussion, we have prepared a time line of the research (see Table 8.1).

Preliminary informant interviews
The funding for the research began in 1980, almost a year before the interviews with the corporate philanthropic elite. At that time we began a series of preliminary, informal interviews to obtain qualitative information on how corporations channeled money to

Table 8.1 Research schedule

Year	Interview	January	February	March	April	May	June	July	August	September	October	November	December
1980	Non-profit			Develop NPO sampling frame →						Draw NPO sample		NPO interviews →	
	Elite									Informal interviews with community informants			
	Corporate												
1981	Non-profit				→ Code NPO data →					Supplementary NPO interviews →			
	Elite		Develop community elite sampling frame					Draw elite sample			Elite interviews →	Philanthropic elite interviews →	
	Corporate											Corporate interviews →	
1982	Non-profit			→ Code NPO data									
	Elite		→ Code community and philanthropic elite interviews →										
	Corporate							→ Code corporate interviews →					
1983	Non-profit	→ Interviews with philanthropic brokers											
	Elite	and professional associations of grant-makers →							Data analysis →				
	Corporate	→											
1984		→ Writing →						1st draft to publisher				Final draft to publisher	
1985			Copy editing →				Page proofs →					Publication	

non-profit organizations. The original proposal had budgeted interviews with a cross-section of the community elite (businessmen, politicians, doctors, lawyers, etc.), but we were unaware of a corporate philanthropic elite prior to our research. It was in the course of these preliminary interviews that we became aware of such a group.

The preliminary interviews began in August, 1980 and the first were with four faculty members at the University of Minnesota who were engaged either in fundraising or with a local non-profit organization. These interviews were the first to alert us to some sort of leadership group among businessmen locally. At the same time we were negotiating a proposal with the Program on Non-profit Organizations at Yale University and John Simon, the director, was also alerting us to the leadership in the Twin Cities. Also about this time we read several very flattering articles on the Twin Cities' business community in *Fortune Magazine*, the *Wall Street Journal* and the *Chicago Tribune* portraying Twin Cities corporations, as progressive and responsive.

In late September, 1980 we began interviewing in the community. Over the next three months the principal investigator (PI) met with the executive director of the Minnesota Council of Foundations, the head of the Charities Review Board, the executive director and director of planning and allocation of the Minneapolis United Way, the executive directors of the St Paul and Minneapolis Chambers of Commerce, the executive director of the Minnesota State Arts Board, the chairman of the board of the Minnesota Opera, the director of the Management Assistance Project, the executive director of the Minneapolis Foundation and representatives of the Dayton-Hudson and Jerome Foundations. Also that fall the PI attended conferences on the funding of hospitals and cultural organizations. During the interviews and conferences there were repeated references to a group of business leaders who were instrumental in finding and providing support for non-profits locally, and this led us to study this elite.

Community elite interviews
We had originally planned to interview only a cross-section of the community elite. The interviews were to be in the spring and summer of 1981. Due to the comments of those interviewed the previous autumn, we thought it a good idea to use the interviews with the community elite to identify the corporate philanthropic leaders. In other words, we would use reputational measures to identify the philanthropic elite with our elite sample as informants.

The sampling frame for the community elite was developed in several steps. First, we scanned Marquis's *Who's Who in America, 1980–81* (1980) for names of people who either lived or worked in the Twin Cities seven-county metropolitan area. There was a total of 820. Because individuals do have the option of not belonging to 'Who's Who' and Marquis's criteria are not clearly defined, we supplemented this list. To ensure that we had the names of all prominent people in the area, we went to key positional leaders in various sectors of the community. We visited the executive directors of the two chambers of commerce (business), the president of the University of Minnesota and the executive administrator of the Minnesota Educational Association (education), the chair of the Metropolitan Health Board and the commissioner of the Minnesota Department of Health (health), the director of the Arts Resource and Information Center and the administrator of the Minneapolis Arts Commission (culture), the dean of the University of Minnesota Law School and the president-elect of the Minnesota Bar Association (law), the mayors of Minneapolis and St Paul (government), sports writers at the Minneapolis and St Paul metropolitan newspapers (sports), and the administrator of the Minnesota Council of Churches and the executive director of the St Paul Council of Churches (religion). These individuals were handed a list of 'Who's Who' names for their sector and asked to add the names of any other prominent people in their sector. All the names mentioned by our informants were added to our list. This gave us a grand total of 1284 names.

We grouped all 1284 people by functional area and drew a 7 per cent stratified systematic sample of 90 names. Business people (35), educators (22), and lawyers (8) were most heavily represented in our sample. Of these 90, we interviewed 80. Seven respondents had moved out of the Twin Cities before we could reach them, and three refused to be interviewed.

The elite sample was interviewed between May and September of 1981. Interviews were face-to-face at their homes or places of business. The interviews lasted between forty-five and ninety minutes. The principal investigator and a research assistant conducted these interviews.

In the course of the community elite interviews respondents were asked to identify 'the individuals who had been most instrumental in raising the level of corporate contributions over the past few years.' Some respondents named no one; others named several people. Individuals who were named three or more times were labelled 'corporate philanthropic leaders'; 30 individuals were thus identified. All but 2 were corporate executives at some point in their careers, 14 were retired, and 2 were deceased. The names generated by this method are listed in Table 8.2.

Having used a reputational measure to generate our list of philanthropic leaders, the question of validity comes immediately to mind. We dealt with this by operationalizing four different indicators of philanthropic elite involvement in fund-raising. First, in interviews with the philanthropic elite (to be described in detail in the next section) we asked each member of the elite to tell us the capital/endowment campaigns which he 'headed up' between 1978 and 1982. Secondly, we obtained the names of the chairs and co-chairs of the ten largest capital/endowment campaigns between 1978 and 1982. All had a goal of $15 million or more. Thirdly, we obtained the names of the chairmen for the 1978 through 1982 United Way campaigns in Minneapolis and St Paul. Finally, we asked each respondent:

'In the past ten years or so (since 1970), what have been some of the most successful . . . fund drives in the Twin Cities on behalf of non-profit organizations? Which of these campaign drives are you most familiar with? Who were the people, the ring leaders, who organized it?'

The results of this analysis are mixed. Of the 23 providing us with information on the first item, 13 reported they had headed a fund-raising campaign between 1977 and 1982, and only 4 stated flatly that they never headed a campaign. However, looking at the campaign chairmanships for the Minneapolis and St Paul United Ways from 1978 to 1982, we found that none of the 30 individuals on our list headed a campaign. Furthermore, we found that only 4 of the 30 men headed a $15 million-plus capital campaign between 1978 and 1982, and 3 of the 4 were co-chairs of the same campaign. The picture is more optimistic when we look at our elite's responses to our items on 'ring leaders' of successful fund drives. Only 18 of the 26 responding elites could (or would) name ringleaders, but 20 of the 30 people on our list were cited as being a ring leader of a successful fund drive. Many of these drives took place early in the 1970s (e.g. Orchestra Hall and the Society for Fine Arts fund drives), others were specific United Way campaigns in the early and mid-1970s, and some were ongoing fund-raising efforts (e.g. the University of Minnesota Foundation).

Table 8.2   *List of corporate philanthropic elite with primary institutional affiliation and number of citations by the community elite*

Name	Primary institutional affiliation (1982)	Total number of citations as corporate philanthropic elite
Kenneth Dayton	Chairman of the Executive Committee, Dayton–Hudson Corporation (former President and Chairman of the Board, Dayton–Hudson Corporation)	14
Elmer L. Andersen	Chairman of the Board, H.B. Fuller Company (former Governor of Minnesota)	12
John Cowles, Jr.	President, Cowles Media Company (former President, Chairman of the Board, Minneapolis Star and Tribune Company)	11
Bruce Dayton	Consultant (former CEO, Chairman of the Board, Dayton–Hudson Corporation)	9
William C. Norris	President, Control Data Corporation	8
Atherton Bean	Chairman of the Executive Committee, International Multifoods Corporation (former CEO and Chairman of the Board, International Multifoods Corporation)	7
Judson Bemis	Retired (former CEO, Chairman of the Board, Bemis Company)	6
Donald Dayton	Retired (former Chairman of the Board, Dayton's)	6
Stephen F. Keating	Chairman of the Board, Toro Company (former President and Chairman of the Board, Honeywell)	6
John S. Pillsbury, Jr.	Retired (former CEO and Chairman of the Board, Northwestern National Life Insurance Company)	6
William H. Spoor	CEO, Chairman of the Board, Pillsbury Company	6
William L. McKnight	Deceased (former Chairman of the Board, 3M Company)	5

Table 8.2   *continued*

Name	Primary institutional affiliation (1982)	Total number of citations as corporate philanthropic elite
Philip H. Nason	Retired (former Chairman of the Board, First National Bank of St Paul)	5
James P. Shannon	Executive Director, General Mills Foundation	5
Curt Carlson	President, Chairman of the Board Carlson Companies	4
Harvey MacKay	President, MacKay Envelopes Company	4
John H. Myers	Retired (former CEO, President, Hoerner–Waldorf Corporation)	4
Jay Phillips	Retired (former President, Ed Phillips and Sons)	4
George Pillsbury	Senator, State of Minnesota	4
Harold Cummings	Retired (former CEO, Chairman of the Board, Minnesota Mutual Life Insurance Company)	3
Archibald Bush	Deceased (former Chairman of the Board, 3M Company)	3
Carl Drake	CEO, Chairman of the Board, St Paul Companies	3
N. Bud Grossman	President, Chairman of the Board, Gelco Corporation	3
Raymond H. Herzog	Retired (former CEO, Chairman of the Board, 3M Company)	3
Norman Lorentzen	Retired (former CEO, Chair of the Executive Committee, Burlington–Northern)	3
James McFarland	Retired (former CEO, Chairman of the Board, General Mills)	3
John Morrison	CEO, Chairman of the Board, Northwest Bancorporation	3
Robert J. Odegard	Executive Director, University of Minnesota Foundation	3
Raymond Plank	CEO, Chairman of the Board, Apache Corporation	3
James Reagan	President, American National Bank	3

In sum, if we look only at $15 million-plus capital/endowment or United Way campaigns between 1978 and 1982, the elite we identified is not well represented. However, when members of the elite reported on their own fund-raising efforts or on the efforts of others in the community, we learned that 23 of the 30 gentlemen had fund-raising experience. Of the 7 which did not have campaign or fund-raising experience, one was the executive director of a corporate foundation, one was a state senator, two were deceased, two were retired executives, and one was an active CEO.

It is difficult to interpret these numbers, but it appears that many on our list had already headed their campaigns in the 1960s and early 1970s. They were older now and not actively leading fundraising efforts. However, they could have been active behind the scenes. Alternatively, the community elite who generated the names for us could have been simply misinformed. They may have been fooled by old family names, corporate titles or personal wealth. Yet several prominent family names received no mention and other extraordinarily successful companies were omitted from our list of philanthropic leaders.

8.3   Interviewing the Corporate Philanthropic Elite

The protocol for interviewing members of the corporate philanthropic elite was straightforward. We began contacting philanthropic elite respondents in August, 1981. Since many on our list were retired we could not contact them directly through their businesses. In many cases their former employer provided us with their office address and telephone number. Sometimes we looked up their home address in the public telephone book. The initial contact was made through a letter inviting them to participate in the study. The letter was written on University of Minnesota stationery; it explained the purpose of the interview; it told who the funders were; it guaranteed confidentiality; and it was signed by the principal investigator. Prior to sending the letters to these people, we had personal contact with only one of them about a year earlier (the chairman of the Minnesota Orchestra), and another had learned about the project through our contact at Yale University. Other than that, we had no prior contact with any of them.

After waiting two or three days for the letter to arrive, we called the office and asked to speak with the respondent. In the course of the conversation with the secretary we identified ourselves and made sure the letter had arrived. If it had not, we excused ourselves, promised to call back, and hung up before making contact with the respondent. If the letter had not arrived a few days later, we sent another. If the letter was there and the respondent had seen it, the secretary either put us through, made an appointment with us, or told us the respondent was unavailable or not interested.

The retirees proved to be much more accessible than active corporate executives, and often set a date within two weeks of the call. The corporate executives were much more difficult to schedule. At times we would be given a date two months after our call. Sometimes both retirees and executives would ask us to call back in three months when they returned from a vacation or especially heavy business travel. In one company, at least, I had to go through a preliminary interview with a vice-president. Four respondents whom I eventually interviewed refused my first request. In general there was never a good time to interview the active executives and dozens of telephone calls were sometimes needed. The minimum amount of time between the first letter and the interview was six days in the case of a retiree, and the maximum was seven months in the case of a corporate executive.

We interviewed 26 of the 30 people on our list. Two people were deceased as indicated in Table 8.2, one was extremely ill, and one simply refused.

8.4   Operationalizing Elite Variables

The crucial data from the elite survey were: the elite's networks to CEOs and other executives within each firm in our study; the elite's recognition of a company as being generous and successful, and the elite's use of and service to each non-profit organization in our study. We will briefly describe how we operationalized each of these variables.

During the interviews with the 26 corporate philanthropic leaders, we gave each of them a list of the 209 publicly held companies headquartered in the Twin Cities and asked them to check off the firms in which they knew personally an officer or a board member, that is, someone they knew on a first-name basis and whom they could call for lunch, drinks, or golf. We then tallied the number of philanthropic leaders who checked a given firm and this was used as an indicator of elite-corporate linkage (minimum = 0; maximum = 26; mean = 6.37; standard deviation = 8.75). A firm's executives were thought to be more integrated into the elite network if more philanthropic leaders checked the firm.

To get a second measure of elite-corporate linkages we scanned the rosters of the area's three major metropolitan clubs (the Minnesota Club, the Minneapolis Club, and the Women's Club for 1978 through 1981) and the two most prestigious country clubs (Woodhill Country Club and Somerset Country Club for 1978 through 1981) for the names of our elite, Company CEOs, or their wives.

We similarly scanned the boards of the eight most prestigious cultural organizations (the Guthrie Theatre, the Minnesota Orchestral society, the Society of Fine Arts, the Children's Theatre, the Walker Art Center, the St Paul Chamber Orchestra, Minnesota Public Radio, and the Minnesota Opera for 1978 through 1981). We selected the eight cultural organizations based on interviews with the chief administrators of 38 Twin Cities cultural organizations in the spring of 1978 (see Galaskiewicz and Rauschenbach, forthcoming). Finally, we examined the boards of the 21 Fortune 500 and Fortune 50 firms (excluding cooperatives) that were headquartered in the Twin Cities area in 1980.

This allowed us to construct a 28 × 98 matrix where the rows represented the 28 living members of the corporate philanthropic elite, the columns represented the CEOs of the 98 largest publicly held firms in the Twin Cities, and the entries the number of clubs or boards a CEO and a member of the elite (or spouse) were both affiliated with. We then tallied down each column giving us the number of clubs or boards where a CEO re-encountered a member of our elite. The zero-order correlation between the elite contact score generated from elite responses and this second elite contact score was 0.717. This led us to do a principal-components analysis combining these two variables in a single construct. We then assigned factor scores to each firm.

To arrive at prestige scores for our firms we again handed a list of all 209 publicly held firms in the Twin Cities to the corporate philanthropic elite and asked them to check off the firms they believed were outstanding in their support of non-profits. Each firm was then assigned a score depending on the number of votes it received (minimum = 0; maximum = 25; mean = 2.44; standard deviation = 5.50; missing cases = 3). Corporate philanthropic leaders also checked off the firms they believed were extraordinarily successful business ventures. Each firm was again assigned a score depending on the number of times it was checked (minimum = 0; maximum = 26; mean = 4.13; standard deviation = 6.67; missing cases = 3). Unfortunately, these items were asked in sequence, and we suspect there may have been some contagion across items. Looking at all 209 corporations on the list, the correlation between a firm's reputation for being generous and successful was .840. To check for a contagion effect more carefully, however, an inter-item analysis for each elite respondent should have been done for these two variables.

The involvement of the elite in non-profit affairs was also drawn from our interviews with 26 members of the corporate philanthropic elite. During the course of these interviews, we handed the respondent a list of 326 non-profit organizations. This was a stratified sample of all public charities in the Twin Cities metro area. We asked them to tell us which organizations they had served personally during the 'past couple of years' and the capacity in which they had served. These capacities included donor, volunteer worker, consultant, board member, officer, and fund-raiser. We subsequently scored each non-profit on the basis of how many members of the elite had served it (in any capacity at all) during the past few years. Considering only the 229 non-profits we subsequently interviewed for the study, the frequency distribution of this variable was highly skewed: only 25.8 per cent of the non-profits had been served by our elite. The maximum number of elites supporting an NPO was 21, and the average number was .89.

We also asked our 26 elite respondents to tell us which organizations they or members of their immediate families had used personally during the past couple of years, by being patients, attending classes, going to plays or concerts, participating in programs, or otherwise using NPO facilities. We subsequently scored each non-profit on the basis of how many members of the elite had used its services during the past few years. Looking again at the 229 non-profits in the study, the frequency distribution of this variable was also highly skewed: only 15.3 per cent of the non-profits had been used by our elite. The maximum was 24, and the mean was .64.

Because both of the above variables were skewed, we did a log transformation of each (assigning zero to cases where the log of zero would otherwise be undefined). The zero-order correlation between them was .919. This led us, in turn, to combine these two variables using principal-components analysis. The principal factor had an eigenvalue of 1.77 and it explained 88.6 per cent of the variance in our variables. The factor loadings for 'service to' non-profits and 'use of' non-profits were both .941. Factor scores were then assigned to our cases.

8.5   Recommendations for Future Research

In retrospect there are several things that ought to have been done differently and which future researchers might heed to. I will discuss what we feel to be better ways of identifying the corporate philanthropic elite, interviewing an elite, and operationalizing elite variables.

Identifying the elite
We believe our introduction to the elite was much too haphazard. First, prior to the funding stage we should have compiled all the newspaper and magazine articles written on the Twin Cities business community from 1970 to 1980. Although not completely reliable sources of information, they would have sensitized us to the role of the elite earlier on. Also, we should have more carefully and systematically selected our preliminary, open-ended interviews. Knowing what we do now about corporations and non-profit organizations we would recommend that the executive directors or staff members of the United Ways, Chambers of Commerce, community foundations, and the largest private and corporate foundations be interviewed first. (Actually, staff proved to be better informants than directors.) After these interviews we would locate the largest non-profit organizations in the area and interview the development officer. Then we would identify two or three fund-raisers who did consulting work for non-profit organizations. These individuals (whom, in fact, we did not interview until very late in the research) proved to be the real insiders and the most knowledgeable about how philanthropy works in a community. We would also identify the largest capital/endowment campaigns (in excess of $15 million) for up to ten years prior to the research and the campaign chairs. Almost always these are successful and well-connected business people in the community. We would then interview those individuals whose campaigns ended at least three to four years prior to the research. Also we would choose campaigns which had attained their goal. If an ongoing campaign or an unsuccessful campaign is chosen respondents will probably not be as likely to 'open up' about the process, since their reputations are still at stake. Finally, we would interview academics and journalists. The appeal of these informants is that they think about philanthropic practices and the role of elites in very analytical terms. However, these informants are seldom directly involved in fund-raising themselves, they never are major donors, and, like the researchers, they are only outsiders trying

to understand the system. Their observations may be insightful but interviews will seldom generate any new data.

Since we consider the preliminary interviews to be so important, let us make some suggestions on how they ought to be conducted. First, the analyst should gather facts from informants – little stories about how some big gift was secured from a corporate donor are invaluable. Capital/endowment campaigns are the major events in the philanthropic world, and everything comes into play as donors, donees, and brokers all get involved. Informants are usually eager to tell their stories because they often see these stories as illustrating an ongoing, underlying process. The analyst, however, should also insist that informants talk about the annual $5 000 to $20 000 gifts as well.

Secondly, the same sorts of questions should be asked of all informants, yet items must be tailored to the individual being interviewed. This point is obvious. One is not going to ask the campaign chairman of a $30 million capital campaign about 'nickel and dime' contributions for operating expenses. Thirdly, there must be room in the interview for informants to depart from the questions and pursue ideas on their own. This is where new and different processes will be identified. Fourthly, the interviewer should never go into an interview without knowing something about the background of the informants and the setting. For example, if interviewing the campaign chairman of a capital/endowment drive, know the dates of the campaign, the goal, the amount raised, the place where the individual works, where he went to school, and any nasty gossip that may have surfaced about the campaign. These data are available from secondary sources and newspapers, and he will expect the interviewer to know this. On the other hand, the interviewee does not expect to interview the investigator, and probably is not too concerned about what she or he thinks. Sometimes it is difficult for the interviewer to resist the temptation of saying something juicy that was learned in another interview. It is tempting, because this could help the investigator look like a fellow insider and may elicit some juicy tales in return. However, by doing this the interviewer jeopardizes his or her credibility as an objective outside observer.

In thinking about the way elites were identified, we are fairly confident that the reputational method is still a reasonable route to go. This discussion over the use of reputational methods is reminiscent of the one which preoccupied the community decision-making literature for years (Aiken and Mott, 1970). Our arguments are similar to those made by the so-called elitists and focus on the behind-the-scenes nature of elite intervention. However, to ensure that we had a better understanding of the nature of a reputation as a philanthropic leader, we would ask community elite respondents to comment briefly on each nominee after he named his list of candidates. No doubt this would take some time. Alternatively, we could follow a strategy similar to Laumann and Pappi (1976) who asked elite respondents to tell them which power resource or personal attribute was possessed by each member of their community elite (e.g. incumbent of an official position, good connections with other influential people). A list of roles in the philanthropic world could be identified and respondents could tell us which role each candidate played. Table 8.3 summarizes some examples derived from our research on corporate philanthropy.

Table 8.3   Roles in the philanthropic process

1	Routinely solicits peers in other firms for contributions.
2	Gives public speeches or writes articles reminding company executives of their obligations to contribute funds to charity.
3	Provides information to funders on prospective non-profit donees.
4	Develops alternative or new means whereby monies are channeled to non-profits (e.g. institutes new giving guidelines, hires contributions staff, institutes employee-matching gift programs).
5	Does matchmaking between donors and donees.
6	Lobbies in the state capital and Washington, DC for legislation to protect and encourage company giving.
7	Provides information to donees on prospective corporate funders.

Interviewing the elite

As noted earlier, not all of our elite respondents were eager to be interviewed. This prompted several improvizations on our part. We pursued vice-presidents and secretaries, showed them the interview schedule, and answered their questions. We wrote second and third letters detailing the purpose of the research, guaranteeing confidentiality, and telling them how the data would be used. We sent a list of those people whom we did interview in order to indicate to the recalcitrants that others were willing to take the time for the interview and that we were 'OK to talk to'. Also this would give the reluctant respondent a list of people to call if she or he doubted our credibility.

Regarding the collection of additional data, we would want to develop a set of items which would uncover the social organization of the elite itself. We collected data on board and club memberships as described earlier, but we never collected information on the personal networks among members of the elite. This is crucial because the elite is a qualitatively different 'elite' if it is highly cohesive or, alternatively, fragmented.

Clearly the major shortcoming in our research is the cross-sectional research design. It makes it almost impossible to sort out a causal ordering among the variables. For example, the correct design would have us measuring the extent to which executives are linked to the elite, the reputation of each corporate donor, and the amount of money the corporation gave to charity at several points in time. This would allow us to see if entering and leaving elite social circles is related to levels of company giving and if giving more is actually related to getting more recognition and applause. As it now stands, we have no way of knowing the true causal ordering among our variables.

8.6 Ethical Issues

There were three areas where ethical matters were a concern: confidentiality in the presentation of results, dissemination of research results, and the accessibility of other academics and non-academics to the data.

Confidentiality in the presentation of results

In all interviews with the elite we guaranteed complete confidentiality. That is, none of the data would be presented in such a way that responses of any one respondent could be identified. In most cases this presented no problem, because the data were aggregated and used in summary form only.

Only in one instance was there a potential problem. We listed the names of the corporate philanthropic leaders in the monograph and then presented quotes from those individuals in the text without, of course, specifically stating who said what. The quotes dealt with why the elite thought companies should engage in corporate philanthropy and how peer pressure worked among executives. We discussed the ethical issues at length with our editor at Academic Press and after consulting with their legal staff she was confident there would be no problem. There was no identifier whatsoever with the quotes, and they contained nothing slanderous aimed at either an individual or corporation. Yet we had to be extremely careful that no one could match the quotes to the names.

Dissemination of research results

In doing large-scale research of this kind, analysts are plagued by the length of time it takes to complete the analysis, write up results, and publish findings. As Table 8.1 indicates, the bulk of the data analysis was done by the end of 1983, but the book was not published until two years later (November, 1985). Given the interest that many study participants had in the results, we were presented with something of a dilemma. We felt we owed the community some feedback, yet the publisher was constantly worried we would disclose too much and thus reduce sales.

We resolved the dilemma by adopting the policy that the Principal Investigator would speak, without fee, to any group who requested feedback; he would host a special colloquium at the university for the nonprofit participants; he would present papers at professional meetings; he would write a sixty-seven page preliminary report to be distributed to the community that would contain only marginal distributions (Galaskiewicz, 1982); but he would not publish any results even in working papers, nor would he give interviews to the press before the analyses were finished.

While there were very few requests for papers presented at professional meetings, there was a major demand for the report. The National Science Foundation had allowed us to budget copying costs in order to disseminate the paper to study participants. This included 229 non-profit organizations, 150 corporations, and about 150 members of the various elites we interviewed. This prompted several requests from around the Twin Cities and from non-profit organizations elsewhere. The Center for Urban and Regional Affairs of the University of Minnesota agreed to copy and mail as many copies as needed, and they eventually sent out 500 copies in addition to the 600 or so that we mailed.

Availability of data

The National Science Foundation has the policy that data collected with the assistance of NSF grants having utility to others shall be made available to users by duplication, or loan for the purpose of duplication (National Science Foundation, 1983). Unfortunately, it takes considerable time and effort to prepare data sets which are usable and, at the same time, protect the anonymity of respondents. Pseudonyms need to be readied, and all identifying data in the file need to be purged. This is very difficult to do when preparing an elite file. For example, a key item in the elite file is the family name and primary corporate or organizational affiliation. This, though, immediately identifies the respondent. Another problem is that an array of general background variables can easily identify an elite member, especially since the names are published. For example, it is easy to spot the person who is sixty-eight years old, a former CEO of a Fortune 500 firm, born in Moundsview, Minnesota, and a member of Woodhill Country Club. The only solution to the dilemma is to exclude all background data from the new file. Although this greatly hinders what analysts can do, it does protect confidentiality.

Another issue is the release of data to non-academic researchers. The data we have may still be of interest to those raising money in the corporate community as well as to those who are evaluating prospective donees. Thus far no non-academics have approached us for data, but our inclination is to refuse them if they do. Our rationale is that the data should be used to benefit the public interest rather than specific individual interests. Even if confidentiality is protected we would think it unfair that one group was able to have this much information simply because it had the staff and resources to analyse the data.

This naturally leads to the issue of using the data for consulting purposes. Even though we have had these data in analysis mode for two years (since June, 1983), we have never been approached by anyone to use the data for consulting purposes (e.g. a corporation considering the proposal of a non-profit that wants to know if its budget to staff ratio is high or low). We suspect this is because most would agree that it would be inappropriate for the principal investigator to sell analyses or information collected with public grant money. Still, PIs typically come to enjoy royalties from books and fees from speaking engagements that were only possible because of NSF funding. Therefore, why should not PIs be allowed to sell data and analyses as long as confidentiality is protected? This is a very difficult issue, and one which we may have to face in the future.

8.7 Conclusion

The purpose of the paper was to describe the research methodology in Galaskiewicz (1985) and to suggest ways to improve upon our earlier efforts. In the course of the paper we provided an overview of the study and its main findings. We also reviewed the methodology in detail. We focused on the identification of the corporate philanthropic elite, interviewing procedures, and the operationalization of variables. Next we discussed the problems we encountered and made suggestions for improving upon our research. Finally, we discussed some of the ethical issues we faced and that we anticipate.

9

Working on directors: some methodological issues

PETER BRANNEN

Social Science Branch, Department of Employment, London

9.1 Introduction

This paper examines a number of issues arising from the process of doing observational research in a setting not much studied by social scientists – the boardroom. The work which is discussed here involved interviewing directors. The focus of the paper is, however, on the research experience of entering and maintaining a presence in the social world of the boardroom. A cynic once commented that some social scientists will do anything rather than study men at first hand in their natural surroundings. To study people at first hand means getting access to those actual surroundings which is more problematic in the case of the powerful than those without power. It is, perhaps, significant that most studies of this kind on the world of work have been undertaken on low status groups (see for example, Lupton, 1963; Brown and Brannen, 1970; Pollert, 1981). Having gained access the nature of the relationship between researcher and subjects is also problematic. The literature suggests that a key aspect of intensive research is absorbing the perspective of those being researched. Elements of the development of the social sciences and the ideological predispositions of individual social scientists make this easier (or appear easier) when the subjects are without power. Finally, and in relation to this, such research and its mode of data collection raises issues of data validity.

I am grateful to Julia Brannen for her critical comments on this paper. Eric Batstone contributed to and commented on an early outline. He, along with Derek Fatchett and Phil White were my co-workers on the project. As all members of the research team and all the actors in the situation studied were male the personal pronoun 'he' is used throughout the text.

This paper focuses on these themes and treats them in an experiential way. One reason for this approach is that there seems to this writer to be very few detailed accounts of the process of observational research and very little literature for the student to turn to. The paper also aims to make some contribution to discussions of positivistic and non-positivistic approaches to observation (Friedrichs and Ludke, 1975). It is based on the experience of negotiating access to four divisional boards of the British Steel Corporation (BSC) and the detailed observation of one of these. At the time of the research, the BSC employed about 250,000 people and each of the divisions was a substantial business in its own right. A full account of the research has been published elsewhere (Brannen *et al.*, 1975; Brannen, 1983).

9.2 Managing Access

The work described here was part of a larger project which used a variety of different techniques of data collection including large scale surveys, observation, in depth interviewing and documentary analysis. This project was set up in 1969 to study worker participation in the running of the steel industry in Britain with special reference to the introduction of worker-directors and the extent to which public ownership (the industry had been nationalized in 1967) had resulted in a significant increase in worker involvement.[1] The worker-directors sat on the divisional boards of the corporation as non-executive part-time directors. The main board, and in particular its chairman, were sponsors of the research. The project was carried out by research staff representing a number of social science disciplines who were based at four British universities. The author of the present paper acted as team co-ordinator. The research team was responsible to a steering committee which was composed of a number of senior academics as well as representatives of the worker directors, the BSC and the trade unions. It is important to note for the purpose of this paper that boardroom observation was not part of the original design of the research agreed to by the BSC.

The management of access to organizations is a political process. In the case of boardroom observation in this project, it had a number of stages. The first stage consisted of getting the support of the academics on the steering committee for this particular extension of the research strategy (i.e. observing divisional boards). It was then important to use their influence to convince the members of the steering committee who were worker directors and those who represented the BSC that, for scientific reasons, access to these boards was essential. The rationale for extending the research strategy in this way was set out in a detailed paper which addressed itself to theoretical, substantive and methodological issues. The worker directors to their credit kept any fears they might have had about being viewed 'in flagrante' well under control and agreed to go along with the general view of the steering group. The BSC member also agreed and was important in getting a hearing for the revised strategy within the organization.

The BSC chairman and the main board personnel director had to be convinced of the legitimacy and need for researchers to have access to divisional board meetings. A document outlining the extended research strategy was sent to the personnel director who put it up to the chairman and managing directors. There was some resistance. The corporation chairman then announced that he would call a meeting of all managing directors to discuss the research, emphasizing his commitment to the project.

Subsequently, the chairman of the steering group and myself were summoned to see the corporation chairman who announced that access had been agreed by all managing directors in principle but that the details of access would have to be negotiated between the research workers and the managing directors. Two members of one divisional board continued to resist; they argued that participant observation was not scientific and that it would disrupt normal board behaviour. In a long meeting with them the scientific integrity of observation and its importance to the project was argued to no effect but in view of the agreement of most of the other directors they withdrew their opposition.

The general strategy of the team was to play the organization by first wooing the person nearest to the chairman and before that wooing the person nearest to that person. Next to use the status and authority of the chairman to obtain the compliance of other actors. Bit by bit key power actors in the situation were won over. This did, however, have some consequences. It meant that effective control over the negotiation was taken out of the hands of the researchers. It also meant that the research workers were being sponsored into the divisional boardrooms by the powerful in a superordinate part of the organization. One further effect was that documentation had to be prepared indicating in some detail why it was necessary to undertake observation and consequently the members of the board were aware of and sensitive to the orientations of the research workers. However, this also had its advantages because the research team were able to emphasize the scientific and professional nature of the exercise. Effectively, however, as the case of the two objecting directors in one division indicated, it was not rational argument but the sponsorship of the powerful that eventually made entry possible.

Rex (1974) argues that sociologists will never be particularly popular if they expose latent functions, but that the degree of acceptability of their findings to those studied may vary with position in the hierarchy. Thus, a factory manager may not wish to know that a particular policy is not operating because of class bias, traditionalism or status bias; his company chairman might, and such a finding might also be of interest to 'more liberal capitalists whom Mills recognized as being capable of taking the wider view because they were men of many interests'. In the BSC case, divisional board-members were willing to accept that research should be undertaken on the worker directors but less happy to have themselves observed. The chairman of the corporation was more open to having his divisional boards observed than the chairmen of those boards.

9.3 Playing the Observer Game

The observer, as Denzin (1978) has noted, has to enter the symbolic world of those he is to observe: he must learn their language, their customs, their work patterns, the way they eat and dress and make himself acceptable. There is an initial period when he must understand what expectations are held of him and when he is taught how he can behave. But he also has to teach respondents so that he can carry out his observer role effectively.

The mode of observation

The approach to data collection within the observer role is not without its problems. Traditional discussions of observational techniques within sociology tend to emphasize the nature of the role the observer will play and its consequences for data collection but little about data recording itself. The stress is on the observer immersing himself in the fieldwork situation, noting in a descriptive way what is occurring, gradually developing hypotheses about what is important which leads to more selective reporting (Gold, 1958; Becker, 1958; 1970). As was mentioned earlier, the team came from different academic backgrounds, were geographically dispersed, and there was no opportunity for more than one observer in the same field situation. This could have meant each researcher employing selective criteria, stressing a different set of events, difficulties in knowing whether differences found in our reports were reflections of each researcher's particular interests and preoccupations or a reflection of the different nature of the board meetings or the worker directors. These problems led us in the direction of an attempt at systematic observation of a limited set of behaviours.

Initially we piloted a detailed recording sheet. We tried this system in a few non-board meetings and decided that it was too complex and too liable to failure. Eventually we agreed that we would use a relatively simple system. Each participant in the board meeting would be given a number and the note of a meeting would indicate who spoke to whom, in what style, answering, addressing, challenging and so on, and the content of that exchange. It was on this basis that reporting was undertaken at the first board meetings though further simplification occurred over subsequent months. I now want to describe some aspects of my own experiences in undertaking the observer role in one divisional board. The general issues raised were, however, common to all four board situations.

Initiation
After permission was gained to observe the board I had a preliminary discussion with the personnel director. I indicated to him that I wished to sit at the table with other board members but that I did not wish there to be any disruption of the normal seating patterns. At the first meeting I attended I arrived ten minutes before the board was due to meet. I was shown to the room by the board secretary who told me that it had been decided that I should sit between the industrial relations director and himself. This had meant moving both the industrial relations director and a worker-director; further changes were possible if I wished. To avoid further disruption I said I was content. The chairman was one of the last into the meeting. He greeted me, as we had already met, and then sat down and the meeting commenced. He opened the meeting by pointing out that I was present 'in order to look at the worker-directors on the board'. He then asked me to say a few words about the research. I was somewhat non-plussed by the fact that a great deal of attention had been drawn to me and in such a way as to directly relate me to the worker-directors. Instead of talking about the board room study I talked briefly about an interviewing programme that we were due to be carrying out at two works within the division. I indicated the size of this programme, its starting and finishing dates. After one further question about reporting arrangements he then turned from me and started the board meeting proper.

This brief description of my board room initiation raises a number of issues. First, the problem of the location of the observer. While we had discussed this within the research team, it was difficult to make exact plans. Effectively, two different locational strategies were discussed which we called 'fly on the wall' and 'one of the lads'. Both were meant to maximize social invisibility. The 'fly on the wall' strategy involved the observer staying at a table to one side of the board table. This technique was adopted by one team member in the situation where there had been some problems over access. In the other strategy positive efforts were made to sit at the board table along with the other board members. It was felt that in this way one would not only be able to observe what was going on but gradually be accounted a normal face around the table. In my own case, I had been located next to the board secretary. The use of a recording technique which attempted to get a verbatim account of the meeting meant that writing had to go on continuously. To be placed next to the secretary who was also engaged in this activity, meant that less attention was drawn to it. It also created a legitimate device for keeping one's eyes down and avoiding facework. This was particularly important in relation to the need to maintain a totally neutral stance in relation to the worker directors.

Neutrality was also part of a wider projection of image. It was useful to emphasise an objective, skilled, professional stance in relation to other directors. This was important both as a form of self/observer protection and fit with the technocratic norms of the directors. While the remarks of the chairman at the beginning of the first board meeting highlighted the role of the observer in a way which had not been anticipated and had not been desired, nevertheless there were some advantages to it. The motivation of the chairman, especially in drawing attention to the fact that the observer was watching the worker directors, was defensive. He was in effect saying to other directors 'we are not under observation, they are'. The effect of the remark was probably at least in some part to reassure the other board members. The effect on the worker-directors was more difficult to calculate. However, there was already an ongoing relationship developed over almost twelve months between the observer and the worker-directors. It is likely that at the first board meeting there was a slight deviation from their normal performance, but no more than that.

Learning the game
In the initial phase a difficult element of observation of board

meetings was to grasp the technology of the meeting. The essential element that was missing initially was the knowledge of the procedure of board meetings and of financial accounting. However, two or three board meetings provided adequate familiarity. Another source of difficulty was getting abreast of 'ongoing stories'. At the first board meeting there were certain assumptions about events that had happened previously. Again after attendance at two or three board meetings the pre-history of the observation could be filled in. While observation of what was said and done was not too difficult, there was rather more difficulty in understanding the ethos of the boardroom, the degree of formality and the basis of the formality, the degree of ritual and the basis of ritual.

Perhaps of greater difficulty for the observer role however was the management of the situation of informal interaction surrounding the board meeting. The central focus of observation was the meeting, but after there tended to be a lengthy lunch preceded by drinks which often lasted as long as the meeting itself. In order to be acceptable in the boardroom it was also important to fit into the informal inter-action surrounding the board meetings. Moreover, it was essential to be acceptable in these locations because of the necessity to maintain relationships with many directors in other situations. It is to some aspects of this control of informal interaction that I now want to turn.

I found the board situation and the norms and values governing behaviour in it strange. There was a natural social distance between myself and full-time board members in terms of a number of factors such as age, life-style and values. The average age of the board members was about fifty, whereas I was in my early thirties. I turned up to board meetings in a battered old small car, while the directors drove Jaguars or similar cars. There was also a difference in terms of life-style more generally which might be summed up from my perspective as 'learning to live with gin and tonic and the problems of eating grouse'. There was also a natural distance in terms of general ideology, political affiliations and more specifically views on nationalization and on worker participation. The board members had a number of background elements in common; a number had gone to the same (public) school, the majority had worked in the same steel companies over a large number of years and had served on the same boards together in the past. They were generally united in terms of their political outlooks and their anti-nationalization views. The same factors also operated to create a natural social distance between myself and the part-time directors other than the worker-directors where there was more affinity in relation to life-style and values.

While some distance between the observer and the observed is necessary and indeed useful, in order that observation is effective it is important for the observer to make himself acceptable. He must move from being a stranger to being accorded the status of provisional member in the situation being observed, otherwise encounters with those he observes are always going to have a degree of performance in them, and are likely to remain at a superficial level. The natural social distance therefore between observer and board members posed some problems. For example, politics quite often entered the discussion, whether they were national politics or the politics of nationalization, and there were strong pressures on the observer to sink his self and to engage in 'passing' practices. These pressures were those of politeness, the need to agree with one's host, but also pressures from the observer role of the need to integrate with and keep in with those being observed. This raised, in crucial ways for the observer, questions of professional and personal integrity.

Overall, the central problem of controlling the form of interaction might be summed up in terms of balancing the level of involvement. It was important to be involved in and take part in conversation but at the same time to avoid being the focus of attention. There was a problem of managing relations with other full-time directors in such a way as not to reveal 'true self' but at the same time not to be seen to be hanging back; there was the problem of maintaining contact with the worker directors but not being seen to be acting either as a social prop or as special buddy. This was particularly important. Relationships were well established with the worker-directors. I had been into their homes, knew their families, shared their ideologies to a greater extent than I shared those of the full-time directors, and knew many more parts of their social network than the full-time directors knew.

I shared certain kinds of information with the worker-directors which were not known to other directors. I also, however, shared information with other directors which the worker-directors were not aware of. As part of the wider research project I was being given information by middle management and by the trade unions and by members of head office staff that neither the worker-directors nor the directors were privy to. At the same time they were occasionally aware that I had categories of information which might be useful to them. The management of information was a crucial element in balancing the level of involvement.

Getting accepted

The board had not been keen to have an observer on it. Indeed, the board had not been keen to have worker-directors on it. Both of these were seen as necessary and evil consequences of nationalization. However, having had to accept an observer, it was important to fit him into the situation, to give him a role and to attempt to integrate him socially. I was initially defined as guest and the full-time directors' behaviour towards me derived from this definition of the situation. After the first board meeting the chairman took up much time ensuring that I had drinks, that I had been introduced to everyone and he took me round again to meet all board members informally and briefly. He then placed me on his right hand side at the dinner table and engaged me in general conversation about the 'state of the universities these days'.

During the period of observation of the board the role definition of the observer changed from that of guest to frequent and familiar visitor. Conversation became less general and external and more familiar and direct. Directors began to satisfy their curiosity as to the kind of person the observer was and his views on what his own activities were about; there was a stage of 'finding out about you'. This in retrospect can be seen as a necessary phase to be gone through before the directors felt able to tell me about themselves. This phase followed and directors' conversation contained a growing content of explanations of the goals and activities of the board and attempts to obtain my assessment of these.

This became difficult for the observer role at points where industrial relations questions were discussed and where it was known that I may well have been with the relevant trade unions in the period before the board meeting. Where the questioning got too insistent I fell back on the ploy of verbally iterating the ethics of my observer stance and pointing out to the directors that, in the same way they trusted me not to pass information from the boardroom through to other parts of the organization, so other parts of the organization and of the trade union movement trusted me not to pass information through to the boardroom. This explanation of the reciprocity of trust was usually readily accepted.

It was also necessary from time to time to block questioning on the worker-directors. Directors were interested in the views of other parts of the organization about the worker-directors scheme, in my views on how the worker-directors were performing and in confirmation of the directors' own views that 'the worker-directors didn't do much good'. Again in these situations I retreated behind a formal definition of the ethics of the observer role. I felt that as well as the ethical undertaking to maintain the confidentiality of boardroom proceedings my position as observer would not have been tenable if I could not be clearly seen by all parts of the organization not to be acting as a channel of informal communication. Again the stance was justified in terms of the professional role. Becker's (1970) question 'whose side are we on' seems to be answerable for the participant observer only at the point before observation begins.

9.4 Problems of Validity

The validity of observational data is one of the main criticisms made of it. I want now to look at a number of threats to validity which emerged in the observation of the board and also to make some comments about those threats.

Effects of the observer on the observed
I mentioned earlier that in attempting to get access to the boardroom for the purpose of observation a number of criticisms were made that the observer would effectively transform the situation which he was observing and therefore the data gained would not be valid. A general argument against the criticism that observer presence causes changes in behaviour of participants is that in ongoing social situations it is much more difficult for actors to change and put on a special performance than it is for them to behave in a normal and natural way. It may well have been possible if the observer had been attending only one or two board meetings for a special show to be put on. Indeed the usefulness of observing for such a short period of time might well be doubted. However, it is difficult to keep up a sustained and consistent performance over seven to eight meetings. Our conclusion, from the analysis of our data, was that there was very little reactive effect to the observer.

Effects on the observer
The opposite side of the coin to the problem of a change in the observed is the problem of change in the observer. This is a more difficult problem to my mind. One of the strengths of the technique of participant observation is the fact that the observer does change in the sense that he grows in his understanding of the social situation of the actors that he is studying. There are stages in the participant observation process, which run from the early stage where the

observer is a stranger, through a stage of initiation in which he becomes partially accepted and then fully accepted within the social situation he is studying. There is also usually movement in the situation from degrees of observer to degrees of participant role. It is possible to move to a fully participant role, that is 'go native' and to entirely drop the observer-scientific role.

This latter situation is unlikely to occur in the observation of the boardroom. Board meetings are not continuous activities; one attends a meeting and its surrounding events and then moves on to other activities. In the worker-director study these other activities were often far removed organizationally and in content from the activities of the boardroom so that one was able to keep board activities in perspective. Nevertheless, the problem of incorporation of the observer was a real one. As I have mentioned earlier, from the perspective of the observed, it is useful to try to incorporate the observer, to make the watcher one of the watched. It is also necessary for the observer to move some way in this direction if he is to enter and understand the symbolic world of the observed in order to increase in breadth and depth the data he is collecting. In the context of doing work on directors pressures to assume 'membership' of the director category arose from both values and life-style.

The general orientation of the full-time directors towards the steel business was that profit was a central objective and all other objectives were secondary to this. The one impartial test of the competence of the board was its ability to make money; all of its activities had to be seen from this perspective. At the board meeting itself the monthly financial report was the pivotal structuring document and financial questions were central to all aspects of the board's discussions. It was crucial for the maintenance of an effective observer role never to query this core value, to think oneself into the set of cognitive categories related to it and to learn to see the world through the eyes of the directors; it is difficult to learn to understand, think and talk in particular value categories without beginning to accept them.

The second set of pressures might be best described as 'learning to live with gin and chauffeurs'. The process of observing directors involved the observer in certain aspects of the life-style of board members particularly those deriving from fringe benefits such as free lunches in private directors dining rooms and the provision of chauffeur-driven cars to deliver one to meetings, to hotels or to trains. Although these fringe benefits may not have been particularly lavish by business standards they were at a different level of life-style to that to which the observer was accustomed and had a certain seductive appeal. They began, after a while, to be taken for granted. There was, however, little chance of effective incorporation, partly, as mentioned earlier, because of the intermittent nature of the activity, and because of the correctives which were provided by other activities; partly because of the observer's own sense of himself and his self-identity, and partly because of an ability to withdraw easily from the field. What was, however, valuable – and I shall return to this later – was an awareness of pressures to change one's life-style, and awareness of learning a new language and along with that new patterns of thought.

Understanding the action setting
Other problems of validity are posed by the degree to which the observer is able fully to understand and comprehend the action setting. Particular problems are posed by the boardroom. First, the board is the end of a management process and is part of a larger organizational process. There is, therefore, the problem of understanding the part within the context of the whole; the problem of the interface between the board and the rest of the organization. If one is interested, as this research had to be, in the decision-making process, this involves a large number of people only some of whom are on the board. Associated with this, decisions often develop over a period of months, if not years, making observation difficult. The board meeting is the end of a process and to understand it one needs to see the preceding social processes. This problem we only partly overcame. The nature of the preceding social processes are of course themselves problematic. Observing part of the process, however, presents the possibility of being able to ask questions, to identify gaps which will lead one on to the rest of the process. The observation of one part of the process then needs to be linked with the investigation of other parts of the process perhaps using other techniques such as interviews and the analysis of documentary material.

There are also problems of understanding the action setting in terms of technical knowledge of the formal rules and the taken-for-granted rules which govern behaviour in the board situation. One major problem in this context was what one might call the camouflaging of conflict. Conflict on the board was of course easy to recognize where people showed emotions and argued in a heated fashion. On the whole, however, the taken-for-granted rules of boardroom behaviour militated against this. There was an emphasis on calmness, on courtesy, on gentlemanly behaviour. Some conflict could perhaps take place on a technical matter where the existence of the conflict would be hidden from the observer unless he understood the technical issues and the variety of technical perspectives on the problem. However, in the case of this piece of research this was not an issue. The major focus was on the worker-directors and the conflict they had with the board. Conflict in which they were involved with other directors would be of a surface kind.

Finally, in understanding the situation one must mention the history of the board and indeed of board members as a guide to understanding current behaviour. Continuous attendance at board meetings meant that the observer picked up more and more of the recent history of the board; interviews with board members and also increasing familiarization with the organization meant that during the process of research there was increasing understanding of the action setting.

Different ways of seeing

I finally want to turn briefly to another problematic area in terms of the validity of observation, that is inter-observer comparability. As I have already indicated this was a central concern to the research team for a number of reasons. The solution to the problem was the adaptation of a formalistic mode of data collection so that each observer had to present a structured report of board meetings. These accounts were then typed up and made available to all other members of the research team for comment and discussion. The constant exchange of research reports meant a standardization of both the reports and also of the focus of observation. However, this relatively tight process of observation in order to deal with the problem of comparability did lead to certain disadvantages and a weakening of the types of data that were collected. I go on to discuss this in the concluding section.

9.5   Conclusions

Participant observation is more than just that. Observation emphasizes entering and understanding the social world of those studied. This means looking at the 'evolution and unfolding of social action through time and across situations' (Denzin, 1978). In this sense observation as a technique also involves and requires talking to people in an unstructured and semi-structured way, as well as the collection of documentary material. It may also require a process of observer introspection. This supplementation of methods was particularly crucial in a board situation. While emphasising the need to use a variety of methodologies in order to comprehend the totality of the process, and also as a means of cross-validating data and interpretation, I want to conclude with a few critical comments on the process of observation as it was carried out in this research.

As I have noted, a systematic data recording approach was used in board meetings. This had a number of advantages. It provided a nearly verbatim record of meetings; it also provided a basis for reliable comparisons between boards and between observers. It had the added advantage of giving an air of technical expertise to our operation which helped to legitimate access and provided a role or work for the observer to do in the board. It acted also as an important check upon impressionistic ideas. It was possible to analyse the material in a statistical manner.

While this form of recording was relatively successful, the observational processes had certain key weaknesses. The focus on the formal board meeting and the emphasis in the research team on systematic ways of recording the meeting meant that the goal of the observational programme became the recording of the meeting. This resulted in an almost total failure systematically to record the informal interaction surrounding the board meeting. The actual meeting for the observers, as for the directors, became the area of work and the observers were drawn into the trap of regarding the lunch and pre-lunch drink times as times of leisure and relaxation. This is not to say that during these periods the observers were not atuned to, or were not picking up, information. It did mean, however, that the formal work requirements on the observers were to produce an account of the board meeting. These accounts were produced, other accounts were not produced in any systematic way.

While there was some written recording of, and much verbal discussion within the research team of the forms of, informal inter-action surrounding board meetings there was no emphasis on, and indeed within the formal research prescription we set ourselves no mention of, the need for observer introspection. Yet in retrospect this was particularly crucial. The worker-directors had in many ways entered the boardroom in similar ways to the observers. They were persons from different backgrounds from the directors who had to move through processes of gaining acceptability to provisional membership and full incorporation. Understanding what was happening to the observers *qua* observers and recording these processes would have increased understanding of the pressures operating on the new worker directors. The failure to keep a detailed diary of the experience of observation was a crucial failure of this part of the research.

In many ways positivistic modes of observation are easier and less demanding on the observer than non-positivistic modes of observation. Watching work is a stressful occupation. There is the strain of 'the outsider' trying to be at least temporarily 'the insider' and added to this the strain of never being able to relax, of having to work even when others are engaging in relaxation. There are tremendous pressures to drop the observer role, temporarily to become what one is observing as a form of release. In addition, one's sense of self and identity are under attack. The good observer is a chameleon changing his colour and fitting into his background so as to be socially invisible. The difficulties and problems of doing this, of maintaining the correct social distance as well as the correct degree of integration, of maintaining a sense of self as well as a sense of observer identity, are very great. To add to this the recording not only of the speech and behaviour of the actors being observed but also the need to be self-aware and to record one's self-awareness is to heighten the degree of strain enormously. This may, however, be a necessary cost of the scientific enterprise of working on work through observation.

Notes

1   It was not felt proper to publish this paper until some considerable time had elapsed and all of the main actors had either severed their connections with the British Steel Corporation or changed their roles in it.

III

Defensive Elites

10

The threatened elite: studying leaders in an urban community

MARGARET WAGSTAFFE and GEORGE MOYSER

University of Manchester

10.1 Introduction

Very few, if any, of those who study elites think it easy or straight-forward. There are arguments over definition, legendary disputes about selection procedures and underdeveloped theories and techniques. However, matters will only improve by a collective self-conscious examination of present procedures and assumptions. It is in this spirit that the present chapter has been written – a reflection principally upon the methodological problems and issues which arose in the course of research on three urban communities. In so far as one of those communities at least posed very considerable problems, the commentary which follows may serve two purposes. First, it may forewarn those who wish to study similar elites in other contexts (and they are probably to be found in major conurbations around the world). Secondly, it raises very vividly, as perhaps only an 'extreme' case can, substantive and methodological questions of general interest in the study of elites.

The questions in view here are quite varied. On the one hand, for example, there is the basic problem of the sense in which the individuals we have studied do or do not constitute an 'elite'. How directly influential or powerful must an individual, or group of individuals, be within the wider polity to be considered an elite? Or is

We wish to acknowledge the financial assistance of the British Economic and Social Research Council for the project on which this chapter is based.

The authors would like to thank Neil Day of Melbourne College of Advanced Education, Melbourne, Australia and Dr David Howell of the University of Manchester for their comments on and suggestions for successive drafts of this paper.

influence within a circumscribed locality, or merely high status within a particular subculture, sufficient? On the other hand, as will be seen below, there are a host of procedural and ethical issues raised by studying those who largely stand outside of, or apart from, the wider society and who are acutely aware of the political dimensions of the production, control and dissemination of information, such as arises from social scientific inquiries. How these matters came to our attention, sometimes traumatically, will become clearer through a brief description of the research that was undertaken (see also Parry, Moyser and Wagstaffe, 1987).

10.2   The Purpose and Context of the Research

In the Spring and Summer of 1981 a number of Britain's major towns and cities experienced outbreaks of civil disorder. These upheavals were characterized by running battles between police and mainly young people. They occurred in multicultural inner-city areas. One such district was Moss Side in Manchester, others included Brixton in London and Toxteth in Liverpool. These places had certain common characteristics such as the depth of poverty and social disadvantage experienced by the citizenry, high levels of unemployment and complex local housing problems. However, there were other communities which were similar but had not hosted angry crowds. Why the difference? What had made some of these districts 'explode' when others had not?

For our research project, we chose to examine the quality of life in three multicultural, inner-city wards, one of which (Moss Side in Manchester) had experienced such conflict and two (Burngreave, Sheffield and Glodwick, Oldham) which had not. Comparing these areas, the question arose: had the tenor and quality of life, before or after the upheavals, been significantly different? Had the traditional community been destroyed and what, if anything, had replaced it? Did the appearance of an angry crowd mean that established forms of political participation were failing to meet the needs of some groups? Is crowd activity a form of political 'dialogue'? If it is, then to what extent do the norms and values of the locality constrain or encourage the activists in the crowd? Did differences in elite attitudes and responsiveness contribute significantly to the outcome (see Burton, 1984)?

In examining these questions we conducted a series of interviews with residents, community activists and political leaders in the three areas. For our elite 'sample', on which we will focus here, we intended to interview city councillors, other political leaders and notables, and those people who, for a variety of reasons, were pre-eminent in their locale. It is to the problems and dilemmas experienced in constructing this group that we now turn.

Between the mainstream political elite which governs the city, and the mass of the citizenry, there is a layer of people who hold sway in their neighbourhood: they are the public spirited; the organizers of campaigns about issues, the workers in political parties, the spokespeople for the grass roots. They are the local elite. Naturally, we desired to have access to these people. This, however, caused problems because many important members of these groups were not disposed to co-operate with our study. These non-cooperators are the people who, for the reasons which are discussed in the following paragraphs, we have designated the 'counter-elite' or the 'threatened elite'.

A counter-elite may be defined in contrast to a conventional elite. Conventional elites (in the West) generally have in common certain characteristics which facilitate research into the nature and concerns of such groups. In so far as the members of these groups are beneficiaries of the social system they are normally supportive and approving of it. They may feel that some or many reforms are needed, but they do not normally wish to dismantle the whole structure and to reconstruct the edifice in its entirety. In addition, they share a common belief in the openness of the system, and readily concede the desirability of free and easy access to the elite for those people who are engaged in research on any relevant subject.

Conventional elites normally regard academic investigation as fruitful and valuable to society as a whole, and will co-operate in the execution of these projects. Moreover, they are prepared to believe that work of this kind can be objective and unbiased and that its findings may provide valuable information which could, in the future, generate important inputs in policy formulation. Perhaps most basically, such an elite and many academics share values, expectations and experiences. For these reasons, members of conventional elites usually give time and assistance to those who wish to engage in elite research. Appointments are not generally difficult to arrange and, during interviews, elite members broadly accept the legitimacy of the researcher's questions as justifiable tools in the search for information. However, when the elite under scrutiny is, in fact, a 'counter-elite', the situation is very different. A research project which depends on the assistance of a counter-elite can be much more difficult to complete than one which centres on a conventional elite.

A counter-elite, almost by definition, does not have a shared conceptual framework with what may be perceived as the representative of a state agency. Research which is publicly funded is often assumed to be conducted for the benefit of what is seen as the establishment. It is widely held by the threatened or defensive elite that social research which focuses on the activities of the deprived is misdirected: that instead attention should be concentrated on the power structures and social arrangements which perpetuate their deprivation (Katznelson, 1973, p. 10). The purpose of the research, indeed, may seem sinister. It may be thought that the findings of the researcher will facilitate social control: that the real (as opposed to given) reason for gathering data on the community is to enable the state, and especially the police, to be fully informed about the community. Why, they may feel, should they co-operate in what they see as their own oppression? This sentiment was expressed to us on a number of occasions during our researches in Moss Side, and was also voiced, although less frequently, in Burngreave and Glodwick. Ironically, this is in many ways the direct opposite of the view taken by more conventional local elites, who are often persuaded to participate in projects on the grounds that communication with outside agencies can be of benefit to the area.

Members of the threatened elite see themselves as guardians of the neighbourhood interest and as bulwarks against threatening or unscrupulous intruders such as media personnel, town hall officials, academics, researchers, and would-be 'do-gooders'. They have taken the role of spokesmen for the less articulate. Usually, they hold their position by virtue of skills or qualities which they are pleased to place at the disposal of the neighbourhood. But they may be very precariously placed, and too insecure to hazard their own standing by co-operating with the 'enemy'. They risk the hostility of their constituency, ostracism and loss of trust. One Manchester activist commented: 'I can't really talk to you any further. I have a good standing in the community but it wouldn't last very long if people thought I was talking [to people like you].'

The more precarious the position of the elite member, the more vulnerable to accusations of co-option into the 'establishment', the less they are likely to jeopardize their standing to facilitate the researches of an academic with no record of involvement in the community, with whom they have no ties, and from whom they expect no benefits.

The 'protectorate' of the defensive elite may well have been subjected to endless research. Indeed, as one experienced community worker observed: 'People feel that they can't walk round the corner without someone popping up to ask them what they think. They are pretty fed up with it.'

The proximity of two of the communities which we studied to major universities had indeed meant that many academic projects had been based in these localities. Such undertakings range in scale and importance from undergraduate essays to large, state-funded social surveys. The process is felt by many to be exploitative and extractive, with no visible benefits to the community. It is not regarded as a pleasant experience. A spokesman for one black community explained how local people felt:

The whole process of answering lists of questions is anxiety laden and distressing to many people because whenever they come into contact with Housing, Social Services, the Education Department, the National Health Service and so on, they must always begin by answering questions. Whatever they do, they always have to answer reams of questions first. Even just buying something on hire purchase involves this. So for you to go to them with your list of questions is itself an oppressive activity. It is associated in people's minds with government and authority, and it threatens them and makes them feel apprehensive and unhappy.

Members of the defensive elite are often reluctant to co-operate because they are cynical about the value of academic research. One activist was very scathing about the process:

Much of what is produced is utter rubbish. Going back as far as 1927, for instance, a woman called Fletcher did a research project on black people. Her report included the sentence: 'Half-caste girls have one white lip and one negroid one'! This project was accepted and validated by the university authorities as a piece of objective, academic research, and still sits on a library shelf and can be quoted [a friend] quoted it in his dissertation, only, I hasten to add, to show what a lot of tripe 'objective academic research' really is.

Some members of the particular 'counter-elites' with which we were concerned expressed a belief that research and information gathered by universities is never neutral, either in its premises, its *a priori* assumptions or its application; that if it is not undertaken from a radical perspective then it must have a liberal-conservative slant. Other members of the defensive elite are not merely cynical about the activity of researchers, but actually hostile to it, believing the process to be of benefit to ambitious academics but positively detrimental to the neighbourhood:

> There is a great deal of anger amongst the politicized blacks of this community about the activities of academics, social workers and other such professionals who have been responsible for the labelling of Moss Side as a problem area. This characterization of the district as 'tough' and 'hard' is bad for Moss Side but, on the reverse side of the coin, has a very positive value for professionals who work in the area. If one has worked successfully in Moss Side, one has proved one's mettle and one's future is assured. So academics designate the area 'difficult', i.e. problematic and needing special handling, and other professionals do not dissent from this assessment, since to do so would detract from their own achievements. Moss Side and 'race' become an industry and a large number of people have a vested interest in keeping it going. But for the people who live there the effects of all this are devastating.

We also found, among our threatened elites, deep seated concern about the possible abuse of findings. Academic research was perceived as manipulative, assuming mass passivity. Also, as the visiting researcher has no stake in the community, he or she cannot be held accountable for his or her action and is immune from any consequences which local people have no choice but to endure. These anxieties were explained thus:

> What you have to try and understand is the fear of the residents of Moss Side concerning what academics and such like will do with the material they extract from the community. Because, in the past, policy makers and media people have used such material to the disadvantage of the community. In an area like Moss Side, indeed in any area of size, there are going to be people with differing attitudes, needs, goals and so on. But the media and the establishment expect the community to speak with one voice, to have one mind. When differences do become apparent, these are then exploited. They are used as an excuse for overriding the wishes of the community and for imposing measures. Policy-makers take the attitude: 'They can't even agree among themselves, they don't know what they want, we have to decide for them.' It is this that the people are so anxious to avoid.

Cause for concern is also occasioned by the reasons for the choice of research target: why, members of the defensive elite are inclined to ask, should this particular community have endless researchers and media people plaguing its members, when other parts of the city go for decades, untroubled by academic or related visitations? Does this mean that this neighbourhood is externally regarded as being strikingly different from those which no one wants to scrutinize? If, as has often in the past been the experience of our research communities, the reason is the presence of a concentration of members of the ethnic minorities, does that imply that the project is underpinned by racist assumptions that local people are different from others and therefore should be examined by academics?

Beyond the worries which were expressed about possible abuse of findings, members of our 'counter-elite' also asked pointed questions about the future security of the material gathered. What, they wanted to know, would eventually happen to the tapes and transcripts? Who would have access to them? How could continued confidentiality be guaranteed? If the researcher's contract was to be terminated in three years' time, and the tapes were to remain the property of the funding authority, how could the researcher give assurances about the safe-keeping of the material, say, five years thence?

A further problem for the researcher who works with a defensive elite is that of impartiality between contending factions (Glasgow, 1980, pp. 26–9). Again, when interviewing conventional elites, while there may be very differing viewpoints, there are usually shared basic assumptions. Thus, for example, while Labour and Conservative MPs may be far apart on how a society should be run, they normally do assume that the kind of society which it is most desirable to run is, indeed, that which is widely described by political scientists in the west as bourgeois or liberal-democratic and, furthermore, give or take a few caveats, that that is the kind of society which exists in Britain today. However, if members of the defensive elite do not share this basic assumption they may believe that the interviewer is working from the perspective of the establishment rather than from that of the respondent, and is thus heavily biased away from the respondent. This is not conducive to the creation of a relaxed and co-operative atmosphere. Such an atmosphere is far more likely to be engendered if the respondent feels that the interviewer is in fact inclined to sympathize with his or her, perhaps less conventional, perspective. However, this simply creates a dilemma for the academic: being 'neutral' in the accepted, scholarly sense of the term inhibits and may even prevent the conduct of the research, but being 'neutral' in the eyes of the respondent may involve a loss of objectivity in the eyes of the scientific community. Sympathetic neutrality may be possible between MPs of different persuasions, but between, say, some factions of an inner-city community on the one hand, and the local police force on the other (where even a known acquaintanceship with either group is sufficient grounds for one to be tainted in the view of the other), is simply not a viable proposition. In this situation, also, the status of the researcher may be significant, in so far as the higher the status of the academic involved, the more likely an automatic assumption about his or her identity of interest with the establishment is to follow. On the other hand, where the researcher is perceived as lacking seniority, it is sometimes felt by members of the counter-elite that they are being expected to deal with an underling. In this case resentment may arise: why doesn't the principal of the project deal with these (elite) members personally? Does this imply disrespect on the part of the principal? Is the community being treated with covert contempt?

Counter-elite personnel, then, feel they have compelling arguments for their hesitance and reserve where research is concerned. This, however, had implications for our project design. It meant that we were unable to replicate our sample as precisely as we had hoped between the three locations, and we had to rely much more heavily on personal introductions and networks than had been our original intentions. None the less we felt, when the project was completed, that we had gathered a sufficiently wide selection of views as to give a reasonably well rounded picture of the collective experiences and concerns of the communities with which we had worked.

It is self-evidently the case that not all researchers receive exactly the same treatment from the defensive elite. Interestingly, despite the hostility often shown to outside investigators, television journalists and programme makers do not normally seem to have a great deal of difficulty in working with local people, including the radicals and activists who form the defensive elite. This may reflect the cumulative effect of several different factors acting to soften resistance to co-operation. Since such teams are often able to take a number of researchers into the area and conduct a fairly widespread survey in a condensed time period, it may be that the project is brought to fruition before local resistance has hardened. Also, it is probably true that the glamour of television undermines determination to remain distant from the research process. Many people are attracted by the chance to appear on television. They may well feel that in a few minutes before the camera they will be able to say volumes on behalf of their community and to a large audience. There is, from our conversations, some evidence that the average citizen has rather more confidence in the fidelity of the camera and crew of a current affairs or news programme than in the reliability of the academic researcher or newspaper reporter. Indeed, one of our respondents, while voicing a very healthy scepticism concerning the veracity of the press, naively observed that the camera cannot lie and that, what one sees with one's own eyes on the television screen, one has to believe. However, in contrast to exciting and glamorous television crews, the would-be researcher will probably have to work very hard to gain access to the elite of a defensive community.

It would be misleading, none the less, to imply that the same degree of resistance will be encountered in any deprived community. Our experience in Manchester was not fully mirrored in Sheffield or Oldham. Whereas we found, in some sectors of the populace of Moss Side, deeply entrenched opposition to our studies, this was far less true in these other cities. There was some scepticism about the benefits to the community of our project in these areas. None the less leaders and activists in the area were rather more favourably disposed toward co-operation with us than those of Moss Side. It should also be noted that the hostility of the threatened elite did not necessarily carry through to those people who were elected representatives and formed part of the elite which governed the city. It would be an exaggeration to imply that all members of the local elite were unavailable for interview or that all members of the city elite were fully accessible. This was not the case. It was simply that it was much easier to have access to, and make interview appointments with, those who were involved in mainstream political life in the city, than those who formed the 'counter-elite'.

10.3 Problems of Elite Identification

When studying conventional elites, there are recognized methods of constructing a sample. Members of such an elite may be identified by the position they hold, or by their decision-making powers, or by reputation. In some cases, the members of the elite are easily identified. If, for example, one wished to study diocesan bishops, as Medhurst and Moyser did (see Chapter 6), the sample is then self-defining. However, where other elites are concerned, the confines or boundaries of the group may be fuzzy and not clearly delimited, and it may be difficult to decide who is, and who is not, suitable for inclusion in the research project.

Constructing a sample of a local elite is fraught with problems. An obvious starting point is the identification, by reputation, of community notables. However, we found that we were dealing, not so much with 'the community' as with a series of locally defined communities, many of which were in some degree hostile to the others. Of course, all communities have their factions, but multicultural communities can have more than most (Suttles, 1972). The divisions in the communities we looked at were sometimes drawn along racial lines, but they were much more often rooted in differences of age and political convictions. For example, in Moss Side, although there were both whites and blacks who expressed antipathetic sentiments to other racial groups, these were not really typical of the factions in the locality. Far more notable were the sharp divides between those generally elderly citizens who expressed faith in the social and political system of which they were a part, and the people, mainly the younger, who voiced cynicism and disillusionment concerning British politics. Both groups further subdivided into the politically active and the passive and, where the active were concerned, the younger people had a spectrum of points of adherence, varying from liberalism or labourism through revolutionary fervour to separatism and isolationism. Constituents of each faction, when asked to name influential people, designated only notables from the section to which they belonged, and did not usually refer to the leaders or activists of other groups. This meant that the construction of a sample by reputational means was seriously impeded.

An alternative way of developing a sample is to identify position-holders. The 'positional' approach was, however, also problematic, because, while this exercise did yield up a collection of notables in the locality, it missed those whose leadership and strength of influence owed more to personal qualities than to any official position. Perhaps, of course, the 'positional' method is most appropriately used on a national scale, thereby missing local leaders. However, it has also been used to identify those people who are powerful and influential in a city. But when the focus of attention is narrowed down to the neighbourhood, position becomes far less significant. It may be that positions of seeming importance are held by those who are well-regarded in the city but who, by virtue of their rise to city prominence, have forfeited the goodwill of their neighbours. Social and political advancement often involve accommodation and negotiation, and sometimes the seekers of office become so compromised in the process that they lose the trust and regard of those citizens whom they originally set out to represent.

How then, is one to identify the neighbourhood elite? It is more or less a process of trial and error. There is a body of local office-holders which makes a good starting point. Statutory and voluntary youth and community clubs and associations can often provide information about who is pre-eminent in the area, and indeed may form the activity base for area notables. Local government officials also wield some influence, and in any case are often good contacts to make because they can form a bridge between the 'inside' community and the 'outside' world. This means that they have access to elite members who may otherwise be hard to contact, yet, by virtue of their outsider status, they are not so disposed to be hostile to researchers and others. Educational institutions can also yield fruitful contacts, especially adult education centres which often form the venue for community and group activities and which also can supply the confident, articulate people who are usually the prime movers in groups and associations. Social workers, with inroads into the very heart of the community, can be helpful if they are convinced of the value of one's enterprise, as can churchmen and religious leaders, who also often have close links with the community.

Once a group of office-holders has been identified, it is necessary to check that the individuals so located are, in fact, important to the affairs of the community in question. This has to be done by word of mouth, and a process of evaluating the reputations of these individuals must be worked through. However, before this task can be undertaken one must gain the co-operation of the community. Where the citizens are not wholly disposed to accommodate a stranger, their trust must be earned.

10.4 Resistant Communities: Obtaining Co-operation

Ideally, one should cease to be a stranger. This means that one needs time to become known to people in the locality, to be seen around, to go to social events, to attend public meetings, to become involved in and to do work on community issues, to develop a personal network. This process will take a minimum of six months (and funding for this period should be built into grant estimates). The importance of gaining the trust of those with whom one wishes to work cannot be overestimated. One researcher who had done this kind of work very successfully for years advised us:

Any community study needs to be preceded by a period of time during which the researchers forge links with the community. To gain the trust of the people in the area you want to study is essential. In order to do that you have to be seen around, go into pubs, go to meetings, become involved in community issues and projects, work for the good of the community. Then, when you have established a network, then you can begin to think about interviews. But not before. If you try to omit the preliminaries, people will just treat you with hostility and suspicion and the whole exercise will be abortive.

This period should also be used to explore ideas concerning ways in which the proposed research can be mutually and reciprocally advantageous to both principal and respondents alike. At this time, personal approaches can be made to community leaders and others in visible positions – group secretaries and organizers, members of tenants' associations, etc. It is generally a good idea to make connections with as many statutory and voluntary agencies as possible. In fact, most researchers in this field find that the best and most fruitful contacts are those which are made through personal networks: friends of friends, or respondents who will provide further introductions.

In elite surveys initial approaches are often made by letter. However, where the elite concerned is a counter-elite, it is probably the case that the recipient is, on the one hand, deluged with paper and on the other lacking in secretarial help and in the position of having to self-finance all use of stationery and post. The need for a reply can be avoided by indicating one's intention to follow up the approach letter with a telephone call. But when the elite is defensive, this can serve as forewarning and give the recipient time to organize a negative response. It is not suggested, of course, that people should be tricked into agreement, but merely that in a personal encounter the researcher is more likely to be able to reassure potential respondents, to allay any anxieties they may have and to win their consent and co-operation.

There are a number of other avenues of approach which can be explored, but all have their pitfalls. Sometimes it is possible to advertise in a local paper for respondents. However, advertisements are usually of negligible value unless some inducement to co-operation can be offered. The notion of public spiritedness may not be applicable to a respondent who sees the interviewer as an agent of a repressive or extractive body. Simply landing on private doorsteps is not advisable. Most of us do not welcome strangers who knock on our doors. Some sort of introduction or link name is needed when describing oneself and one's project. When making contacts, short, honest explanations are essential. Networks in such communities are close-knit, and word spreads. Anything short of total frankness will encourage suspicion and reduce one's chances of getting co-operation. Once labelled as shifty or dishonest, one might as well give up. Also, one is vulnerable to events over which one has no control – other research agencies may publish findings concerning the target area, for example, and one is then immediately accused of duplicity and intrigue. But the more scrupulously honest one has been, the less likely this is to apply. Where it is most difficult to gain access, then obviously some degree of persistence is indicated before that particular avenue of exploration is abandoned. But great care is needed, for where counter-elites are concerned, persistence can in fact have the effect of hardening attitudes and entrenching opposition, if the researcher is not very careful to avoid arousing hostility.

Good places to develop links are the local political parties (but see Parry, Moyser and Wagstaffe, 1987, section 2). Party agents can provide connections with both mainstream politicians and fringe activists, and often have links with the grass roots. Also the local libraries can provide information about what is going on, and sometimes too, access to organizers. However difficult access seems, the researcher should remember that 'the community' is actually a conglomerate of groups and factions, and there is always some dissent, and there are always some who will talk about the affairs of the neighbourhood.

Field workers should bear in mind the fact that potential inter- viewees, especially if heavily involved in voluntary activity, may have very little time to spare. It is best, when making interview appointments, to ask for between a half hour and an hour. Often, if the respondent is enjoying the experience, it will go on longer. Interviews on our project were originally envisaged as a process of working through a list of open-ended questions grouped into a series of topics. However, this format soon proved to be unsuitable as it stood, and in need of modification. Respondents, in answer to early questions, would often develop their answers in such a way that they pre-empted the researcher and included other topics. Then, when in due course those topics were reached, would indicate, sometimes with a show of impatience, that those areas had already been dealt with. Furthermore, experienced researchers in the field suggested that the use of a list of questions was probably inhibiting respondents to some degree. In the circumstances it seemed sensible to abandon the questionnaire and to opt for a semi-structured interaction based only very loosely around a cluster of discussion topics.

Interviewers need to arm themselves with as much background information as possible before venturing to begin the survey. The importance of full use of secondary sources, documentation and archival material cannot be over-emphasized. Demonstrations of ignorance of the issues which historically and currently are the concerns of the elite in question, can only serve to emphasize one's non-community status. This has the effect, where the elite is defensive, of inhibiting the flow of information. People are often willing to discuss areas of shared knowledge but defensively reluctant to volunteer new facts, especially in sensitive areas. The degree of willingness to talk is also affected by other factors. Where the respondent in question is part of an organization, that institution's own traditions of openness or secrecy will have considerable bearing on the attitude of the potential source. The respondent may also be affected by others present, or even by being seen to be approached by a known researcher.

Once the problem of access has been settled, one must turn one's attention to the location of the interview, and the method of recording to be adopted. Venue is crucially important, the general rule being that the quieter and more private the place, and the less susceptible to interruption, the more satisfying the encounter will be to all concerned. Privacy allows the respondent to speak without fear of being overheard by others who may be hostile to co-operation, or more fearful, and who have not experienced the process of reassurance which normally precedes the interview. It also allows better concentration. Themes can be developed without interruption and loss of train of thought. On the other hand, the more public the meeting, the more probable it is that distractions will impede the smooth flow of the interview. Offices and private dwellings provide good locations, not only for the above reasons but also because the respondent, being on 'home ground', will probably feel relaxed and confident. Furthermore, it is usually possible to have more control over the level of background noise, which can be crucially important when one comes to transcribe the tape. Of all the interviews we recorded, those made in youth clubs where the speakers vied with practising reggae musicians or steel groups were the most difficult to transcribe.

So far as the problem of keeping a record of what the respondent says is concerned, the choice lies between note taking and tape recording. Note-taking is often preferred by respondents who might feel shy or inhibited by the use of a tape recorder, but it does have drawbacks. Sometimes, when people see what they have said printed in black and white it strikes them as being too bald. If they then deny that that was what they said, and one has only a collection of sketchy notes of the interview, it is difficult to withstand the *volte face*. An additional handicap where the use of notes is concerned is that, however quickly the interview is written up, much valuable material will be irretrievably lost in the process. Comparative exercises show that an interview generating 8–10 pages of typed material from hand-written notes, would normally produce 20–25 pages of transcript. This is not to say, however, that tape recording interviews is an ideal method: it, too, has its disadvantages. The first and most obvious is the natural reluctance of many people to commit to tape information which they consider to be sensitive or in some way liable to backfire. Even those who are fairly confident and comfortable with a tape recorder tend to drop their voices, mumble or cover their mouths with their hands when discussing anything of a controversial nature. Alternatively, some people will instruct the researcher to 'turn that thing off' before elaborating on a delicate issue. And this in itself raises difficulties: information given 'off the record' in this fashion, crucial though it may be to the concerns of the interviewer, cannot be directly quoted for publication, although it can be used as background material. It is true that where note-taking is the chosen method of recording, respondents will sometimes say 'don't write this down', but it tends to happen rather less often than when a tape is being made.

One advantage of using a recording machine is that one is more able to confine one's attention to the response one is getting than when one is taking notes. It can be rather difficult to listen carefully to what is being said in order to respond naturally, and at the same time to be ready with further questions which will direct the interview along the preferred avenues of exploration. Furthermore, one simultaneously has to make a mental note of, and remember, unexpected points which the interviewer has raised and which one wishes to have elaborated. When, in addition to all this, the researcher is hurriedly trying to scribble down as much of what is being said as possible, the whole process tends to flow less smoothly.

Something which must be learned from experience is how to pace the interview. Obviously, not all respondents proceed at the same speed. Some are windy and verbose, and may use all the allocated time discoursing on the first of the cluster of topics that one wishes to explore, leaving no time for the rest. Others are economical of speech, or even abrupt, and will cover the prepared ground rapidly. In these circumstances, one needs to have developed a flexibility of approach which can be tailored to suit the situation of the moment. One way of doing this is to have a group of primary topics to explore, but, within each section, to have a collection of sub-sets of issues or themes which can be developed at more or less length as time dictates.

Sometimes, the duration of the interview is a function of the style adopted by the interviewer. While it is obviously essential to try, as far as possible, to avoid introducing bias and to refrain from asking leading questions, it can be necessary to cue the respondent. Completely open-ended questions can result in frustration, bafflement or irritation. Questions which contain some guidance for the respondent usually elicit a discussion of the case for and against any proposition contained therein. Potential field workers should note, therefore, that although totally neutral inquiries are methodologically sound in that they avoid drawing the respondent towards the bias of the researcher, they are not necessarily the most fruitful or productive. It is a dilemma which has to be worked through on each individual case. Also, flat contradictions of the speaker's points do not normally help to maintain a good atmosphere. A better way to introduce awkward issues of controversy is to use some softening and distancing device, such as 'What would you wish to say to those people who have an opposing viewpoint?' This is especially true where the speaker is not very socially confident or sophisticated, or possibly slightly intimidated by the researcher.

Another dilemma which has to be resolved, when researching a defensive elite, is the legitimacy of pressing inquiries into areas which are felt to be especially sensitive or inimical to the interests of the community. Social networks, in this context, can be problematic. Obviously, it is of importance to the researcher in terms of developing contacts and also it is significant to our understanding of how elites function. However, questions about personal networks, contacts and social arrangements can be perceived as intrusive by those who feel that their community is under siege. One activist responded:

The questions you want to ask are not harmless. They are positively dangerous. Whenever the police come to one of our houses they go through our personal papers, books, diaries. They want to know who our friends are, who our contacts are, where we go, what groups we are in, what activities – social and political – we take part in. Whether you intend it or not, and I'm quite prepared to believe that you don't, but the end result is the same, the information you want to gather is just the kind of information they seek.

Having recorded an interview, one must address oneself to the necessity of making a transcription. The difficulties that one may encounter here should not be underestimated. Common sense will dictate that the best available quality of technical equipment is used. Even this, however, cannot compensate for the obstacles created for the transcriber by respondents who swallow syllables here and there (and these are the norm, not the exception), the drone of traffic and the thumps and bangs which regularly drown out key words. These problems are compounded when the respondent does not necessarily share the culture of the interviewer. Heavily accented English can make transcription very laborious. Furthermore, with a respondent of a different background the whole interaction can assume an unexpected structure. A very simple example of this is drawn from our research into individual involvement in group activity. Occasionally, the question 'Do you belong to any groups?', referring, of course, to voluntary citizens' or pressure groups, would elicit the answer: 'No, I leave that sort of thing to teenagers. And, anyway, I'm not musical.' When the exchange does not develop in predictable ways, filling in the gaps in an indifferent recording through a combination of memory and common sense is a much more time-consuming process than where the logic of the answer follows the logic of the question as one might expect to be the case in conventional elite research.

In view of these complicating factors, the decision concerning who is to undertake the transcriptions is one which needs careful thought. Obviously if one is able to delegate this time-consuming business to an efficient audio-typist one can devote one's energies to good advantage elsewhere. But with some interviews, even where precautions have been taken to ensure as good a quality of tape as possible, the stenographer's skills will not compensate for the fact that memory cannot be brought into play to supply the deficiencies of the recording. One therefore may feel obliged to transcribe one's own material. This is said by Dexter to take roughly ten hours for each hour of tape, but that is in fact a very loose guide (Dexter, 1970). Patterns of speech vary considerably. Some people drawl, others hold forth at high speed. And again, background noise, unusual sentence structure and word choice, accented English and irregular inflexion can all increase the time taken to obtain an accurate account of the interview. In these cases the ratio of translation to recording time can be fifteen hours to one, or even higher.

Whether to transcribe the whole tape or not is another dilemma. Obviously, there is some verbiage which could be dispensed with. We found, however, that comments and observations which, on the early tapes, we had not considered notable, eventually were proved to have considerable significance. Had we not made complete transcriptions, many of the themes which we later came to consider important, would simply not have emerged.

As it is desirable that tapes should be processed as quickly as possible, it is not normally a good idea to make too many appointments in a short period of time. If the transcription of tapes proceeds apace, one can constantly monitor one's interviewing technique, and can learn to be prepared for those accidental arrangements (such as the relative positioning of the involved parties *vis-à-vis* the recorder) which can make life easier or more difficult for the transcriber. Also one can take up from one interviewee points and issues which can then be explored with others. Once the transcription has been completed, the researcher may or may not wish to submit a copy to the respondent for ratification, or enlargement. Whatever process is followed is by arrangement between interested parties. It should be borne in mind, however, that the more protection that is offered to the source, in a study of this nature, the more forthcoming that source is likely to be. Conversely, if confidentiality and anonymity cannot be guaranteed, respondents will be constrained by the possibility of adverse reactions to their participation and their observations.

10.5   Evidence and Interpretation

Once the material has been gathered, there is a process of verification to be worked through. When working with a conventional elite, where much of what has been said is 'on the record', material can often be ratified from printed sources, such as newspaper archives and local government documents. Where the counter-elite is concerned, this is not necessarily the case. Documentary material is less voluminous and, even where it has been created, is less likely to be complete or archived in a retrievable manner. One must rely more for substantiation on processes such as triangulation, whereby the statements made by one respondent are (anonymously) tested on another.

However, even with a 'counter-elite', there is always some

secondary source material which can be used to verify, supplement and support the primary data. Census records give much valuable background for this type of study. Information concerning the socio-economic status of residents, type of housing and density of occupation, the age profile of the local population, etc., can be derived from this source. Publications issued by city councils on local and regional trends in housing, education, health, law enforcement, employment, personal income and expenditure, etc., are all available, usually for the asking, to students and researchers. The diligent investigator will collect material from local newspapers and magazines and will obtain transcripts of television and radio programmes concerning the research target. Adult education centres, libraries and community meeting places may have archival material including the findings of previous surveys and projects. Not to be neglected is the local senior citizens' meeting place, which can be an invaluable source of oral history of the area.

Finally, with reference to an issue which is of crucial importance, we would wish to direct the attention of the researcher to the ethical and moral issues involved. Will the research findings be damaging to the community? What potential for use and abuse arises from the report? Will policy decisions be affected, and if so, how? Can the researcher safeguard the interests of respondents and at the same time maintain the integrity of the project?

10.6 Conclusions

Researching a threatened elite can be a difficult and problematic process. It is almost axiomatic that the success of any given research project is closely associated with the appropriateness of the chosen methodology. In elite research, a variety of approaches is available to the student. These range from the large-scale survey by question-naire, through structured or semi-structured interviews to oral history and phenomenological investigation, and can draw on a wealth of secondary and archival material. Counter-elite watchers, however, can be sorely constrained by the nature of their subject. Much more time is needed to develop a network of respondents than when one is working with a conventional elite. Respondents are likely to be defensive and constrained. The dearth of secondary sources and archival material is a serious drawback. The philosophical issues which arise are knotty and difficult. None the less, with a suitable research topic, the right approach and persistence, it can be done.

11

Elite studies in a 'paranocracy': the Northern Ireland case

PAUL ARTHUR
University of Ulster

11.1 The Context

Northern Ireland's constitutional status has always been ambiguous. It was created by the Government of Ireland Act, 1920, which was intended to be a temporary expedient pending a permanent solution to the Irish crisis. In fact, the 1920 Act was, according to a distinguished constitutional lawyer, a 'legislative ruin within seven months of its passing' because its provisions 'were dictated with a view to political pacification rather than administrative efficiency'. Moreover, the Government of Ireland Act was designed for the whole of Ireland, and when the Irish Free State broke away from British rule, had to be amended to be applicable to Northern Ireland alone. But it was not changed substantially, so that powers were delegated to Northern Ireland which had been drafted to meet a different situation. No regard was paid, for example, to the needs of Northern Ireland as a separate political and economic unit, and the Act was not revised to take account of the changing role of the state, economic crises or social and political conflicts.

The 1920 Act had one obvious advantage – it quarantined the Irish issue from British domestic politics, but at a price.

In respect of substance, the 1920–1 Anglo–Irish settlement had one aspect, so evident as to be deserving of comment . . . It was that no reduction in the number of parties involved was achieved as a result of it. They remained as before, their conceptual approaches fundamentally unchanged, though now there were two sovereign states and a subordinate government, where there had been a sovereign state, a national movement and a minority resistant to it. (Mansergh, 1978, p. 45)

Sixty years of devolved government have not changed these conceptual approaches one iota but have added to the complexity of the problem, so that now we refer to two sovereign states, one fragmented majority community with receding attachments to one of these states, and a disillusioned minority with allegiance to the other. Anyone engaged in elite interviews concerned with the Northern Ireland question has to consider all four parties, each of them carrying their own selective political memories.

Until the mid-1960s it was fashionable to examine Northern Ireland as a peculiar form of devolution within a unitary state: in fact, the first Minister of Finance referred to the province as 'an autonomous state with a federal relationship to the United Kingdom'. It was seen, too, as an example of 'governing without consensus', a recognition of the fact that it did not enjoy full legitimation. Stability was ensured by a security policy in which citizens became accustomed to the belief that the rule of law must always be suspended, and by a philosophy of 'let sleeping dogs lie' by Westminster. As the Kilbrandon Commission on the Constitution (Cmnd. 5460, 1973, para. 1303) frankly acknowledged: 'the intractability of the "Irish problem" and the uncomfortable lessons of history provided every inducement to the Government in London to keep Northern Ireland out of United Kingdom politics'. The result was that Stormont, the site of the local parliament and government, became more authentically than Westminster the centre of the province's political life and a potential focus for allegiance. A former Prime Minister, Brian Faulkner (1978, p. 26), admitted that Stormont 'led politicians in Northern Ireland into illusions of self-sufficiency, of taking part in a sovereign parliament. It created unspoken separatist tendencies.' He accepted that both sides were responsible for that situation.

Westminster's limited control tended to be at administrative rather than political level. One recent study has concluded that, until recently, 'Northern Ireland was the divided responsibility of the Home Office, the Ministry of Defence, the Foreign Office and, sporadically, the Cabinet Office'. In addition, 'Westminster's supervision over Northern Ireland's legislative process was more concerned with constitutional propriety than with political desirability' (Birrell and Murie, 1980, pp. 287 and 9). The result was a reasonably successful example of administrative devolution in which strong departmental links were established between certain Stormont and Whitehall officials concerning overall financial responsibility, social security, agriculture, the public health service and industrial development. Two factors arose from this arrangement. There was no informed Whitehall view of the more controversial aspects of Northern Ireland politics. Secondly, no real consideration had been given to the personnel of the local Civil Service beyond a recognition of their administrative competence – in other words, no real thought had been given to the peculiar political circumstances in which they worked – such as the fact that they had served only one political party continuously since 1921, and that from their earliest days their very recruitment had been a matter of political controversy.

These problems were pushed to the forefront of the political agenda in 1968. The genesis and activity of the civil rights movement have been amply documented. Suffice to say that (largely Catholic) demands for basic civil (i.e. British) rights were perceived by the authorities as being a fundamental challenge to the political system itself. Communal rioting became so severe that Westminster, exercising its sovereignty under Section 75 of the 1920 Act, intervened to force a reform programme through Stormont. From August 1969, two senior officials (one of whom had been Ambassador to Denmark from 1966 to 1969) were dispatched to Belfast to oversee British policy and to report directly to London. These 'visiting firemen', who occupied rooms adjacent to the Prime Minister and the Minister of Home Affairs, created resentment among the indigenous Civil Service, and placed the hapless Prime Minister in the role of a surrogate. As well, this form of direct rule by proxy allowed the Whitehall officials to familiarize themselves with administrative procedures and decision-making processes at Stormont should the moment ever arrive when direct rule would need to be imposed.

A complicating factor was the increasingly active role played by the Irish Republic. It had claimed Northern Ireland's territory since 1921 and wrote this irredentism into its 1937 Constitution. By the 1960s, however, it had recognized that there could not be Irish unity unless the two communities in Northern Ireland were reconciled. So the Republic had begun to stress functional co-operation rather than nationalist rhetoric. This cautious strategy was shattered by the communal rioting of 1968–69 when the Dublin government was forced into the role of 'second guarantor' of the reform programme. London reacted angrily by declaring that the Northern Ireland problem was purely an internal affair, especially after attempts were made to place the issue on the United Nations agenda. This public brawling raised the tension within Northern Ireland so that as time went on London and Dublin could do little more than respond to the latest atrocities.

Neither the reform programme nor waves of coercion returned stability to the province and finally, in March 1972, Stormont was prorogued and direct rule was imposed. Increasingly Britain had found itself 'reduced to using the instruments of warfare, rather than those of civil administration' (Miller, 1978, p. 150). Following an incident known as Bloody Sunday (when paratroopers opened fire and killed unarmed civilians in Londonderry on 30 January 1972) the Catholic population withdrew compliance from the state and London got sucked into the Irish quagmire once more. A Secretary of State for Northern Ireland, William Whitelaw, was appointed to govern the province. First impressions were not favourable, and he is alleged to have told Cecil King (1974, p. 194) that 'the Augean stables were nothing to the mess he found at Stormont. Disproportionate salaries for Ministers; jobs for the Protestant boys; every power of the Government used to depress the Catholics.' Additionally, Westminster politicians soon appreciated that the Northern Ireland problem did not fit into the usual parameters of British political practice, so that since 1972 we have had six successive sets of institutions: direct rule with an appointed advisory council; devolved coalition government; temporary direct rule; a constitutional convention; temporary direct rule again, and the current experiment in 'rolling devolution'. Only the coalition government which lasted for five months in 1974 held out any real prospect of stability. It was composed of representatives of the two communities, it was answerable to London, and it had an Irish (Dublin) dimension added to it. It encompassed, therefore, the four contending parties and it was a cautious attempt to probe their fundamental conceptual approaches. Its collapse raised serious doubts about any form of lasting settlement.

11.2 Conflicting Interests

Those who work on the Northern Ireland problem, especially those who have lived in the province over the past fifteen years, are conscious that they carry their ethnic and emotional baggage with them. In a face to face society they will be known by the political actors. A psychologist, Ken Heskin (1980, p. 100) had described Northern Ireland between 1921–72 as a 'paranocracy' in which the basis of power 'was the successful appeal to paranoid fears in the Protestant electorate about the political, social, philosophical and military potential of their Catholic neighbours'. The change of administration in 1972 has intensified those fears because it has inexorably shifted the problem from the 'narrow ground' of Northern Ireland to the broader canvas of Anglo–Irish relations.

In addition, Northern Ireland has existed in a state of political pathology. Since 1968 the crime rate has soared almost six-fold: Northern Ireland has proportionally the largest prison population in Western Europe. The death toll arising from civil disturbances approaches 2500 and it has been calculated (New Ireland Forum Report on the Cost of Violence, 1983, p. 19) that 39 000 jobs have been lost because of the violence between 1979–80. These statistics illustrate a political culture based on bitter mistrust.

Researchers engaged in elite interviews to elicit confidential information must respect such confidences absolutely. It has not always been so. For example, a doctoral student of International Relations had two interviews with Clive Abbott, an Assistant Secretary at the Northern Ireland Office, during 1981. He had not disclosed that he had worked for a Unionist MP at Westminster as a research assistant, and he proceeded to release what he alleged was a verbatim transcript of the interviews to Enoch Powell MP. In a parliamentary debate during the Report Stage of the Northern Ireland Bill (whereby the Secretary of State was attempting to impose his 'rolling devolution' scheme) Powell declared that Abbott's remarks were further evidence of a continuing attempt by Whitehall to thwart the government's wishes to bring Northern Ireland more fully into line with Great Britain, and that it was part of a secret deal between Dublin and London.[1] Such allegations caused considerable consternation and led to an inquiry by a high-ranking official.

The incident did little to smooth the path of others working in the field. My research over the past decade has been concerned, *inter alia*, with analysing the objectives, performance and character of British governmental action in Northern Ireland since 1972, and, in particular, examining the constraints and opportunities emanating from mainland Britain, the Irish Republic and the province itself.

The constraints imposed by the Republic in British policy involves two considerations: the attitude of Dublin governments to the North needs to be seen alongside internal political and economic developments in the South; and the changing nature of Anglo–Irish relations and the consequences for Northern Ireland have to be assessed. At United Kingdom level the changing role of the Northern Ireland

Office has to be considered. This entails an investigation of how the changing personnel of the NIO familiarized themselves with the problem, and how their perceptions about the problem changed over time. The creation of the NIO raises questions about the tension and conflicts between the NIO and the Northern Ireland Civil Service (NICS); tensions between the British departments of state created by differences of approach to Northern Ireland; and the roles of the various Secretaries of State pursuing their individual strategies. All of this treads very sensitive ground.

An examination of such a contentious contemporary problem relies on the availability of sources and at first glance there appears to be no shortage of relevant official documents. Chronologically these documents illustrate British policy-makers' growing awareness of the complexity and intractability of the Northern Ireland problem. We are fortunate too in having the memoirs of several key decision-makers. Four British Prime Ministers have been intimately concerned with the issue over the past decade and two of these have written accounts of their role. Harold Wilson's memoirs are marginal to the problem, but James Callaghan has written revealingly about his overlordship of the reform programme. In addition, one Secretary of State, Merlyn Rees, has written two short accounts of his time in Northern Ireland as has one junior Minister, Lord Windlesham. These are supplemented by a host of books dealing with various aspects of the problem, including one by a former Northern Ireland Prime Minister, Brian Faulkner, and by a former senior civil servant, John Oliver (Oliver, 1978). Finally, several well-informed journalists have produced a steady stream of 'insider' information since 1972. Much of this is very valuable, but the tradition of the 'unattributable leak' makes much of it dubious as a research resource.

The success of the project, therefore, depends on going beyond these sources and arranging elite interviews with key politicians and senior civil servants in London, Belfast and Dublin as well as knowledgeable commentators in the three capitals. I have had some limited experience interviewing local political leaders in an attempt to explain the collapse of the power-sharing experiment of 1974. Interestingly enough, those interviews were concerned with the nature of elite behaviour since they relied on Arend Lijphart's consociational model. That project has little to offer the present research because, as one respondent put it, local politicians see 'Ulster as the navel of the world'. In other words, with two notable exceptions they have not the vision to lift their heads above their own parapets.

The outsider is immediately struck by the closed nature of the British political system. The tenacious researcher constantly confronts an invisible barrier entitled 'the Official Secrets Act'. In their illuminating study of the Treasury, for example, Heclo and Wildavsky (1974, p. xix) commented that probably 'less is known about the characteristic behaviour of civil servants and their political masters than about the fertility cults of ancient tribes'. During a period of recession when civil service morale is allegedly low, a desire to enlighten academics may be furthest from their minds, particularly if they feel that security issues could arise.

The academic seeking interviews with Northern Ireland civil servants must realize that he or she is dealing with a bureaucracy under stress. The same might be said about interviewing mainland officials transferred to the NIO. It is noteworthy, for example, that no fewer than eight of the twelve divisions of the Belfast office of the NIO were concerned with matters of law and order; and it is patently obvious that constitution-making in Northern Ireland is a very frustrating exercise. But two factors may make a spell in the NIO more exciting for imported officials. One is that it might be a good testing ground for permanent secretaries. And complementing that is a view of the NIO as an adventure playground for bureaucrats in terms of constitution-making and of simply keeping the show on the road. The interviewer, therefore, brings a different psychological approach to officials from the two administrative sites.

That may appear to be a fairly minor problem. What is of fundamental significance is the knowledge that

in Ulster, the great permanent question of political philosophy – the moral basis of authority, and of the right to resist authority, the relationship between law and force and that between nationality and political allegiance – were being debated. (Utley, 1975, p. 7)

And it may well be that a major barrier to a solution lies in the fact that our political masters suffer from 'a blinkered empiricism, a philosophical and political narrowness of imagination about the passions that can move men in politics' (Crick, 1972, p. 215). In other words, the Ulster question is simply the most intractable in contemporary British politics, and it may be that the emperor has no clothes. Elites are not noted for displaying their nudity.

This has been a tortuous way to say simply that the context is the problem. The imposition of direct rule has destabilized politics fundamentally within Northern Ireland and potentially within the island itself. It has removed the local legislature and executive and has left a political vacuum – filled from time to time by another 'solution'. Ironically it has removed departmental contact between Belfast and Dublin, thereby increasing the homogeneity of the Republic and depriving its leaders of the opportunity to learn how to cope with a truly pluralist society. Simultaneously, and paradoxically, it has brought about an improvement in Anglo–Irish relations because it persuaded the then Taoiseach (Prime Minister) that it was repudiation of Britain's insistence that the Northern Ireland conflict was a matter for the United Kingdom alone, indeed an admission that partition was unworkable.

It is in this maelstrom of conflicting ideologies and emotions and interests that the researcher is placed. And there is, of course, the subjective factor: 'the "personal equation" suggests that the perceptions and interpretations of the research will be contingent on the values of the researcher' (Burton, 1978, p. 167). I am a product of a Catholic upbringing and education in the Bogside area of Londonderry – 'Derry' to its nationalist residents, who bitterly resent the British appendage to an ancient Gaelic site. My political education was forged as a member of the Northern Ireland Labour Party when it went through an ecumenical phase in the early 1960s appealing to Catholic and Protestant on the basis of class politics; and of close involvement in the civil rights' campaign in 1968 and 1969.

The biographical data are relevant. One approaches an interviewee with certain pre-conceptions. One assumes that the interviewee is aware of one's ethnic background and reacts accordingly. One may attempt to use that background to curry favour with a political actor from a similar environment. In more mundane language, the researcher is conscious that he operates in a system concerned with political survival. His instinct advises him who are friends and who are enemies, who will be accessible and who will procrastinate. In all of these assumptions he may be mistaken, but they are part of the psychological baggage he takes with him into an interview.

11.3 Manipulation by Elites?

It may be a misnomer to describe the process to date as 'elite interviewing'. Undoubtedly it has been an important research tool in unravelling the complexity of a contemporary problem. But one's experience suggests that it is part of the wider phenomenon of 'participant observation' – 'the empathic and analytic immersion into a social world' (Burton, 1978, p. 165). With the exception of the indigenous political and administrative elite – and the imposition of direct rule in 1972 was a recognition that they had failed to solve the problem – research on the Northern Ireland question inevitably entails examination of London and Dublin perceptions. Since both these actors had adopted a policy of distancing themselves from the problem before 1968 they came fresh to the issue: in fact, 'fresh' is a euphemism for 'ignorant'. Dublin had been strong on rhetoric but weak on constructive practical action; and London had exercised a wise and salutary neglect of the province. A shared ignorance was challenged by a competition in national psyches. Urgency required the collection and analysis of detailed and accurate knowledge.

All of this can be explained by examining briefly the course of my research. Originally, I was engaged in a two-year Social Science Research Council (SSRC) funded project entitled 'Direct Rule in Northern Ireland'. The path of that research did not always run smoothly. A list of potential interviewees was drawn up and approached by letter, for formal interviews. The first list consisted of fifteen Westminster politicians who had served in Northern Ireland between 1972–79, in addition to three former Prime Ministers (Messrs Heath, Wilson and Callaghan) and two Unionist MPs. The initial response was disappointing, seven acceptances out of twenty, only one of whom had been Secretary of State, Merlyn Rees. Senior officials were approached more tentatively. Since politicians are 'on the record' virtually continuously they can be approached with confidence based on sound information. It was hoped to learn the ground rules through these interviews. Besides, we were advised by relatively junior administrators to steer clear of their superiors for as long as possible. In fact, this advice represented bureaucratic conservatism.

The initial project had not envisaged a Dublin input but the course of political events and the perceived reluctance of some of the principals in the 'Direct Rule' research suggested that a more fruitful approach might be to broaden the parameters of the project. It carried, too, an implicit threat: if Dublin was prepared to co-operate could elements in London procrastinate in participation?

Approaches to politicians and officials in Dublin have been much more successful. No one has refused assistance. Meetings have been arranged literally in some cases at thirty minutes notice and very often they have been done through telephone calls rather than formal written requests. There has not been any insistence that prior notice of questions be supplied (as there was in some instances in Belfast and London) and generally the atmosphere has been relaxed and welcoming. There may be an ethnic explanation for this. My own religious and political background would suggest to Dublin contacts that I could be trusted. There is also the fact that the Irish Republic has a political culture based on patronage and brokerage which has made the bureaucracy more open and the political system more sensitive to the public. Finally, there are political considerations in that the desire for unity entails a willingness to meet and listen to all shades of Northern opinion.

The element of trust cannot be exaggerated. Heclo and Wildavsky (1974) discovered at a very early stage that 'mutual trust was the leitmotif of all working relationships and that in order to be accepted into our chosen political community we had to show ourselves trustworthy'. Their study of the Treasury can be used as the classic manual of the interview technique, its successes and limitations. Trust is based on authority, the authority of the informed:

> The moment the interviewer shows unfamiliarity with the subject (though why else would he be there?) he will begin to feel himself on the smooth slipway to the outer office . . . Hence the researcher's dilemma: to learn more he must already know much; he cannot get information without at least a small fund to begin with and he has trouble obtaining that without prior knowledge'. (Heclo and Wildavsky, 1974, p. xviii)

In fact, that very dilemma may be a plus for the interviewer who is attempting to secure a 'worm's-eye' view of administration. The outsider's modesty encourages the insider's own *amour propre*. If modesty can be combined with a perspective (based on wide reading) which is novel then the interview can be very satisfactory for both sides.

Modesty may not be too easy to attain with political interviewees. The politicians' vanity and vulnerability can induce a degree of contempt on the part of the academic. Unlike the official, the politicians' actions are so patently public that a barometer of success can be constructed and one can more easily measure perceptions of reality. Of course, Ireland has been the graveyard of political careers in the past and one is very conscious of the constraints and limitations within which the politician operates. So allowances need to be made. I must say, however, that even with the most generous construction placed on the politician's motivations, interviews conducted at

Westminster tended to be, with one notable exception, time-consuming and irrelevant. A few reasons suggest themselves. One is a curious nostalgia which many politicians adopt towards the province. The result tends to be a desire to have a cosy chat about the peculiar circumstances of Northern Ireland and its people, thereby avoiding answering some of the more pertinent points. More importantly, Northern Ireland has given some London-based politicians their first real grasp of power and one which would not damage them with their constituents if their policies failed; culpability would lie with the unfortunate Irish. In a few instances it became difficult to keep the interview on the rails because respondents wanted to talk incessantly about taking 'big decisions' and 'being on your own' as these decisions were being taken. This element of 'macho' politics did not square with the sometimes timid and wrongheaded advice which the record shows they had often followed. There was, too, a strange notion of Northern Ireland being 'out there' as if it had assumed some extra-terrestrial dimension.

One should not be too dismissive of these interviews. The politicians' prejudices are an important aspect of the question. In one particular instance, a meeting with a senior Unionist MP, the value of the interview technique became evident. No sooner had the interview begun than it had become clear that this politician does not suffer fools gladly. When trust was established, he was expansive and incisive in his answers, so much so that less than two of five agreed topics had been covered by the time the interview had to finish. An immediate agreement to talk to me at much greater length at a mutually convenient time and place suggests that this interview was a success, particularly since our political beliefs are miles apart. Two general points arise from this meeting. One is that the location of meetings is important. This was the only parliamentary interview conducted in a private office; others were held in the lobby and it became impossible to hold the politician's attention completely. So many distractions occurred on one occasion that my contact offered me another meeting within a week. Secondly, all my interviews have been held in the hope that I can arrange a follow up meeting within a year. Experience teaches that no matter how well briefed we may be, we are unlikely to pick up all the nuances on the first meeting. Besides that, as the list of interviewees is extended it is likely that facts and interpretations have to be re-examined. In every instance I have been offered a second meeting and most of these have been unsolicited.

These general points have been borne out in interviews with 'ex's': 'the important men who are no longer active community members

... Today's details are different, but yesterday's spirit is likely to be very much alive' (Heclo and Wildavsky, 1974, p. xviii). I have held only three meetings with ex-members of the Northern Ireland civil service, but all three were long, generous and fruitful. They were held in the comfort of the interviewees' homes – all of them, incidentally, living in England for security reasons – and conducted after being entertained lavishly. The relaxed atmosphere contributed enormously to the success of these interviews. Recently retired officials are a huge source of information: they continue to exercise the discretion of the service, but within these limitations they are happy to unburden their thoughts and it is a great advantage that they are no longer concerned with the minutiae of policy.

One final comment on the conduct of interviews. Officialdom represents a closed community with its own informal network of communications. The interviewer must display both a degree of sensitivity and honesty. The latter quality may pay dividends because one soon discovers that the network is informed about the project and individuals may react through non-cooperation if they feel they are not receiving full information. My own experience suggests that interviews should be as open-ended as possible. When, for example, I have been asked for a list of questions in advance, I have offered instead a broad view of the areas I would like to cover. No one has refused to see me because of this approach, and interviews have tended to be discursive, an extended conversation where the interviewer is more than a mere cipher. It allows for a breadth in the conversation which might throw up some unusual information or interpretation. There is the danger, however, that minute but important details will slip through this broad net. Only a fairly wide ranging series of interviews can overcome that difficulty.

All of the above indicates that it may be too melodramatic to consider that elite interviewing is about manipulation. Undoubtedly politicians and officials will attempt to suggest that they are the fount of all wisdom. It was not unusual, for example, to find that a politician had at the ready a copy of a speech he had made – often many years earlier – in anticipation of a question; or that an official would steer the conversation away from awkward areas. But if the nature of the project is wide-ranging then it may be more sensible to think in terms of elites rather than a monolithic elite. It is the conspiracy theorist who thinks in terms of monoliths, whereas the evidence would suggest that the institution may as easily be shaped by events as vice-versa. It is the task of the interviewer to establish that which is documentary evidence and to discard that which is propaganda.

That task may be easier where he is dealing with defensive elites, 'defensive' not simply in terms of their past activity but in relation to their intermittent attention to the issue. The elite(s) come with detailed knowledge of discrete areas of policy. Rarely do they have an overview. Where they are being questioned by one who has observed and participated in the process (at different times and in different intensity, it needs to be said) then a separate issue arises: that of the objectivity of the researcher.

11.4   Conclusions

Northern Ireland may be *sui generis*. A study of direct rule goes well beyond the question of public administration. It is concerned with fundamental constitutional issues, with intra- and inter-state relations and with security and defence. This last touches on foreign affairs and international relations, and allows conspiracy theories[2] to thrive. Is the Irish Republic prepared to abandon its tradition of neutrality and join NATO in return for a promise of Irish unity? Is the Foreign Office contemptuous of Britain's greatness and undermining it through the Irish imbroglio? The study also raises ethical questions. Should we lend credence to terrorist organizations by interviewing and publicising spokesmen from their front organizations? At an early stage of my research I made a value judgement that I would not talk to anyone from Provisional Sinn Fein but that I would interview a spokesman for the UDA. The decision was based on the well-publicised position of Sinn Fein that it unequivocally supported the armed struggle of the IRA, whereas the UDA appeared to be entering a political phase by probing the potential support for Ulster independence. Time will tell whether the latter was no more than a smokescreen to gain respectability so as to avoid proscription by the authorities. Subsequently I decided to use their material only as 'background'. In either case one is erring on the side of caution and is open to the charge of self-censorship.

As a practical exercise it raises delicate matters. Some of my interviewees have had constant security protection; indeed, one retired prematurely after a bomb was discovered underneath his car. Some have been officials in the NICS, conscious that, after 1968, they were under scrutiny as being politically suspect. Equally, Whitehall officials may not relish being questioned on their state of knowledge about Northern Ireland before 1968 nor about the tensions which arose with the indigenous officials when direct rule was imposed.

Finally, Northern Ireland raises questions about British and Irish statecraft. In an era of decolonization what has gone wrong with this 'little local difficulty'? Is a blinkered empiricism part of the problem? Is it nostalgia for Empire? Does the Republic's faltering attempts at containing the problem devastate the illusions of rhetoric?

Of course, all of these questions are pointed at the elite(s). What of the interviewer? He could, of course, declare his prejudice but should be conscious that it is open to conversion. He needs to be aware that he is not used as a megaphone to convey others' prejudices. Perhaps the only means to overcome this is to interview as widely and as frequently as possible; that is, the longer the time-span of the project the greater should be his capability for spotting manipulation. Crucially, he must realize that interviews are but one segment of the research process.

Elite interviewing may be a crude, but necessary tool. The first requirement is an elite to interview. A reluctance on the part of some key witnesses to come forward undermines the exercise in this instance. It may be that a policy of attrition will produce results in the end. Undoubtedly, some vital meetings have occurred because kindred souls in high places in Dublin and London have lent their names to the project. The foregoing suggests that there may be a large element of chance in such a project. What cannot be challenged is that it is a time-consuming business and one often feels that one's time would be better spent in a library. The second requirement is that interviews are conducted in as ideal conditions as possible. And that is very difficult to gauge. The interviewer brings his prejudices with him, his vanity, his egotism, his voyeurism. These may even be substitutes for proper groundwork. What may not become obvious until it is too late is that the illusion of activity may be bearing little fruit, or that the interviewer may be being led up cul-de-sacs.

Ideally, elite interviewing should act as a complement to the published material as one tries to build up as accurate and objective a picture as possible. The academic can trade off his information against his respondent's expertise. The result can be fecund, but it may be flatulent.

Notes

1 See *Belfast Telegraph*, 2 July, 1982.
2 A good example is J. Enoch Powell, 'Dev and devolution', *The Spectator*, 8 January, 1983, pp. 19–20.

12

The study of Soviet and East European elites

CHRISTOPHER BINNS
University of Manchester

12.1 Elitism and the Principles of Communist Politics

Communist theorists have always rejected the applicability of elite theory to their societies, on the ground that the communist party represents not an instrument of elite domination but the most perfect channel for the true interests of all working people, who are actively involved in the elaboration and implementation of policy. This outright rejection is also understandable in view of the anti-Marxist orientation of most elite theory, particularly of the founding fathers. Yet there appears to be a strong *prima facie* case for the application of elite theory to communist politics: decision-making is highly centralized and concentrated and, moreover, many of the central principles and mechanisms of communist politics would seem to be blatantly 'elitist' in character. Our first task in this paper will be to elucidate the implications of these principles and to show the main variations in their development and in their contemporary operation in the Soviet Union and Eastern Europe.

One of the most basic principles of communist politics is that of the 'vanguard party', first adumbrated by Lenin in his 'What is to be done?' (1902). He argued that in Russian conditions of that time a mass party of the type of the German SPD was inappropriate. What was needed was a 'cadre' party, a small, highly disciplined party of 'professional revolutionaries', recruited from among the most active and 'conscious' elements of the working class and intelligentsia. Enlightened by its understanding of the 'scientific' theory of Marxism which enabled it to discern the long-term 'objective' interests of the working class, this vanguard had the right to 'guide' the working class along the correct revolutionary path: if left to their own devices the workers would be diverted by the promise of piece-meal economic and social reform into mere 'trade-union conscious-ness'. Thus, in its origins, Bolshevism was quite openly elitist in character.

After the Bolshevik revolution the character of the party inevitably changed with its new dominant power position. At the time of the revolution there were some 200,000 members. This number doubled after Lenin's death in 1924, and from the later 1920s the numbers inexorably rose as Stalin recruited the 'new technological intelligentsia' for his industrialization drive, reaching nearly four million by the late 1930s. After the Second World War there was another steep rise in recruitment to reach some seven million members by Stalin's death in 1953. Since the 1950s numbers have risen at a steady rate to the present figure (1986) of some 19 million, representing nearly 7 per cent of the total population but, more importantly, over 14 per cent of the working population. The communist parties of Eastern Europe have exhibited similar trends. Yet the CPSU is still a cadre party: membership is by invitation and recruitment, not by controlled voluntary entry, and a high degree of commitment is expected of all members.

Moreover, the party has retained its 'vanguard role', now expressed in the principle of 'the leading role of the party' in society. During the phase of the 'dictatorship of the proletariat' in the Soviet Union the party used force to ban other political parties and to crush its class enemies. Since the completion of this process (roughly marked by the Stalin constitution of 1936) the party has been the 'vanguard' not just of the industrial proletariat but of the whole people, compromising the 'non-antagonistic' classes of the urban workers and the collective peasantry. In the communist regimes which developed in Eastern Europe in the 1940s a plurality of parties was often maintained in a nominal 'popular front' system, but all the non-communist parties accept the 'leading role' of the communist party and are heavily controlled by it. The communist party exercises its 'leading role' through a heavy saturation of party members, especially at the senior levels, in all non-party institutions such as ministries, elected assemblies, trade unions, youth organizations, military and economic units. Since the primary responsibility of party members is to their party organization not their working institution, this is an effective method of controlling non-party activity. In addition all responsible, decision-making posts throughout society are subject to the party's *nomenklatura*. This vitally important mechanism, which we shall discuss in detail later, consists of a list of all those key positions which are subject to party appointment or approval (non-party members may be trusted with such posts) by the relevant level of the party hierarchy. This is the ultimate expression of the 'cadres decide everything' principle so often praised by that expert in personnel management, Joseph Stalin.

12.2   The Identification of the Elite

Having established that there is a *prima facie* case for applying elite theory to communist politics, we now have to identify the elite structure to be investigated. The term 'elite' is only useful if we can give a concrete operational definition of it. While, as noted above, official Soviet criticism has always rejected the concept, the idea of a 'ruling class' or 'power elite' has been much discussed by Marxist and non-Marxist analysts of Soviet and East European socialism.

Marxist criticism has tended to identify either the 'bureaucracy' or the 'intelligentsia', or both together, as an exploitative 'stratum' or class. The exiled Trotsky in his *The Revolution Betrayed* (1937) was a major influence here. He argued that, while the USSR was still basically a 'workers' state' in view of the crucial step of the socialization of the means of production, this state had become 'degenerated' by the usurpation of an exploitative party bureaucracy led by a dictator (Stalin) – a process aided by Russia's economic and cultural backwardness and the temporary failure of international revolution. Trotsky never took the step of calling this 'parasitical stratum' a 'ruling class'. This move was made in the 1950s by Milovan Djilas, once Tito's right-hand man in Yugoslavia, who argued that the party bureaucracy, with their privileged life-style, were a 'new class' in Marxist terms in that they controlled the means of production in their own interests even though the technical owner-ship remained nominally in collective hands (Djilas, 1957). Djilas was influenced by the views of the former Trotskyist James Burnham who, in his famous work *The Managerial Revolution* (1941), influenced by elite theory, argued that what matters in modern industrial states is not formal ownership but control of the means of production and that the new managerial elite formed a crucial controlling group. More recently the East German dissident Rudolf Bahro (now in West Germany) has written of a 'polit-bureaucratic dictatorship', in which the political and administrative bureaucrats form a stratum of special interests which stands in an 'antagonistic' (i.e. exploitative) relationship to the primary producers

(Bahro, 1978, p. 240). Other critics have held that it is the 'intelligentsia', from which the political elite is allegedly recruited, which constitutes the ruling parasitical stratum (Parkin, 1971; Giddens, 1973; Konrad and Szelenyi, 1980).

The trouble with these structural approaches to the problem of a ruling class or stratum is that their referents are far too ill-defined for analytical purposes. The terms 'bureaucracy' and 'intelligentsia' both include large numbers of people who have very little effective political power – minor clerks on the one hand and graduates in non-political professions (doctors, teachers, etc.) on the other. The functional approach has in fact offered more concrete possibilities. A. G. Meyer (1964) adapted C. Wright Mills' 'positional power elite' model in his suggestion of a political elite consisting of the party professionals (the *aktiv*), military and police officials, industrial and administrative executives and leading academics and opinion-makers (e.g. journalists). A. Nove (1975) developed this idea by suggesting that the 'ruling class' might be defined by the party professionals plus the *nomenklatura* officials, appointed or approved by the party. We now have a pretty good idea of the composition of this list (see Harasymiw, 1969 and Voslensky, 1984 for the USSR, and MacShane, 1981, Appendix 5 for Poland), so the idea is quite operationally precise. Bahro's 'polit-bureaucratic dictatorship' appears to refer to much the same group: 'This social group essentially embraces the higher offices of all political, state and "social" managerial pyramids, including the military police and ideological branches, i.e. . . . . party, state and economic officials in the broadest sense' (Bahro, 1978, p. 240).

There is now a considerable degree of consensus among Marxist and non-Marxist scholars in applying this 'positional power elite' approach based on the *nomenklatura* to communist political systems, and it has been the *de facto* basis for much useful empirical work, as we shall see. Nevertheless, conceptual problems still remain when we try to place this notion of a 'power elite' within a general model of Soviet society. First, some problems about the nature of the elite: to what extent is there a single, unified elite in Soviet-type societies? At one time it was fashionable to argue that there was an inchoate form of 'bureaucratic pluralism' in the USSR, with competing elite groups on the Mills model (e.g. Hammer, 1974). The objection to this is that party saturation of non-party institutions and the overlap of party and non-party posts at the top level (e.g. the Defence Minister is always also in the party Politbureau) means that there is no such thing as competitive group or institutional autonomy in Soviet-type systems; even though from time to time 'localist' or 'compartmentalist' deviations do arise, they are exceptions which prove the rule. Disagreements between departmental heads undoubtedly occur, but they are like the bargaining which takes place in a British cabinet, operating within a general discipline of collective governmental responsibility. Nor does the multi-national character of a state (e.g. the USSR) generally affect the political unity of the central elite: in general we have to steer a middle course between accepting the public monolithic front of Soviet-type elites at face value and discerning Western-type pluralist divisions within them.

But what about the relation between this elite and the rest of society? The first point to make is that we are not just dealing with a central, national-level elite, but rather with a hierarchy of elites extending down to local level, as the *nomenklatura* system does. Secondly, what are the implications of elite recruitment and maintenance? Is there evidence of a new 'middle class' of 'eligibles' from which the elites are recruited? There does seem to be much *prima facie* evidence in favour of this view. Education is undoubtedly the key instrument of social mobility in Soviet-type states. An awareness of this has inevitably led to the use of 'connections' and unfair pressure to gain access to the highly competitive higher educational institutions. There is also plenty of evidence to show that, as in the West, children from white-collar backgrounds have more chance of gaining access to higher education than those from blue-collar backgrounds. All the same, the process of forming a 'middle class' is still in its early stages: it is still not possible to claim 'class rule' by the 'intelligentsia'. In the USSR, for example, over 60 per cent of all graduates come from working class or collective farmer backgrounds (Matthews, 1982, p. 159) and, while it is true that virtually all top leaders are graduates, many of these have graduated from the technological faculties of provincial universities or from the 'higher party schools', where working-class recruitment is far higher than in the arts or pure science faculties of the more prestigious universities. We are certainly not dealing with an educational-administrative elite of the apparent homogeneity of the French *grands écoles* graduates. On the whole, the Soviet elite has taken care to ensure considerable permeability from below. There has been little evidence of the transmission of political privilege across generations, though there is evidence of the transmission of social privilege: children of top leaders tend to eschew the uncertainties of politics in favour of cushy jobs in the cultural intelligentsia, professions or foreign trade missions. So if there is a ruling class it is a class of the 'democratic' rather than the 'aristocratic' type, to use Mosca's terminology, at any rate in present circumstances.

Next there is the problem of the relation between the political elite and the communist party mass membership. A recent study computes the total size of the *nomenklatura* in the USSR at all levels at some three million (Voslensky, 1984, p. 95), not all of whom are party members. Since demotion from *nomenklatura* rank is very rare (Voslensky, 1984, pp. 81–8), this means that the vast majority of ordinary party members will never be members of the political elites in the sense we have defined them. One could look on the mass membership as a more plausible candidate for the class of 'eligibles' than the 'intelligentsia', though it would not be a perfect one (because some *nomenklatura* posts are filled by non-party people). But there is a deeper problem here. The elite model presents a confrontational, divided picture of society: elites, eligibles, mass. Yet one of the great strengths of the communist system, as best demonstrated by the long-standing stability of the USSR, is its integrative capacity. There is no question of an inert mass: all sectors of society are mobilized and integrated into a centrally-directed system. People at the lower levels certainly do not have much political decision-making power as we see it, but they are to a much higher degree than in Western societies involved in a supportive role either by rituals of public commitment or by involvement in the implementation of policies. This is particularly true of communist party members (though 'involvement of the masses' ranges much wider than this). To regard the mass communist party membership simply as being composed of pliant careerists (Voslensky, 1984, pp. 96–100) is too cynical a view. The vast majority of them, as has been argued by one of the USSR's severest *émigré* critics (Zinoviev, 1981), are just good, solid, establishment figures, who gain little material benefit, in career or goods, from their membership, but rather the non-material advantages of increased status within the workplace or district, the excitement of belonging to an exclusive club with its secrets and rituals, of being associated with an enormously powerful institution even if one's own role within it is miniscule: a cross between a masonic society, an established church and an Old Boys' Association. The mass membership of the party provides a cementing network, a capillary system which, if it avoids sclerosis, lubricates and integrates the political system.

The positional power elite model can, nevertheless, provide a useful operational research strategy provided that we do not forget its limitations. Elite theory, like other political science models, is a blunt, imperfect instrument which can only highlight certain important aspects of a complex picture, and in Soviet-type societies this picture is even more complex to describe and analyse than in liberal-democratic states.

12.3   Elite Research in Soviet-Type Systems: Problems and Achievements

We have argued so far that the fundamental principles of communist politics do exhibit definite elitist tendencies and that, with certain reservations, it is possible to delineate in a fairly concrete way a positional power elite within Soviet-type systems which is worth investigating. We now proceed to consider what progress has been made by Western researchers in this direction and what problems they have encountered.

The vast majority of Western elite studies of Soviet-type systems deal with the question of elite recruitment and maintenance and derive virtually all their material from published documentary and secondary sources. This is no accident; indeed, it is dictated by the general context of conducting research in such societies. The basic fact is that it is impossible for Western scholars to carry out major and fully representative surveys, by questionnaire or by interview, on general elite opinion in these countries. It is generally also impossible to gain access to unpublished party and non-party archives which would enable scholars to fill out the serious gaps which still remain in documentary or statistical publications and secondary sources. For this reason the opening up of Soviet and East European countries to exchange agreements involving access to these countries by Western scholars during the 1960s did not lead to the anticipated revolution in Western studies of Soviet-type political systems: what it is possible to do in this area can still mainly be done at home if there is good access to published material. Nevertheless, we shall argue that direct work in the countries concerned is indispensable for gaining an understanding of the cultural context in which the elite operates and that interviewing and other research methods can shed light on elite decision-making processes within specific areas from which a broader picture of elite functioning may be derived.

However, much has been achieved by the judicious use of published material. The pioneering study in this field was John Armstrong's *The Soviet Bureaucratic Elite* (1959), which analysed recruitment and turnover in the Ukrainian party apparatus. Armstrong later supplemented this work by interviews with some

seventy West European public administrators and private businessmen who had been in close contact with the Soviet bureaucracy
(contributing to his study *The European Administrative Elite*, 1973)
– an interesting early example of the effective use of confirmatory
interviewing, to which we shall return later. Another pioneering
study was that by Peter Ludz of the Socialist Unity Party in the GDR
(Ludz, 1968–72). Ludz vigorously defends his use of what scholars
working in more accessible fields might argue was 'secondary'
material, on the grounds that systematic techniques of content
analysis and cross-checking can produce results which meet high
scholarly standards (Ludz, 1972, pp. 19–20). He is undoubtedly right
in general terms, but it remains the case that research based on
selective published material is bound to be rather tentative in its
conclusions. While it is true that since the Khrushchev period
published statistical materials are much fuller and more reliable than
they used to be under Stalin, there are still tantalizing gaps: for
example, our information on minor officials is very limited and the
information on the vitally important deputy chairmen of particular
bodies is often very patchy. But trying to bridge these gaps by the use
of newspaper and journal articles, which, of course, quote
information selectively, usually based on access to a secret party
archive, is obviously a very risky procedure. It is often difficult to
assess whether the information at one's disposal is complete enough
for any firm conclusions to be drawn. Hence it is pointless going over-
board on theoretical constructions and data manipulations if the
original data are thin or incomplete. This was the weakness of the
behaviouralist work on elite attitudes and their relation to the official
ideology (Lodge, 1969; 1971; Kanet, 1971; Beck *et al.*, 1973).

All the same, one should not detract from the value of this
prosopographical work on elite recruitment and turnover. Our
knowledge of the working of the party and its relationship to society
has been greatly extended by the work of Rigby (1968), Hough (1969)
and Gehlen (1969) on the CPSU (Communist Party of the Soviet
Union) and on more specific aspects of elite recruitment by
Churchward, Frank, Hill and Rigby (see Bibliography). In more
recent years impressive work on regional elites has been done by
Miller (1977), Hill (1977) and Hodnett (1978) and on the
nomenklatura by Harasymiw (1984) and Voslensky (1984).

However, the use of confirmatory or contextual interviewing *in
situ* for this type of research has probably yet to be fully exploited by
Western researchers, who are all too often put off by the initially
daunting nature of the task. It is worth quoting in this regard the

experience of one Western researcher who has produced one of the most impressive recent studies of regional elites. The study of Moldavian party elites by Hill (1977) is almost entirely based on material gathered from local and regional newspapers and Soviet secondary sources, even though Hill spent the session 1967–68 in Tiraspol (Moldavia). Hill explains this as follows:

> Even interviews with local officials in Tiraspol itself proved to be of only marginal value from an academic point of view: those interviewed clearly wished me to come away with the standard, legally-based official viewpoint, and all state officials showed a manifest reluctance to discuss relations with the party committee. In general it proved impossible to penetrate the propaganda facade of the security-minded bureaucrats, so contacts with local political leaders were of little real worth in this study. (Hill, 1977, p. 5)

He experienced similar frustration when trying to gain access to archives which would illuminate the decision-making processes of Moldavian elites:

> Details such as these [of decision-making processes] – which may perhaps be regarded as the very stuff of politics – simply are not available to researchers, and one is obliged to use different approaches and perhaps concentrate on slightly different aspects of political life. (Hill, 1977, p. 6)

Occasionally one encounters rather happier experience of on-the-spot interviewing by western researchers (see, for example, Frolic, 1971 and Taubman, 1973, both, perhaps significantly, studies of local politics), but Hill's experience is undoubtedly shared by many, including, to some extent, myself. But my view is that Hill is too dismissive of the value of interviewing. Certainly, this is never going to be a major information source, particularly on elite recruitment. But one also suspects that there were deficiencies in Hill's aims and methods. This leads me to make some observations based on my own experience. During the period from August 1976 to July 1977 and from September to December 1978, I was attached to Leningrad University as an exchange researcher. The subject of my research was the development by the party in the late 1950s to early 1960s of a new policy introducing an organized system of secular life-cycle rites and festivals, partly as an anti-religious measure, partly as a positive measure to revive what was seen as flagging political commitment among young people by promoting colourful and impressive communal symbolic events (see Binns, 1979; 1980). Since many elements in this policy were quite new and controversial and involved the setting up of new institutional mechanisms, it was very important for me to understand the decision-making processes of senior officials of the party, the soviets, Komsomol, etc., in developing this policy. It was hoped that this would also reveal much about elite decision-making in general.

Undoutedly elite decision-making is much more difficult to study in Soviet-type states than elite recruitment, for the reasons Hill gives. Yet, with the right approach and expectations, interviewing can, I believe, yield important information. Much depends, firstly, on a judicious choice and presentation of the research topic. Here an indirect rather than head-on approach will often produce best results. For example, suppose you bluntly state that you want information about relations between the party and the soviets in political decision-making. This is such a general topic that it is very easy for interviewees to waffle away without giving much concrete information, and at the same time it confronts very directly a highly controversial question (party–soviet relations) which rarely gets aired in public, and on which the interviewees, playing safe, will give a standard party-line statement. I suggest that a better approach is to select some concrete policy in which you know by secondary sources that both party and soviets were actively involved. Since this is more specific, it is harder for interviewees to dodge the issues, and the controversial issue of party–state relations can be approached indirectly, by implication, rather than in a head-on assault. In any case there have been so many studies of general elite recruitment that what we need now is specific studies of the development and implementation by elites of particular policies. Some Western research topics are either not going to be accepted by the authorities in Soviet-type states or are going to yield very scanty results. One often has to propose a subject which is researchable but which will yield indirect information about the real subject of one's research. Also, presentation is very important. This involves translating the summary of the research topic into the cultural concepts of the country under research. Thus, if one was interested in studying possible group-conflict between party and military hierarchies in defence policy-making, this subject would be impossible *tout court*, but might be accepted in terms of 'The stimulation of the defence-readiness of the country in the context of the all-round development of the national economy', and then applied to a particular policy. My own research topic, for example, was presented as: 'The educative role of new Soviet, non-religious festivals and rituals in the formation of the new Soviet man'. This sounds corny, but in fact represents an important and necessary cultural re-orientation.

Secondly, there is the problem of selection of interviewees. This is a very difficult problem for a Western researcher. As much preparatory work as possible should be done before coming to the country, since it does help if there are at least some initial names with their locations on the initial application made through the exchange agreement; if the application is accepted these names can then be used as a minimum start. It is virtually useless applying to the Foreign Departments of universities after arrival in the country for recommendations of names of people who might be interviewed: they will do nothing. It is the researcher's responsibility to find out the names of the appropriate people. This involves often prolonged detective work, since there are no available statistical handbooks listing the staffs of particular institutions (including universities and research institutes) and since telephone directories are available only to private subscribers, never in public boxes. One method is to use a sort of 'snowball' technique, by asking one's initial contacts to recommend others in the area, and so on, gradually building up a related network. The other indispensable method is *svyazi* – 'connections'. In a bureaucratically dominated system personal links provide vital human lubrication, and never more so than in the USSR. Personal connections, even if they are totally unrelated to your research topic, may, as local citizens, often be able to find out names and locations for you. In the same way, once you know whom you want to interview, connections can often smooth the way to actually gaining 'access' to the person concerned. A direct approach through the Foreign Departments or by telephone can often lead to defensive stone-walling, but if you can cite the name of a mutual connection, doors can be opened. Altogether, researchers must be prepared to expend considerable effort and patience in seeking out and gaining access to interviewees; good connections will ease, but not remove the problem.

Thirdly, we should consider the conduct of the interview. It is extremely rare for people to consent to be tape-recorded in Soviet-type societies, so careful preparation of questions and good note-taking are essential. Where you do succeed in taping an interview, it is advisable to transcribe the material immediately, since capricious border guards are liable to confiscate or destroy any taped material even if you have a document of official permission for it. Sometimes an interviewee will demand to see a list of questions in advance and stick to that list. In any case it is a good idea to give the interviewee a good idea of the general course of your interview questions beforehand. It is essential to prepare plenty of supplementary questions in case the original ones do not 'work', and also to design indirect questions which will test the consistency of the interviewee's responses and may elicit information which a more direct question might not yield. It is, unfortunately, often the case, as Hill's experience quoted above suggests, that an interviewee, particularly a party official or a relatively subordinate person, will give totally standard and uninformative answers to your questions. Even so, such interviews are rarely completely useless. It is impossible in a face-to-face situation to conceal all hesitations, slips of the tongue, significant asides and emotional responses which are all part of the significant data to be obtained from an interview and should be noted if possible. Also, standard, uninformative responses are often the product of badly designed questions. One important point is to demonstrate that you are thoroughly acquainted with your subject, which will show that you will not be fobbed off with the party line. Wherever possible you should try to arrange a supplementary interview. I found that where this was possible the first interview was mainly useful for establishing an atmosphere of trust, while the second was where the real interchange took place.

The creation of trust and goodwill is a vital component of elite interviewing in Soviet-type systems, as with all defensive elites, and it pervades all stages of the process. We have seen that a suitable cultural re-orientation plus the judicious use of personal connections aids this development of trust. Western researchers must prepare themselves to meet often with a very hostile reception, particularly when their research concerns a politically sensitive area (as mine did – I found out that Trotsky had originally proposed the policy I was investigating back in the 1920s, and its revival was somewhat embarrassing). I was several times denounced before other people as a representative of Western bourgeois anti-Sovietism intent on mocking the Soviet state. These outbursts sometimes depend on political pressures subject to the current state of East–West or Anglo–Soviet relations, but often they are the product of genuine fears about the use of data by the researchers, over which, of course, the suppliers of data have no control. Unfortunately, there have been occasions in the past where Western researchers have written sensationalist accounts of their stays in the USSR in the mass media after they have returned or where the attitude of researchers towards their Soviet hosts has been openly politically hostile. The researcher needs to reassure Soviet interviewees about his or her intentions and to take initial hostile outbursts calmly. Curiously enough, the use of the native language in interviewing (which in the USSR is indispensable anyway because not many elite members know English) is not always conducive to building up trust. Indeed, relative fluency in the language by a foreigner can be greeted with intense suspicion on the grounds that he or she may be trained by MI6 or represent an *émigré* organization.

Research is a parasitical occupation, and your task is definitely eased if you can perform some small service for the people who are helping you, not just by giving jeans and tights (though these may help!), but, for example, by putting them in contact with other Westerners in their field, by promising to obtain Western books or even just by taking time to present your own viewpoint in discussion. People naturally like receiving something in return. When I was in Leningrad I gave some help at the English faculty at the university, assisting Russian researchers with translation problems in English, discussing British politics and society with people specializing on the United Kingdom, and so on. If you build up an atmosphere of goodwill, particularly in the institution to which you are primarily attached, reports on this fact will be made to the higher authorities who will be more disposed to granting you interviews and communicating information.

Finally, the importance of 'informal, off-the-record contacts' must be stressed. Naturally, there is a problem with using off-the-record information as evidence, but it can give you very important leads which can be followed up in formal interviews or in published sources. Interviewees often become totally different people when they are off-the-record in an informal social situation, particularly when lubricated with a little vodka. In one case I can remember somebody who had given the appearance of being a hostile cold warrior in public turned out to be an extremely nice and cultivated person who just felt he had to put on a hostile facade in front of his colleagues.

The above advice applies to 'normal' research conditions in all Soviet-type states. Very occasionally, of course, the curtain is lifted in an exceptional period of liberalization. It was in such a period when the famous United States–Yugoslav Carnegie opinion-making elites project was conducted in Yugoslavia in 1968 (see Barton *et al.*, 1973). Significantly, it was not followed up by similar projects in the more restrictive atmosphere of the 1970s. Nevertheless, the project remains a remarkable and unique monument to what might be possible if such circumstances returned, in spite of the limitations of its research design and analysis (see e.g. Welsh, 1976). Yugoslavia is in any case the country of Eastern Europe most accessible to Western research and has the longest and widest experience of public opinion surveys. In all 517 'opinion-leaders' were interviewed out of an original pool of 1423 derived by a 'snowball' method out of a positional base. A long prepared questionnaire of 80 items (pre-tested by open-ended interviews) was administered by Yugoslav social psychology students (untaped), a rather unfortunate mediation between the researchers and their data – particularly as there were disturbances at Belgrade University at the time, which coincided with the *événements* in Western Europe and the Prague Spring and invasion of Czechoslovakia! This, though, is said not to have distorted the results. All the same this East–West co-operative project was a major achievement and its experience deserves close analysis by every researcher in Soviet-type systems.

Unfortunately, such circumstances rarely occur in Eastern Europe. A more promising research tool for the elite researcher in recent years is presented by the interviewing of émigrés. Clearly there are dangers here: a random group of people emigrating or being expelled from their country cannot be a representative sample either in social composition or in political outlook. Nevertheless, if these factors are taken into account, émigré interviewing can be a most valuable supplementary tool for the elite investigator. In particular the post-1970 wave of Jewish emigration has presented many opportunities here, since many of these émigrés belonged to the intellectual and artistic elite with links to the political elite. Already there have been individual Western surveys on samples of varying size (Gitelman, 1977; White, 1979, pp. 95–7; 1980), and major surveys are being conducted under the aegis of the United States and Israeli governments. In recent years, there has also been an increasing trickle of defections from quite high levels of the political elite (ambassadors, central committee officials) which are potentially of great value (provided that the information from them is disseminated beyond the secret service of the recipient country!). A recent interesting example of work on elites arising from personal experience is Michael Voslensky's book on the Soviet *nomenklatura* (1984). Interviewing of émigré elite members was also used by Matthews (1978) as a supplementary method in his study of elite privilege and life-style in the USSR (see his discussion of methodology in Matthews, 1978, pp. 186–8).

In general, however, it must be admitted that the direct interviewing of elites, whether it is carefully organized in the country concerned or uses émigré respondents, is in present circumstances in Soviet-type systems no replacement for the basic method of interpreting published primary and secondary material. The basic reason for this, apart from the unpredictability of the results, is the impossibility of securing a truly representative sample and information which is sincerely and honestly given. Nevertheless, I do believe that with persistence and care Western researchers can derive much useful information from formal and informal elite interviewing as a confirmatory and interpretative instrument.

12.4 Conclusions

I have argued above that there is a strong *prima facie* case for the relevance of the concepts of elite theory to some of the fundamental principles of communist politics. To a large extent this was borne out in detail when we tried to identify a political elite in Soviet-type systems and plausibly discovered it in a positional power elite model based on *nomenklatura* posts, though we noted that this model did not satisfactorily explain the role of the mass membership of the communist party or account for the integrative character of communist systems. We then argued that many valuable studies had been made of Soviet and East European elites based largely on published sources. Despite the problems which direct interviewing in the country poses we argued that this was an invaluable instrument which, though at the moment inevitably supplementary in character, had not in general been fully exploited by Western researchers. What is needed now is more systematic research of elite decision-making in specific policy areas, and in this task elite interviewing could furnish valuable material, which could also be supplemented by the interviewing of émigrés.

In general, we hope to have shown that the conceptual and methodological problems of Soviet-type elite researchers merit serious consideration and study by scholars working on other defensive elites and even by those working in liberal-democratic societies. The practical difficulties encountered in elite interviewing (access, establishing trust, etc.) turn out to be not dissimilar in kind to those experienced in other societies, but their dramatically enhanced magnitude brings the problems into clearer focus while at the same time offering the non-communist elite researcher great consolation when the going apparently gets hard. Furthermore, the conceptual problems of applying elite theory to communist systems raise important questions about the universal applicability of the elite model. Nevertheless, if we take a pragmatic and flexible view of the elite approach as a rough and ready heuristic device, we do find that it illuminates some key principles of communist politics and that the resultant body of empirical work has greatly advanced our understanding of the working of communist political systems and, thereby, of politics in general.

13

Interviewing political elites in Taiwan

MOSHE M. CZUDNOWSKI
Northern Illinois University

13.1 Introduction

This is the report of a student of political elites in Western political systems who was given the opportunity to conduct research on political elites in a developing country with a quasi-single-party regime, the Republic of China on Taiwan. The report focuses essentially on strategy and tactics in elite research under the constraints of a first-time experience in both a different culture and a different type of political system. As such, it is exploratory and tentative, and intended merely to share with the community of students of elites some of the insights of this experience. It should be added, however, that many of these insights – though in different contexts – have been previously noted in Dexter (1970, especially ch. 2) and Moyser and Wagstaffe (1985).

13.2 A General Model of Elite Interviews

Interviewing political elites is considered in this discussion as a research technique for gathering data about certain political phenomena. The concept of the elite is left unspecified, and has to be defined by the researcher in terms of the specific purposes of his inquiry. The discussion refers only to face-to-face interviews and it

This report is based on research conducted in the Republic of China on Taiwan which was made possible by a 1983/84 Fulbright Award, a Research Grant from the Pacific Cultural Foundation in Taipei, and a Visiting Professorship at National Taiwan University in Taipei. The author gratefully acknowledges this support and the hospitality of his sponsors and hosts in Taiwan.

will be assumed that they are individualized, i.e. they each involve only one political actor. Collective interviews involve 'public' rather than anonymous statements as sources of information and are usually not considered an appropriate research technique in the study of elites.

So defined, an interview consists of an interaction between a researcher and a respondent; more specifically, it is a series of purposive actions (questions, answers, comments) by each of the participants involved. For part of an interview, researcher and respondent may pursue the same purpose (e.g. establishing the detailed chronology of certain events); for other parts, their purposes may partly overlap and partly diverge (e.g. the respondent volunteers or acknowledges some aspects of his involvement in an action, but deliberately omits other aspects in which the researcher is equally, if not more, interested). This latter type of situation can develop into a quasi-adversary interaction (e.g. the respondent denies a fact which the researcher nevertheless knows to be true), but the researcher has to contain the adversary aspect at the analytical level, i.e. bear it in mind without allowing it to be externalized and interfere with the trust he has tried to build up in the respondent's attitude toward the research and toward the researcher himself. In the areas lying between such clear alternatives are the instances in which the two actors offer somewhat different formulations, interpretations or emphases on which they may or may not reach agreement.

The 'trust' component is essential for the success of the interview and of the entire research project, and has to be viewed against the background of a basic, constitutive, asymmetry in the political interview situation. For the respondent, his image, his reputation, his past, present and perhaps future career are being, or could be, exposed to the interpretation of an 'outsider', the researcher, who, unlike the lawyer or the psychotherapist, is not professionally bound by an oath of confidentiality. The entire purpose of the interview, for the researcher, is to obtain information that he or she can and will use. Only the source of the information, i.e. the respondent's name and position, is usually given the protection of anonymity; the contents of the interview, in so far as the source is not identified, are not confidential, unless there is agreement to the contrary on certain items at the request of the respondent. While the reputation of the interviewing scholar, concerning his skills and professional integrity, are also at stake, the scholar is not accountable to the general public, and certainly not to the respondent's constituency or his or her superiors.

This does not mean that the researcher should not keep the political elite in mind in the exercise of his profession, if he wants to maintain credibility and future research access to the elite; in any specific interview, however, the asymmetry is obvious and often acknowledged: for the respondent, his political profile is totally at stake, whereas for the researcher, the respondent is only one case in the population or sample studied.

It is therefore important that the respondent be genuinely convinced that the researcher is unbiased toward him and the subject of the study in general, and that he will not use the information obtained in the interview for political rather than scholarly purposes.

This basic description of the interview situation is probably generally valid, though many variables will intervene to determine the specific degree of researchability of political elites or of a specific member of a given elite. Among these, the political regime and the political culture are no doubt the most important. The empirical study of political elites has relied almost exclusively on the expertise gained in Western or Western-type political systems with a more or less well-established democratic political culture. The research strategies, methods and techniques developed in these studies are no reliable guideline for research among elites in 'second world' and 'third world' regimes, should such elites become more accessible to empirical research. What accessibility denotes, in this context, is the openness of office holders and politicians to personalized questions and their ability and willingness to offer personal responses, as opposed to official 'party line' or 'governmental policy'. The existence of a competitive party system is not a necessary condition for some degree of openness among political elites, as my recent experience in the Republic of China on Taiwan has taught me. Despite a quasi-authoritarian, quasi-single-party regime, criticism outside the ruling Kuomintang (KMT) party is tolerated within certain limits, and while on most policy issues the KMT remains a rather monolithic party, there is a perceptible 'loosening' in what probably was previously a more strictly enforced conformism across the various levels of party elites. If these are indeed changes in comparison to the earlier years of KMT rule on Taiwan, they seem to indicate an impending transformation in the political culture.

Within any specific political culture with some degree of research access to elites, a second variable which seems to influence the openness of members of such elites is seniority: senior members of the elite are politically more secure and therefore more likely to feel free to offer personal opinions. One could also argue, however, that at higher levels of the political system far more sensitive and consequential issues are involved, on which politicians would prefer to abstain from revealing information or dissenting opinions. This author's research experience indicates that the more 'closed' a political culture is, the greater the difference in openness between senior and junior political actors: only senior party or government officials, who have apparently reached the top levels of the political ladder, will not feel threatened by volunteering personal opinions (while observing, of course, more discretion about sensitive issues than about those that can be publicly discussed). In more 'open' political cultures these differences between higher and lower levels, or senior and less senior political actors, tend to weaken considerably and seniority as the distinguishing concomitant of openness is replaced by what it actually stands for even in 'closed' cultures: personal independence. The politician who is able to resign from his position or even exit from politics altogether should he so decide, without being economically or otherwise dependent on the government or his party, will generally be more 'open' in research interviews. While this seems to be a generally valid tendency, one has to bear in mind that much will always depend on the respondent's political office (e.g. officials responsible for security or defence matters will usually be less 'open' than policy-makers or chief administrators in areas such as education, commerce or labor relations), the idiosyncratic characteristics of his or her personality and, last but not least, the description of the research topic.

As a general rule of thumb, research topics should not be narrowly defined if one seeks personal, face-to-face interviews. The respondent should be persuaded that the imposition on his or her precious time is warranted by a justifiable need to obtain his or her views on issues of broad socio-political consequences. The description of the research topic should also avoid terms conveying involvement in a highly controversial and hotly disputed issue, if such involvement is likely to deter a respondent from agreeing to be interviewed or from discussing the issue. Such problems can sometimes be avoided by using a smoothing, conciliatory, terminology. One of the purposes of my study of elites in Taiwan was to measure the extent and intensity of elite cleavages. I described it as a study of elite integration. This appealed to the ruling KMT party, interested in demonstrating the overtly acknowledged progress in integration which had been achieved; it also left the door open to the dissenting opposition in its attempts to convince me that cleavages were real, persistent and not easily surmountable.

13.3   The Republic of China on Taiwan: A Social, Economic and Political Overview[1]

When the Chinese Nationalist Government, retreating from the Mainland, established itself on the island of Taiwan in 1949, it found there an underdeveloped, essentially agricultural society, in which educational opportunities had been severely limited during decades of Japanese rule. Thirty years later, in 1980, Taiwan had a diversified society and a booming economy. The estimated per capita GNP in 1984, at 1980 prices, was US$3361, with an average annual GNP increase of 8 per cent for 1980–84. Although the population increased rapidly (net natural growth in 1979 had been 19.7 per cent and the total 1984 population reached 18 500 000), the number of agricultural workers decreased by 17 per cent between 1971 and 1979. Labor-intensive light industry was developed in the 1960s with production growing at an average annual rate of 18 per cent as low labor costs enabled Taiwanese products to successfully penetrate major world markets. In the following decade the emphasis was on capital-intensive heavy and petro-chemical industries. The free-market economy, in which the share of the private sector in total production reached 81 per cent, did not prevent the ratio between the average highest (top 20%) and the average lowest (bottom 20%) per family disposable income from reaching a low 4.34:1 in 1979.

In the 1980s, as other developing countries in East Asia, such as South Korea, began successfully to compete with Taiwan's light industry exports on the world markets, political and economic leaders in the Republic of China (RoC) understood that they had to shift the emphasis to high-technology-intensive industries. Continuing economic development based on successful foreign trade also became a political imperative for the regime on 'Island China', embattled and isolated on the international political scene, especially since the 'de-recognition' of the RoC by the Carter administration at the end of 1978. The appointment of Yu Kuo-hwa, a financial expert widely respected in international banking circles, as Prime Minister of the RoC in 1984 was an overt recognition of the primacy of the economic imperative.

In Taiwan, embarking on a political career involves an achievement orientation and risk-taking. Even when he or she works within the strongly centralized organization of the ruling KMT, the political office holder has to be a skillful and often improvising co-operator and co-ordinator; these requirements are probably even more important for holders of elective positions. Many of the younger members of the political elite have obtained advanced degrees from United States and other Western universities and have acquired a good understanding of how Western democracies work; this does not necessarily predispose them favourably toward an accelerated Westernization of the political system in the RoC, but it no doubt helps them in their evaluations of the regime. The individual who runs for office as an independent – or 'non-party' – candidate takes on even greater risks, since a 'non-party' candidate is usually in opposition to the KMT and, to put it mildly, the ruling party will not extend a warm welcome to his or her often very harsh criticism of its policies.

Formally, all policies are decided by the Standing Committee of the KMT Central Committee, a body of thirty-one holders of high-ranking government and party positions, presided over by the Party Chairman who is also the President of the RoC. The detailed planning and legislative, regulatory or administrative implementation of policies is conducted by the various branches of the National Government and facilitated or co-ordinated by the party organization which has its offices and officials at every level of the government structure: from the Legislative Yuan to City Councils, with regional coordinators at the level of the Province.

In elections to the Legislative Yuan, with their multi-seat districts, the KMT allocates its candidates to specific neighbourhoods in usually successful attempts to ensure the necessary spread of votes which will lead to the election of all its candidates. 'Non-party' candidates cannot benefit from such grass-roots organization since, according to the 'martial law' in force, the formation of new political parties is prohibited. Moreover, there has been considerable factionalism among 'non-party' leaders and their supporters. Yet, in successive elections to the Legislative Yuan, 'non-party' candidates have accumulated about 30 per cent of the total vote, though, given the electoral system, this has not entitled them to more than 9 seats out of the 52 'supplementary' seats from territorial districts of Taiwan in 1983.

'Supplementary' seats are those for which elections are held in Taiwan (and the adjacent small islands) and they represent a temporary solution to a fundamental problem the KMT government has to face. As direct continuator of the Nationalist Government established on the Mainland, and guardian of the 1946 Constitution, the Government of the RoC on Taiwan claims to be the only holder of legitimate authority over the entire Chinese nation, while Mainland China is considered to be in a temporary 'period of

Communist rebellion'. Unwilling to relinquish this claim, and probably unable to do so without endangering the stability of its government and of the power structure on Taiwan, the Government of the RoC is maintaining the legislators elected to the First Legislative Yuan in 1947 on the Mainland in their positions until a new legislature can be elected nationwide, i.e. *de facto* for life. They are the living evidence that this is the government of all China, except that age and death are taking their toll. At the same time, the KMT needed to demonstrate and broaden its legitimacy on Taiwan. Hence the 1969 decision to create 'supplementary seats' and to hold elections for these seats in Taiwan, starting with 15 additional members in 1970. The number was subsequently raised to 52. In the legislature, however, these members elected in Taiwan are greatly outnumbered by the 'legislators-for-life' who are still active and participate in the sessions of the Legislative Yuan. Although the gradual extinction of the legislative contingent elected on the Mainland is only a matter of time, the KMT government has not yet proposed a solution that would give a future Legislative Yuan the appearance of representing the entire Chinese nation – if such a solution does indeed exist.

A parallel process of partial 'Taiwanization' takes place through recruitment to the Provincial Government and to the National Executive. While the Provincial Assembly is entirely and directly elected by the population on Taiwan, the Provincial and National Executive are appointive bodies. The Vice-President, the Deputy-Premier, the Governor of Taiwan Province, several cabinet ministers and deputy ministers, as well as the mayors of Taipei and Kaohsiung (these two cities are under the direct authority of the National Government) are chosen from among experienced native Taiwanese government or party officials, according to what seems to have become an unwritten convention. Since these are appointive positions in a highly centralized political system, it is difficult to assess whether selection to such positions carries with it sources of personal influence other than the authority of the office.

Mainlanders dominate the senior positions – e.g. the offices of Premier, Defence, Foreign Affairs, Finance, National Security Council, to name only the most important. At some earlier time in their careers, some of them had been personally recruited by the late President Chiang Kai-shek, or, if they are somewhat younger, by his son, first Premier and now President Chiang Ching-kuo. The recruitment of Taiwanese, at the lower and intermediate levels of government, proceeds through the party organization; the Taiwanese, too, seem to have been personally recruited by the President and Party Chairman when they became candidates for higher-level offices.

Thus, the recruitment system seems to be highly centralized and highly personalized. It is therefore of interest to note that next to the 'economic miracle' on Taiwan, the recruitment of a very able political personnel has possibly been one of the most outstanding achievements of the KMT.

Some members of the young Taiwanese intelligentsia (especially lawyers), mostly of modest origins, as well as several families and factions which by virtue of wealth or education had dominated certain local and regional governments, found themselves outside the recruitment network of the KMT. For reasons as diverse as the protection of local interests, opposition to the centralization and monopolization of power by the KMT, or a latent Taiwanese 'nationalism', some of these elites eventually became an active and bitter opposition to the KMT government, capable of mobilizing the support of certain strata which had either not yet benefited from the economic development policies of the KMT, or after having benefited, thought it would be wise to try to contain any further growth in support for the ruling party. Although 'tolerated' as independent ('non-party') candidates and elected office holders, these opposition leaders complain of being harrassed by the KMT during election campaigns and still consider the 1979 police intervention against a demonstration, and the subsequent stiff jail sentences against some of their leaders, as evidence of an authoritarianism which remains a major source of political cleavage, distrust and, in some isolated cases, openly admitted apprehension. While there are occasional demands for a more conciliatory attitude from within the KMT elites, the cleavage remains real, at least in the perceptions of the opposition, although it surfaces only periodically.

What this implies for the foreign researcher is the need to convince both the ruling party and members of the opposition of his ability to position himself in a neutral but friendly observation point, while recognizing the consequences of partially conflicting scales of priorities. Having said this, one must also emphasize the fact that – although many of the suspicions prevailing in a relatively closed political culture have to be overcome – the political elites in Taiwan have become researchable in many aspects of their involvement and this, by itself, indicates an opening-up of what seems to have previously been a more closed political system.

13.4   Learning to Cope with the Political Culture

The fact remains, as stated above, that one first has to overcome suspicions. Personal trust and personal recommendations are the keys for opening doors. For a first-time visiting researcher, this presents some problems. Common sense suggests that one should seek an introduction to two or three highly positioned and influential officials, and convince them of his purely scholarly motivations and ethics, including the absence of any political prejudice on his part; the rest would hopefully follow rather easily on the basis of their recommendations. There is only one flaw in this: how does one get introduced to such highly influential officials in the first place?

One fallacious assumption leading to the hope that one may be able to bypass this problem is the belief that being sponsored by a local university (let alone the most prestigious university), and by United States and Chinese research foundations, is synonymous with having obtained 'political' approval for the proposed research project. Approval perhaps, but actually you are on your own!

An experienced researcher would not make the success of his project dependent on the anticipated hospitality and goodwill of his hosts; he needs professional logistics and an *entrée* to political circles. What better precaution and planning could there be than asking for an interested collaborator and co-investigator from among the senior scholars at the host university? Long before his travel to the research site, the researcher will correspond and consult with a collaborator recommended to him and discuss division of labour, methodology, sampling, etc. All those involved in the process have been trained in the United States and have a perfect command of English, and no problems of communication arise. Needless to say, they are also supportive of the project. There is only one problem to which the unsuspecting foreign researcher has not been alerted: there is no senior professor of political science in Taiwan who has not written articles on politics in Taiwan for local newspapers, magazines or other periodicals, and thus involved himself in the political process. Consequently, he is either a member of the KMT and supporter of the government, or a critic of the government and its policies. In the first case, his presence on the team will make opposition members reluctant to talk; in the second, the 'establishment' will refuse to co-operate and perhaps even deny access to certain decision-making centres. Again you are on your own, with the additional problem of having to relinquish a negotiated collaboration.

There is no general advice on how to solve such dilemmas. I was fortunate to obtain access, through academic channels, to a high-level official at Central Party Headquarters who apparently was interested in research. He agreed to offer advice and help in interviewing government and party leaders. Although it was still very much a matter of following the lines of specific political networks, starting from the centre was a distinct advantage and doors began to open. It should be added, however, that some very high government officials eventually agreed to be interviewed without party intervention or personal recommendations, at least as far as I could tell. They were all of relatively advanced age, in top positions, and had served in important offices for many years. Crossing the political cleavage line into the territory of the opposition had to be similarly 'engineered', but only after firmly advancing my research within the government and ruling party sector.

It is admittedly difficult for a foreigner, unfamiliar with either Chinese political culture or the detailed political history of Taiwan in the last thirty-five years, to evaluate the relative importance of facts, events, personalities and relationships. However, being 'on my own', as a foreigner, also had its advantages. Pleading ignorance and a desire to learn as much as possible can be used as a device for asking for facts and explanations. In one particular type of circumstance I found it repeatedly necessary to plead ignorance of the Chinese political culture, which most of the time was a perfectly candid and true admission. This refers to occasions when respondents appealed to traditional culture in their explanations of actions and attitudes. I was hesitant to accept cultural 'explanations' when they did not seem politically convincing in terms of stated purposes, conditions or rationality. One way of challenging such references to tradition was to ask explicitly what purpose was served by resorting to 'traditional behaviour'. In other instances it proved necessary openly to confront the respondent with his own claim – that his was a modern and modernizing government which had successfully proven its efficiency and rational decision-making; how, then, could he justify what seemed to be non-rational action (or inaction) by reference to tradition? Were there not other components of the situation that he had omitted to mention, which could explain the action in rational terms?

I would not question symbols or non-political cultural patterns, but after some time, when political behaviour was 'explained' to me in terms of 'tradition', I developed a Pavlovian reflex warning me that I might not be told the whole truth. In many cases, it turned out to be a matter of unquestioning loyalty to the leader (or leadership), provided the leader protected the interests of the people (which included 'his people'), and that is characteristic of Chinese political culture. In certain respects, however, such behaviour had some of the characteristics of 'party loyalty', 'party discipline' or 'machine politics' in Western government systems. The major difference seemed to consist, at least in some cases, in the inability of political machines to justify their actions by reference to an ancient cultural tradition.

Certain traits of a political culture sometimes reveal themselves in the terminology of political discourse. One of the purposes of my study was to learn about the motivations (i.e. the expected consequences) of seeking or accepting political office: were they oriented toward extrinsic or intrinsic rewards? Governmental office carries with it high esteem in the Chinese culture, but remuneration for such service, in Taiwan, is relatively low, and influence (especially in collective bodies such as city or county councils, and the more so in much larger Provincial and National legislatures) depends on party guidelines and coalition-forming among members on issues of local, regional or special interest. Moreover, those who are seeking security and upward mobility through the political system are more likely to find such rewards in appointive office in the party or government bureaucracy, even if the party sometimes 'trains' promising candidates for higher office by encouraging and nominating them for elective office. The fact remains that city, county and Provincial legislators often initiate their candidacies by organizing support and seeking party nominations or running as non-party independents. Among those who succeed in getting elected, many more will stand for re-election several times than will look forward to and seek higher elective office. What motivates these people? It is through the answer to this question that I learned the symbolism of political discourse.

Government service is held in high esteem, but the most frequent answer was phrased in somewhat different terms: 'Being a councilman (or Assemblyman) enables me to help my people.' The Western political scientist would interpret this as 'constituency service', but the constituency service of the British MP or the United States Congressman is a means for generating, maintaining or increasing support for re-election; it is the 'price' to be paid for gaining seniority and advancing in the system. The elected official in Taiwan does not consider such service as a 'price'; rather (at least such are the terms he uses) it is the purpose of his involvement. Is politics in Taiwan a not-for-profit social welfare activity? When the 'helping my people' answer began repeating itself, I knew I was missing a central point. Responses to follow-up questions, such as 'What kind of help could you offer?', were not very fruitful: helping someone who had problems with the bureacracy or the police, finding a job for an unemployed relative of a neighbour, etc. Was 'fixing a traffic ticket' for a friend a political motivation?

The meaning of 'helping my people' (apart from such ordinary constituency service) soon revealed itself when it appeared that the most popular city, county or Assembly committees were those dealing with 'construction' and 'public works'. Economic development in Taiwan has been facilitated by heavy government investment in the building of a modern infrastructure: airports, roads, schools, 'industrial parks', civic centres, etc. Moreover, there were the 'regular' licensing and regulatory powers of the various levels of government. Government investment and regulatory powers created many profit-making opportunities for citizens and companies. 'Helping my people' meant allocating, or helping to allocate, such opportunities. Was the elected official who facilitated such allocations himself a beneficiary? In many cases respondents denied any personal profit, but some openly admitted that they had personally invested money in the construction company of a friend, or that the direct beneficiary from government contracts was a close family member. In one case, a construction company was owned by the respondent's wife, but one has to bear in mind that even the extended family is a tightly knit institution in Chinese society. On an overpopulated island, zoning regulations could make even a small landowner a rich person, if his property was located in the proximity of urban or industrial development areas. Thus, 'helping my people' meant providing benefits to my family and friends, who – in anticipation of such shared benefits – had often contributed money and services to the candidate's election campaign.

None of this was considered immoral, let alone illegal. Party and government officials confirmed this to me; problems of illegality arose only when the services or goods supplied to the government were faulty or below specifications. Is this the political morality of a traditional society? (Banfield, 1958). Undoubtedly yes. However, there seemed to be some uneasiness in admitting it to a Western researcher. 'Non-party' opposition members accused KMT officials, in general, of corruption, but according to one senior KMT office holder in a large city, opposition members, once elected, easily follow the same pattern and 'help their families and friends'. In the final stages of my research I raised the entire issue with a prominent KMT official; he admitted it was a 'problem' the party had to address. From this and other discussions I concluded, however, that this 'political morality' was not merely traditionally accepted, but also constituted a policy instrument for gaining and strengthening support for the regime. *Enrichissez-vous!* has apparently survived quite well as a governing device.

13.5   Problems of Strategy and Tactics in Interviews

The interview format
Recording the interview is essential in order to give the interviewer the freedom to engage in a smoothly flowing interaction with the respondent. Permission to record should be obtained (not necessarily ahead of time), but when the reason for recording is explained and anonymity is guaranteed, there is usually no objection to it. Even in Taiwan there was only one case in which I was asked not to record certain segments of an interview, and although no explicit reason was given I was led to believe that the respondent was not convinced that my tapes would be safely sheltered from inspection by individuals not involved in the research project. Sometimes, when a respondent indicated an intention to volunteer information on what I considered could be a 'delicate' issue I would stop the recorder myself for a few minutes, or indicate my willingness to do so, in order to encourage him to proceed.

It has been my repeated experience in interviewing elites in different countries, including Taiwan, that a useful way to begin an interview is to ask for the respondent's biography, starting with a brief description of the parental home in economic, cultural and political terms during the period of the respondent's adolescence, even when the research subject is only remotely related to early socialisation. Moreover, it is useful to occasionally demonstrate curiosity for certain details in order to emphasize that the researcher takes an interest in the respondent's experiences and interactions with his environment from a broader perspective, beyond the frequent monotony of a narrowly defined political chronology. Such questions can be improvized as the biography unfolds. The purpose is primarily to create a degree of 'intimacy' in the interview situation, and I have yet to meet the respondent who does not enjoy telling me part of his life story. More often than not the probing researcher will be also rewarded by some politically relevant details or insights into the respondent's personality. The only possible disadvantage of this technique is that some respondents may spend too much time on the biographical profile they wish to project, but that is also an indication that the researcher has succeeded in motivating the respondent into a friendly and hopefully trustful co-operation and has stimulated his interest in the interview. As for the time factor: with only infrequent exceptions, even rather busy cabinet ministers and other high political executives, in Taiwan and elsewhere, who had warned me at the beginning that they were available for only one hour because they had another appointment, were still eagerly talking two and some-times three hours later showing no sign of an intention to terminate the conversation (after they had duly postponed 'the other' appoint-ment, or forgotten they told me they had one!). This should be evaluated in the light of the theoretical model of a potential adversary interview situation, and of the fact that in the later and final stages of the interview one discusses political issues and not college athletics.

Generally speaking, the interviewer's ability to succeed in maintaining an atmosphere of trust is greatly enhanced by having done his or her 'home-work' properly. The respondent should be made aware of the fact that one is not wasting his time with questions about facts included in the published information available on his career. If possible, this should be supplemented by information gathered from other sources, including previous interviews conducted with other politicians; needless to say, the latter have to remain anonymous. This will allow the interviewer to concentrate on the perspectives and emphases the respondent attaches to his answers and comments, and to interject follow-up or probing questions which should sound as spontaneous and context-responsive as possible. At all times, however, the interviewer should bear in mind the details of the structured part of his or her questionnaire, e.g. what specific details about education or first job, etc. have to be obtained, with great emphasis being placed on dates in order to establish the age of the respondent at the time a particular event occurred – something which occasionally presents a problem in Taiwan, because the twentieth-century calendar in the RoC begins in 1911, the year of the establish-ment of the Republic. The interviewer should also bear in mind the categories and variables he or she has decided to use in the analysis and interpretation of answers to open-ended questions. In any exploratory research, however, such categories and variables should be made amenable to subsequent refinements.

Dealing with controversial issues or potentially embarrassing situations
Refusal to answer a question is embarrassing; in the Chinese culture it

is equivalent to 'losing face'. The respondent may then prefer to offer the interviewer a plausible but misleading answer. If the interviewer knows that the respondent has been disingenuous, he should not immediately insist on obtaining additional details or other versions of the event. If the event is sufficiently important to warrant further probing one may resort, after briefly passing to another subject, to imputing a statement contradicting the respondent's answer to a member of the opposition: 'Now, I know that he may not be telling the truth, but a member of the opposition claims that . . . Could you comment on this?' If the interviewer is not sure that the respondent is concealing the truth or part thereof, but the event warrants a further probe, he may ask a seemingly 'neutralizing' question, such as: 'Who else could offer me some additional insights into this matter?'

In the political culture of Taiwan, some high-level policy dilemmas are not being publicly discussed. One of these, for example, concerns the long-term implications of the claim, by the government of the RoC, that it is the legitimate government of all China, including the mainland.

To raise the issue in elite interviews I projected it into a hypothetical future. 'Suppose the status quo continues for another generation, do you think your children will accept, as you do, the policy stand of the RoC government and its claim that it is the government of all China?' Since the answer to this question did not involve personal stands or commitments, opinions were quite frank and divided, with all the necessary caveats for uncertainty and hypothetical conjecture. Perhaps the most interesting comment was that of several highly educated KMT politicians who had studied at Western universities and who explicitly stated that they did not feel uncomfortable with the inconsistencies between political myth and realities, as long as realities remained unchanged. Such responses make one wonder whether there is any difference in cynicism about politics and the use of power between the Chinese and Western political cultures.

If generalizations were possible from the limited experience of one researcher, they would probably have to include the following items: First, establish credibility and trust as a friendly foreign observer who wishes to understand the system and identify achievements and problems. Do not hesitate to ask 'difficult' questions, provided they do not imply criticism or advice. At the middle and higher levels you are dealing with a highly sophisticated elite, and its members are well equipped to understand the underlying purpose of your question.

Secondly, use projective techniques, whenever necessary and

possible. The most controversial issues can be discussed using such procedures. Questions raising doubts about the interpretation given by a respondent should be attributed to anonymous critics. None of this is a deceptive device, since the foreign researcher will have actually been offered a number of critical viewpoints in preceding interviews, sometimes from respondents of the same political persuasion.

Thirdly, at the higher levels of the elite, when interviewing individuals who are likely to be 'insiders' to the decision-making process, or at least very close to it, the researcher may decide to share with the respondent some of his own tentative analysis based on a long series of information-gathering interviews, as a means for verifying his understanding of the system or of some complex issue. Some respondents may be eager to find out how much the foreigner has learned about their system. Within the boundaries of the political culture, and depending on the sensitivity of the issue, the response will be factual, frank and oriented toward getting a point across to the Western communities of political analysts.

13.6 Research Under Exploratory Conditions: Some Substantive Issues

In rapidly changing societies, research designed on the basis of existing knowledge may face a need to reassess some of its substantive assumptions when it encounters the subtle and sometimes not so subtle transformation tendencies in such societies. This need is even more evident when 'existing knowledge' is fragmentary and to a certain extent impressionistic, and the non-academic literature consists of either government documents or ideologically and polemically inspired journalism. When my own 1983/84 findings are published, I suspect they will not considerably modify most of these characteristics of existing knowledge about the RoC on Taiwan.

It would be erroneous to assume that political elites in a transitional society promote either modern or traditional policies. The ability to translate modern approaches into acceptable policies is a political variable, and elites may be guided by political consider- ations constraining their preferences for modernization, especially in a system in which a modernizing governing elite needs to maintain (if not increase) the legitimizing support of a population in which certain traditional groups may perceive innovation as threatening to their interests. Only in fields in which innovation can be shown to have immediate beneficial results, such as industrial technology, can modernization proceed more swiftly. In other fields, modernizers may have to learn to live with the frustrations of ambiguities and contradictions.

One of the cleavages my research was intended to investigate, in order to measure the degree of political integration, was the postulated differences between the mainlanders who had settled on Taiwan with the retreating armies of the Nationalist government, and the native Taiwanese. Previous research (Appleton, 1970; 1976, and the earlier studies discussed there) seemed to suggest that integration was likely to proceed along generational lines. As Taiwanese youth and the children of mainlanders grew up together and went to the same schools and colleges, they were likely to develop similar attitudes. Moreover, rapid urbanization had transformed the Taiwanese from a predominantly agricultural to a middle-class industrial and business society, and mass higher education had opened for them access to teaching positions at all levels, to government offices and to high-technology industry. Finally, intermarriage had blurred many of the earlier distinctions and apprehensions. Was it possible that my initial assumption about a mainlander/Taiwanese cleavage in politics was no longer valid?

The detailed answer to this question constitutes part of the substantive report on my research in Taiwan. Strategies in exploratory research design depend on substantive assumption, but they are essentially a methodological problem and I should therefore report here that the original formulation of a unidimensional cleavage turned out to be an oversimplification. Three dimensions had to be added: elites versus masses, older versus younger elites, and overt versus latent differences. Moreover, in explaining such differences, economic factors and emigration to the United States also had to be considered. At the mass level, integration between mainlanders and Taiwanese is highly advanced, with the exception of the older age groups. At the elite level, the KMT has implemented an overt and wide co-optation policy, recruiting Taiwanese politicians into the national government structures. At the Provincial level, Taiwanese elites now constitute the overwhelming majority in elective and appointive offices. Their authority, however, is greatly dependent on the policies and allocations of the national government which is dominated, in the majority of the important offices, by members of the older generation of mainlanders. There is no overt mainlander/Taiwanese cleavage at the elite level, although certain positions are 'traditionally' reserved for mainlanders. Finally, at this institutional level, there is the dilemma about the composition of the Legislative Yuan after the gradual extinction of the mainland-born legislators. Most of the Taiwanese political elites also belong to a younger generation; this compounds the origin differential with a generational differential. The possible interaction between these two factors and attempts to identify such latent interaction against the background of overt consensus necessitated the ongoing development of interview tactics adapted to parameters not foreseen in the original research design.

The second cleavage the research project was intended to investigate was the overt opposition between the KMT and the 'non-party' politicians. The somewhat unexpected result was that once the historical, human and personal components were set aside ('Suppose Martial Law had been revoked, the organization of an opposition party had become legitimate, and your party would have won a majority in a free election; what would you do differently than the KMT government?'), no significant policy differences emerged. There were references to a more welfare-state oriented policy, but essentially the response was: 'We would pursue approximately the same policies, but in a more efficient manner.' The reason for this may very well be the fact that any government of the RoC (KMT or otherwise) does not and would not have much freedom of action on the international political scene. With only minor differences in domestic programs (once the restrictions on the freedom to organize political parties were removed) the 'non-party' opposition could be defined as a group contesting the KMT's monopoly of political power. The claim is, of course, legitimate in Western democratic terms, but there is hardly any substantive cleavage present other than that between the 'ins' and the 'outs', with the 'outs' protesting the 'rules of the game'. This account does not exhaust the political issues, since there were many nuances in the political platform of 'the opposition', but for the purposes of illustrating the need for flexibility in interview strategy and techniques it should suffice.

13.7 Conclusion

This report suggests that the actual research of elites in the RoC was more complex and more frequently subject to revisions in interview strategy and techniques than had been anticipated. One should bear in mind, however, that the project had been conceived and carried out with the explicit knowledge – on the part of the researcher and his sponsors – that it would be an exploratory study in what was an area previously not easily accessible to systematic empirical research.

Having said this, it seems likely that the interview strategies and techniques described in this report could be profitably applied in other research contexts. This researcher has satisfactorily used projective techniques in Western democratic systems, and flexibility in elite interview techniques is strongly recommended, provided the definitions of, and the measurement scales applicable to, the researched variables are scrupulously kept in mind while improvising contextually determined adaptations. A structured questionnaire, with pre-coded categories for the interpretation of open-ended questions, is always a good frame of reference to bear in mind, even if such categories have to be subsequently refined.

If there is any general insight that this experience in interviewing political elites in a non-Western political culture provides for further research, it can be summarized as follows. Political, cultural and other variables may turn out to be more frustrating than anticipated. None of these frustrations should make the researcher oblivious to the fact that he has to leave doors open for subsequent research, either his own or that of others. Western research in developing countries should be future oriented. Create new 'bridges' and extend them, without burning old ones. Any single research project is merely one link in a chain; try always to view your own more or less narrowly defined research objectives in the light of such longer-term consequences.

Note

1   The data presented in this section are extracted from different publications of the Government of the Republic of China. The most comprehensive is the Annual Review of Government Administration. Amongst non-governmental sources, the major study of economic development is Fei *et al.*, 1979. For the 1983 legislative elections result and other 1983/84 political events, the section draws on the Taipei English daily newspaper, *The China Post*.

Bibliography

Aiken, M., and Mott, P. E. (eds) (1970), *The Structure of Community Power* (York: Random House).
Allen, C. H. (1979), 'The study of Scottish politics: a bibliographical sermon' in H. M. and N. L. Drucker (eds), *The Scottish Government Yearbook 1980* (Edinburgh: Paul Harris), pp. 11–41.
Anderson, L. F., Watts, M. W., and Wilcox, A. R. (1966), *Legislative Roll Call Analysis* (Evanston: Northwestern University Press).
Appleton, S. (1970), 'Taiwanese and mainlanders on Taiwan: a survey of student attitudes', *China Quarterly*, no. 44, pp. 38–65.
Appleton, S. (1976), 'The social and political impact of education in Taiwan', *Asian Survey*, no. 16, pp. 703–20.
Armstrong, J. A. (1959), *The Soviet Bureaucratic Elite: A Case Study of the Ukrainian Apparatus*, Praeger Publications in Russian History and World Communism, no. 76 (New York: Praeger).
Armstrong, J. A. (1973), *The European Administrative Elite* (Princeton: Princeton University Press).
Bachrach, P., and Baratz, M. S. (1962), 'The two faces of power', *American Political Science Review*, vol. 56, pp. 947–52.
Bachrach, P. (1967), *The Theory of Democratic Elitism* (Boston: Little Brown).
Bahro, R. (1978), *The Alternative in Eastern Europe* (London: New Left Books).
Bailey, S. K. (1950), *Congress Makes a Law* (New York: Vintage Books).
Banfield, E. (1958), *The Moral Basis of a Backward Society* (New York: The Free Press).
Barber, J. D. (1966), *Power in Committees* (Chicago: Rand McNally).
Barker, E. (Jr) (1946), *The Politics of Aristotle* (Oxford: Clarendon Press).
Barnes, J. (1979), *Ahead of His Age: Bishop Barnes of Birmingham* (London: Collins).
Barnes, S. H. (1977), *Representation in Italy* (Chicago: University of Chicago Press).
Barton, A. H., Denitch, B., and Kadushin, C. (1973), *Opinion-Making Elites in Yugoslavia* (New York: Praeger).
Barton, A. H. (1985), 'Background, attitudes, and activities of American elites', *Research in Politics and Society*, vol. 1, Studies of the Structure of National Elite Groups, G. Moore (ed.), (Greenwich: JAI Press), pp. 173–218.
Beck, C. *et al.* (eds) (1973), *Comparative Communist Political Leadership* (New York: McKay).
Becker, H. S. (1958), 'Problems of inference and proof in participation observation', *American Sociological Review*, vol. 23, no. 6, pp. 652–60.
Becker, H. S. (1970), *Sociological Work: Method and Substance* (Chicago: Aldine).
Beetham, D. (1977), 'From Socialism to Fascism: the relationship between theory and practice in the work of Robert Michels', *Political Studies*, vol. 25, nos. 1 and 2, pp. 3–24, 161–81.

Beetham, D. (1978), 'Reply to Bennett', *Political Studies*, vol. 26, no. 4, pp. 489–90.

Bennett, R. J. (1978), 'The elite theory as Fascist ideology – a reply to Beetham's critique of Robert Michels', *Political Studies*, vol. 26, no. 4, pp. 474–88.

Berrington, H. (1973), *Backbench Opinion in the House of Commons* (London: Pergamon).

Binns, C. A. P. (1979-80), 'The changing face of power: revolution and accommodation in the development of the Soviet ceremonial system', *Man* (N.S.), Part I, vol. 14, pp. 585–606, Part II, vol. 15, pp. 170–87.

Birdwhistell, R. L. (1971), *Kinesics and Content: Essays on Body-Motion Communication* (London: Allen Lane).

Birrell, D., and Murie, A. (1980), *Policy and Government in Northern Ireland: Lessons of Devolution* (Dublin: Gill & Macmillan).

Blakenship, L. V. (1964), 'Community power and decision-making: a comparative evaluation of measurement techniques', *Social Forces*, vol. 43, pp. 207–16.

Bogdan, R., and Taylor, S. J. (1975), *Introduction to Qualitative Research Methods* (London: John Wiley).

Bolland, J. M. (1984), 'The limits to pluralism: power and leadership in a non-participatory society', *Power and Elites*, vol. 1, no. 1, pp. 69–88.

Bottomore, T. B. (1966), *Elites and Society* (Harmondsworth: Penguin).

Brady, D., Cooper, J., and Hurley, P. (1979), 'The decline of party voting in the US House of Representatives', *Legislative Studies Quarterly*, vol. 4, no. 3, pp. 381–401.

Brady, D., with Stewart, J. (1982), 'Congressional party realignment and transformations of public policy in three realignment eras', *American Journal of Political Science*, vol. 26, no. 2, pp. 333–60.

Braley, E. F. (1950), *Letters of Herbert Hensley Henson* (London: SPCK).

Brannen, P., Batstone, E., Fatchett, D., and White, W. (1975), *The Worker Directors* (London: Hutchinson).

Brannen, P. (1983), 'Worker directors – an approach to analysis: the case of the British Steel Corporation', in C. Crouch and F. A. Heller (eds), *International Year Book of Democracy* (New York: Wiley).

Brown, R. and Brannen, P. (1970), 'Social relations, and social perspectives amongst shipbuilding workers', *Sociology*, vol. 4, nos. 1 and 2, pp. 71–84, 197–211.

Bryman, A. (1984), 'The debate about quantitative and qualitative research: a question of method or epistemology', *British Journal of Sociology*, vol. 35, no. 1, pp. 75–92.

Bullock, C., and Brady, D. (1983), 'Party, constituency and roll-call voting in the US senate', *Legislative Studies Quarterly*, vol. 8, no. 1, pp. 29–43.

Burnham, J. (1942), *The Managerial Revolution: What is Happening in the World* (New York: Putnam).

Burton, F. (1978), *The Politics of Legitimacy. Struggles in a Belfast Community* (London, Routledge & Kegan Paul).

Burton, M. G. (1984), 'Elites and collective protest', *The Sociological Quarterly*, vol. 25 (Winter), pp. 45–66.

Burton, M. G., and Higley, J. (1984), 'Elite theory: the basic contentions', American Sociological Association Meeting, San Antonio (August).

Bush, T., and Kogan, M. (1982), *Directors of Education* (London: Allen & Unwin).

Cannell, C. F., and Kahn, R. L. (1953), 'The collection of data by interviewing', in L. Festinger and D. Katz (eds), *Research Methods in the Behavioural Sciences* (New York: Dryden Press).

Chamberlain, L. H. (1946), *The President, Congress and Legislation* (New York: Columbia University Press).

Chadwick, W. O. (1983), *Hensley Henson: A Study in the Friction Between Church and State* (Oxford: Clarendon Press).

China, Republic of, Government Publications:

Annual Review of Government Administration, Research, Development and Evaluation Commission, Executive Yuan.

Ten-Year Economic Development Plan for Taiwan, Republic of China (1980-1989), Council for Economic Planning and Development, Executive Yuan, March 1980.

Educational Statistics of the Republic of China, Ministry of Education, 1982.

Monthly Key Economic Indicators of Taiwan, The Republic of China, Directorate-General of Budget, Accounting and Statistics, Executive Yuan.

Churchward, L. G. (1966), 'Soviet local government today', *Soviet Studies*, vol. 17, no. 4, pp. 431–52.

Churchward, L. G. (1968), *Contemporary Soviet Government* (2nd edn, 1975) (London: Routledge & Kegan Paul).

Churchward, L. G. (1973), *The Soviet Intelligentsia* (London: Routledge & Kegan Paul).

Clausen, A. R. (1967), 'Measurement identity in the longitudinal analysis of legislative voting', *American Political Science Review*, vol. 61, no. 4, pp. 1020–35.

Clausen, A. R. (1973), *How Congressmen Decide: A Policy Focus* (New York: St. Martin's Press).

Clubb, J., and Traugott, S. (1977), 'Partisan cleavage and cohesion in the House of Representatives, 1861–1974', *Journal of Interdisciplinary History*, vol. 7, no. 2, pp. 375–401.

Cohan, A. S. (1977), 'The question of a united Ireland: perspectives of the Irish political elite', *International Affairs*, vol. 53, no. 2, pp. 232–54.

Cooper, J., and Brady, D. (1981), 'Institutional context and leadership style: the House from Cannon to Rayburn', *American Political Science Review*, vol. 75, no. 2, pp. 411–25.

Cooper, J., Brady, D., and Hurley, P. (1977), 'The electoral basis of party voting: patterns and trends in the US House of Representatives' in J. Cooper and S. Maisel (eds), *The Impact of the Electoral Process* (Beverley Hills, Calif.: Sage).

Cornford, F. M. (Jr) (1941), *The Republic of Plato* (Oxford: Clarendon Press).

Crewe, I. (1974), 'Introduction: studying elites in Britain' in I. Crewe (ed.), *British Political Sociology Yearbook, Volume I: Elites in Western Democracy* (London: Croom Helm).

Crick, B. (1972), *Political Theory and Practice* (London: Allen Lane).

Czudnowski, M. M. (1982), 'Does who governs matter?', *International Yearbook for Studies of Leaders and Leadership*, Vol. I (De Kalb, Ill.: Northern Illinois University Press).

Dahl, R. A. (1961), *Who Governs?* (New Haven: Yale University Press).
Davidson, R. H. (1981), 'Subcommittee government: new channels for policy making' in T. E. Mann and N. J. Ornstein (eds), *The New Congress* (Washington: American Enterprise Institute).
Denzin, N. (1978), *The Research Act in Sociology: A Theoretical Introduction to Sociological Methods* (New York: McGraw Hill).
Dexter, L. A. (1970), *Elite and Specialized Interviewing* (Evanston: Northwestern University Press).
Djilas, M. (1957), *The New Class: An Analysis of the Communist System* (London: Thames & Hudson).
Domhoff, G. W. (1967), *Who Rules America?* (Englewood Cliffs, N.J.: Prentice-Hall).
Domhoff, G. W. (1971), *The Higher Circles* (New York: Vintage Books).
Domhoff, G. W. (1979), *The Powers that Be* (New York, Vintage Books).
Duggan, M. (1983), *Runcie – The Making of an Archbishop* (London: Hodder & Stoughton).
Dunleavy, P. (1981), 'Professions and policy change: notes towards a model of ideological corporatism', *Public Administration Bulletin*, no. 36, pp. 3–16.
Easton, D. (1969), 'The new revolution in political science', *American Political Science Review*, vol. 63, no. 4, pp. 1051-61.
Edinger, L., and Searing, D. (1967), 'Social background in elite analysis: a methodological enquiry', *American Political Science Review*, vol. 61, no. 2, pp. 428–45.
Faulkner, B. (1978), *Memoirs of a Statesman* (London: Weidenfeld & Nicolson).
Featherstone, K. (1982), 'Elite interviewing amongst West European parliamentarians: some reflections from personal experience', ECPR Joint Sessions, University of Aarhus.
Fei, J. C. H., Ranis, G., and Kuo, S. W. Y. (eds) (1979), *Growth with Equity: The Taiwan Case* (New York: Oxford University Press).
Fenno, R. (1966), *The Power of the Purse* (Boston: Little Brown).
Fenno, R. (1973), *Congressmen in Committees* (Boston: Little Brown).
Fenno, R. (1978), *Home Style: House Members in Their Districts* (Boston: Little Brown).
Fenno, R. (1986), 'Observation, context, and sequence in the study of politics', *American Political Science Review*, vol. 80, no. 1, pp. 3–15.
Ferejohn, J. (1974), *Pork Barrel Politics* (Stanford: Stanford University Press).
Field, G. L., and Higley, J. (1980), *Elitism* (London: Routledge & Kegan Paul).
Field, G. L., and Higley, J. (1982), 'The states of national elites and the stability of political institutions in 81 nations, 1950–1982', Annual Meeting of the Sociological Association of Australia and New Zealand, Sydney, 26-28 September.
Fiorina, M. P. (1974), *Representatives, Roll Calls, and Constituencies* (Lexington, Massachusetts: D. C. Heath).
Fisher, L. (1985), *Constitutional Conflicts Between Congress and the President* (Princeton, N.J.: Princeton University Press).
Frank, P. (1971), 'The CPSU Obkom First Secretary: a profile', *British Journal of Political Science*, vol. 1, no. 2, pp. 173–90.

Freeman, L. C., Fararo, T. J., Blomberg Jr, W., and Sunshine, M. H. (1963), 'Locating leaders in local communities: a comparison of some alternative approaches', *American Sociological Review*, vol. 28, no. 5, pp. 791–798.

Friedrichs, J., and Ludke, H. (1975), *Participant Observation* (Farnborough: Saxon House).

Frolic, P. (1971), 'Decision-making in Soviet cities', *American Political Science Review*, vol. 66, no. 1, pp. 38-52.

Galaskiewicz, J. (1982), 'Corporate-nonprofit linkages in Minneapolis-St. Paul: preliminary findings from three surveys', unpublished paper (Minneapolis, MN: Department of Sociology, University of Minnesota).

Galaskiewicz, J. (1985), *Social Organization of an Urban Grants Economy: A Study of Business Philanthropy and Nonprofit Organizations* (Orlando, FL: Academic Press).

Galbraith, J. K. (1969), *The New Industrial State* (Harmondsworth: Penguin).

Gallie, W. B. (1955-6), 'Essentially contested concepts', *Proceedings of the Aristotelian Society*, vol. 56, pp. 167-98.

Gehlen, M. P. (1969), *The Communist Party of the Soviet Union: A Functional Analysis* (Indiana: Indiana University Press).

Giddens, A. (1973), *The Class Structure of the Advanced Societies* (London: Hutchinson).

Giddens, A. (1974), 'Elites in the British class structure' in P. Stanworth and A. Giddens (eds), *Elites and Power in British Society* (Cambridge: Cambridge University Press).

Gilbert, A. D. (1980), *The Making of Post-Christian Britain* (London: Longman).

Gill, R. (1975), *The Social Context of Theology: A Methodological Enquiry* (London: Mowbray).

Gill, R. (1977), *Theology and Social Structure* (London: Mowbray).

Gitelman, Z. (1977), 'Soviet political culture: insights from Jewish emigrés', *Soviet Studies*, vol. 29, no. 4, pp. 543–64.

Gittings, R. (1978), *The Nature of Biography* (London: Heinemann).

Glasgow, D. G. (1980), *The Black Underclass* (London: Jossey-Bass).

Goffman, E. (1972), *The Presentation of Self in Everyday Life* (Harmondsworth: Penguin).

Gold, R. L. (1958), 'Roles in sociological field observations', *Social Forces*, vol. 36, no. 3, pp. 217–23.

Gouldner, A. W. (1975), *For Sociology* (Harmondsworth: Penguin).

Goyder, J., and Leiper, J. M. (1985), 'The decline in survey response: a social values interpretation', *Sociology*, vol. 19, no. 1, pp. 56–7.

Gray, J., McPherson, A. F., and Raffe, D. (1983), *Reconstructions of Secondary Education: Theory, Myth and Practice Since the War* (London: Routledge & Kegan Paul).

Habgood, J. (1983), *Church and Nation in a Secular Age* (London: Darton, Longman & Todd).

Hagger, M., and Wolters, M. (1981), 'Ideology and roll-call behaviour at Westminster', Political Studies Association Annual Meeting, Hull.

Hammer, D. P. (1974), *The USSR: The Politics of Oligarchy* (Hinsdale, Ill.: Dryden).

Hansen, S. (1975), 'Participation, Political Structure and Concurrence', *American Political Science Review*, vol. 69, no. 4, pp. 1181–99.

Harasymiw, B. (1969), '*Nomenklatura*: The Soviet Communist Party's leadership recruitment system', *Canadian Journal of Political Science*, vol. 2, no. 4, pp. 493–512.

Harasymiw, B. (1984), *Political Elite Recruitment in the Soviet Union* (London: Macmillan).

Heclo, H., and Wildavsky, A. (1974), *The Private Government of Public Money. Community and Policy Inside British Politics* (London: Macmillan).

Henson, H. H. (1942–50), *Retrospect of an Unimportant Life*, 3 Vols (London: Oxford University Press).

Heskin, K. (1980), *Northern Ireland: A Psychological Analysis* (Dublin: Gill and Macmillan).

Higley, J., Deacon, D., and Smart, D. (1979), *Elites in Australia* (London: Routledge & Kegan Paul).

Higley, J., and Moore, G. (1981), 'Elite integration in the United States and Australia', *American Political Science Review*, vol. 75, no. 3, pp. 581–97.

Hill, K. Q., and Hurley, P. A. (1979), 'Mass participation, electoral competitiveness and issue-attitude agreement between congressmen and their constituents', *British Journal of Political Science*, vol. 9, no. 4, pp. 507–11.

Hill, R. (1973), 'Patterns of deputy selection to local soviets', *Soviet Studies*, vol. 25, no. 2, pp. 196–212.

Hill, R. (1977), *Soviet Political Elites: The Case of Tiraspol* (London: Martin Robertson).

Hodnett, G. (1978), *Leadership in the Soviet National Republics: A Quantitative Study of Recruitment Policy* (Oakville, Ontario: Mosaic Press).

Hoffmann-Lange, U., Neumann, H., and Steinkemper, B. (1980), *Konsens und Konflikt Zwischen Führungsgruppen in der Bundesrepublik Deutschland* (Frankfurt: Lang). Abridged English translation: 'Conflict and consensus among elites in the Federal Republic of Germany' in G. Moore (ed.), *Research in Politics and Society*, Vol. 1, Studies of the Structure of National Elite Groups (Greenwich, JAI Press, 1985), pp. 243–83.

Hoffmann-Lange, U., Kutteroff, A., and Wolf, G. (1982), 'Projektbericht: die Befragung von Eliten in der Bundesrepublik Deutschland', *Zumanachrichten*, no. 10, pp. 35–53.

Holsti, O. (1969), *Content Analysis for the Social Sciences and Humanities* (Reading, Mass.: Addison-Wesley).

Hough, J. (1969), *The Soviet Prefects: The Local Party Organs in Industrial Decision-Making* (Harvard University Press).

Hunter, F. (1953), *Community Power Structure: A Study of Decision Makers* (Chapel Hill: University of North Carolina Press).

Ionescu, G. (1975), *Centripetal Politics: Government and the New Centres of Power* (London: Hart-Davis, MacGibbon).

Iremonger, F. A. (1948), *William Temple* (London: Oxford University Press).

Kadushin, C. (1968), 'Power, influence and social circles: a new methodology for studying opinion-makers', *American Sociological Review*, vol. 33, no. 5, pp. 685–99.

Kanet, R. E. (ed.) (1971), *The Behavioral Revolution and Communist Studies* (New York: The Free Press).

Kariel, H. S. (1961), *The Decline of American Pluralism* (Stanford: Stanford University Press).

Katznelson, I. (1973), *Black Man, White Cities* (Chicago, University of Chicago Press).

Kavanagh, D. A. (1971), 'The deferential English: a comparative critique', *Government and Opposition*, vol. 6, no. 3, pp. 333–66.

Keller, S. (1983), 'Celebrities as a national elite', in M. Czudnowski (ed.), *Political Elites and Social Change: Studies of Elite Roles and Attitudes*, International Yearbook for Studies of Leaders and Leadership, Vol. II (De Kalb., Ill.: Northern Illinois University Press).

Kelsall, R. K., Poole, A., and Kuhn, A. (1972), *Graduates: The Sociology of an Elite* (London: Methuen).

Key, V. O. (Jr) (1966), *The Responsible Electorate* (Cambridge, Mass.: Harvard University Press).

King, Cecil (1975), *The Cecil King Diary 1970–74* (London: Jonathan Cape).

Kingdon, J. (1973), *Congressmen's Voting Decisions* (New York: Harper and Row).

Kogan, M. (1971), *The Politics of Education* (Harmondsworth: Penguin).

Kogan, M., and van der Eyken, W. (1973), *County Hall* (Harmondsworth: Penguin).

Konrad, G., and Szelenyi, I. (1980), *Intellectuals on the Road to Class Power* (New York: Harcourt Brace Jovanovich).

Krippendorff, K. (1980), *Content Analysis: An Introduction to Its Methodology* (London: Sage).

Knoke, D., and Kuklinski, J. H. (1982), *Network Analysis*, Sage Quantitative Applications in the Social Sciences, No. 28 (London: Sage).

Kurtz, D. M. (1984), 'Institutions, leaders and interlocking in a southern state: Louisiana', *Power and Elites*, vol. 1, no. 1, pp. 51–68.

Larson, D. W., *Land of the Giants: A History of Minnesota Business* (Minneapolis, MN.: Dorn Books).

Laumann, E. O., and Pappi, F. U. (1976), *Networks of Collective Action: A Perspective on Community Influence Systems* (New York: Academic Press).

Leijenaar, M., and Niemöller, K. (1982), 'Elite interviewing: sailing between Scylla and Charybdis', ECPR Joint Sessions, University of Aarhus.

Levine, D. H. (1978), 'Venezuela since 1958: the consolidation of democratic politics', in J. J. Linz and A. Stepan (eds), *The Breakdown of Democratic Regimes* (Baltimore: Johns Hopkins University Press).

Lijphart, A. (1968), *The Politics of Accommodation: Pluralism and Democracy in the Netherlands* (Berkeley, Calif.: University of California Press).

Lijphart, A. (1977), *Democracy in Plural Societies: A Comparative Exploration* (New Haven: Yale University Press).

Lindblom, C. E. (1968), *The Policy-Making Process* (Englewood Cliffs, N.J.: Prentice-Hall).

Lipset, S. M., Trow, M., and Coleman, J. (1956), *Union Democracy* (New York: Anchor Books).

Lodge, M. C. (1969), *Soviet Elite Attitudes Since Stalin* (Columbus, Ohio: Merril).

Lowell, A. L. (1902), 'The influence of party upon legislation', *Annual Report of the American Historical Association*, no. 1, pp. 321–543.

Ludz, P. C. (1972), *Parteielite im Wandel* (Köln), translated and revised as *The Changing Party Elite in East Germany* (Cambridge, Mass.: MIT Press).

Lukes, S. (1974), *Power: A Radical View* (London: Macmillan).

Lupton, T. (1963), *On the Shop Floor* (Oxford: Pergamon).

Mackenzie, W. J. M. (1967), *Politics and Social Science* (Harmondsworth: Penguin).

MacRae, D. (Jr) (1958), *Dimensions of Congressional Voting* (Berkeley: University of California Press).

MacShane, D. (1981), *Solidarity: Poland's Independent Trade Union* (Nottingham: Spokesman).

Makin, G. (1982), 'Elite interviewing and Argentinian politics: a forced option', ECPR Joint Sessions, University of Aarhus.

Mansergh, N. (1978), 'The prelude to partition: concepts and aims in Ireland and India', *The 1976 Commonwealth Lecture* (Cambridge: Cambridge University Press).

Marcus, G. E. (1983), ' "Elite" as a concept, theory and research tradition' in G. E. Marcus (ed.), *Elites: Ethnographic Issues* (Albuquerque, N.M.: University of New Mexico Press).

Matthews, M. (1978), *Privilege in the Soviet Union: A Study of Elite Life-Styles under Communism* (London: Allen & Unwin).

Matthews, M. (1982), *Education in the Soviet Union* (London: Allen & Unwin).

McIver, J. P., and Carmies, E. G. (1981), *Unidimensional Scaling* (Beverley Hills, Calif.: Sage).

McPherson, A. (1983), 'An angle on the geist: persistence and change in the Scottish educational tradition', in W. M. Humes and H. M. Paterson (eds), *Scottish Culture and Scottish Education 1800–1980* (Edinburgh: John Donald).

McPherson, A., and Raab, C. (forthcoming), *The Making of Scottish Educational Policy* (Edinburgh: Edinburgh University Press).

Medhurst, K. (1984), *Church and Labour in Columbia* (Manchester: Manchester University Press).

Medhurst, K., and Moyser, G. (1982), 'From princes to pastors: the changing position of the Anglican episcopate in English society and politics', *West European Politics*, vol. 5, no. 2 (April), pp. 172–91.

Medhurst, K., and Moyser, G. (1985), 'Lambeth Palace, the bishops and politics' in G. Moyser (ed.), *Church and Politics Today* (Edinburgh: T. and T. Clarke).

Meisel, J. (1958), *The Myth of the Ruling Class* (Ann Arbor: The University of Michigan Press).

Meyer, A. G. (1964), 'The USSR incorporated' in D. W. Treadgold (ed.), *The Development of the USSR: An Exchange of Views* (Seattle: Washington University Press), pp. 21–8.

Michels, R. (1959, originally 1911), *Political Parties: A Sociological Study of the Oligarchical Tendencies of Modern Democracy* (New York: Dover).

Miliband, R. (1969/1973), *The State in Capitalist Society* (London: Weidenfeld & Nicolson/London: Quartet Books).

Miller, D. W. (1978), *Queen's Rebels: Ulster Loyalism in Historical Perspective* (Dublin: Gill & Macmillan).

Miller, J. (1977), 'Cadres policy in nationality areas: recruitment of first and second secretaries in non-Russian republics of the USSR', *Soviet Studies*, vol. 29, no. 1, pp. 3–36.

Miller, W. (1983), *The Survey Method in the Social and Political Sciences* (London: Pinter).

Miller, W. E., and Stokes, D. E. (1963), 'Constituency influence in Congress', *American Political Science Review*, vol. 57, no. 1, pp. 45–56.

Mokken, R. T., and Stokman, F. N. (1976), 'Power and influence as political phenomena' in B. Barry (ed.), *Power and Political Theory. Some European Perspectives* (London: Wiley), pp. 33–54.

Moore, G. (1979), 'The structure of a national elite network', *American Sociological Review*, vol. 44 (October), pp. 673–92.

Moran, M. (1985), *Politics and Society in Britain: An Introduction* (London: Macmillan).

Morgan, D. (1969), 'The social and educational background of Anglican bishops: continuities and change', *British Journal of Sociology*, vol. 20, pp. 295–310.

Mosca, G. (1884), *Teorica Dei Governi e Governo Parlamentare*. English version published in 1939 by A. Livingstone (ed.), *The Ruling Class* (New York: McGraw-Hill).

Moyser, G. (1979), 'Voting patterns on "moral" issues in the British House of Commons, 1964–69', British Sociological Association Conference, unpublished paper, London School of Economics.

Moyser, G., and Wagstaffe, M. (1985), *The Methodology of Elite Interviewing*, Report No. H0025003 (London: Economic and Social Research Council).

Nadel, S. F. (1956), 'The concept of social elites', *International Social Science Bulletin*, vol. 8, no. 3, pp. 413–24.

National Science Foundation (1983), *Grant General Conditions* (Washington, D.C.).

New Ireland Forum (1983), *The Cost of Violence Arising from the Northern Ireland Crisis Since 1969* (Dublin: The Stationery Office).

Nordlinger, E. (1981), *On the Autonomy of the Democratic State* (Cambridge, Mass.: Harvard University Press).

Norton, P. (1981), *The Commons in Perspective* (Oxford: Martin Robertson).

Nove, A. (1975), 'Is there a ruling class in the USSR?', *Soviet Studies*, vol. 27, no. 4, pp. 615–38.

Oliver, J. (1978), *Working at Stormont* (Dublin: Institute of Public Administration).

Oppenheim, A. N. (1966), *Questionnaire Design and Attitude Measurement* (New York: Basic Books).

Oppenheimer, B. (1974), *Oil and the Congressional Process* (Lexington, Mass.: D. C. Heath).

Ornstein, N. J., Mann, T. E., Malbin, M. J., Schick, A., and Bibby, J. F. (1984), *Vital Statistics on Congress, 1984–1985 Edition* (Washington: American Enterprise Institute).

Pahl, R. E., and Winkler, J. T. (1974a), 'The economic elite: theory and practice' in P. Stanworth and A. Giddens (eds), *Elites and Power in British Society* (Cambridge: Cambridge University Press).

Pahl, R. E., and Winkler, J. T. (1974b), 'The Coming Corporatism', *New Society*, vol. 30, no. 627 (October), pp. 72–6.

Pareto, V. (1923), *Trattato di Sociologica Generale*. English version published in 1935 by A. Livingstone (ed.), *Mind and Society* (New York: Harcourt, Brace).

Parkin, F. (1971), *Class Inequality and Political Order* (London: MacGibbon and Kee).

Parry, G. (1969), *Political Elites* (London: Allen & Unwin).

Parry, G., and Moyser, G. (1983), 'Political participation and community in Britain: conceptual and methodological issues', APSA Annual Meeting, Chicago.

Parry, G., and Moyser, G. (1984), 'Political participation in Britain: a research agenda for a new study', *Government and Opposition*, vol. 19, no. 1, pp. 68–92.

Parry, G., Moyser, G., and Wagstaffe, M. (1987), 'The crowd and the community: context, content and aftermath', in G. Gaskell and R. Benewick (eds), *The Crowd in Contemporary Britain* (London: Sage).

Parry, G., Moyser, G., and Day, N. (forthcoming), *Participation and Democracy: Political Activity and Attitudes in Contemporary Britain* (Cambridge: Cambridge University Press).

Peabody, R. L. (1969), 'Research on Congress: a coming of age' in R. K. Huitt and R. L. Peabody (eds), *Congress: Two Decades of Analysis* (Baltimore, MD: Johns Hopkins Press).

Plummer, K. (1983), *Documents of Life*, Contemporary Social Research Series, No. 7 (London: Allen & Unwin).

Pollert, A. (1981), *Girls, Wives, Factory Lives* (London: Macmillan).

Poole, K. T. (1983), 'Recovering a basic space from a set of issue scales' Working Paper No. 44-82-33, Pittsburgh, PA: Graduate School of Industrial Administration, Carnegie-Mellon University.

Poole, K. T., and Daniels, S. (1985), 'Ideology, party and voting in the US Congress, 1959–1980', *American Political Science Review*, vol. 79, no. 2, pp. 373–99.

Poole, K. T., and Rosenthal, H. (1984), 'The polarization of American politics', *Journal of Politics*, vol. 46, no. 4, pp. 1061–79.

Poole, K. T., and Rosenthal, H. (1985), 'A spatial model for legislative roll call analysis', *American Journal of Political Science*, vol. 30, no. 1, pp. 357–84.

Poulantzas, N. (1969), 'The problem of the capitalist state', *New Left Review*, no. 58, pp. 67–78.

Pridham, G. (1981), *The Nature of the Italian Party System: A Regional Case-Study* (London: Croom Helm).

Pridham, G. (ed.) (1986), *The Theory and Practice of Coalition Behaviour: An Inductive Model for Western Europe* (Cambridge: Cambridge University Press).

Pridham, G. (1987), *Political Parties and Coalition Behaviour in Italy: An Interpretative Study* (London: Croom Helm).

Purcell, S. K., and Purcell, J. F. H. (1980), 'State and society in Mexico: must a stable polity be institutionalized?', *World Politics*, vol. 32, no. 2, pp. 194–227.

Putnam, R. (1976), *The Comparative Study of Political Elites* (Englewood Cliffs: Prentice-Hall).

Putnam, R. D. (1973), *The Beliefs of Politicians: Ideology, Conflict and Democracy in Britain and Italy* (New Haven: Yale University Press).

Raab, C. D. (1980), 'The changing machinery of Scottish educational policy-making', *Scottish Educational Review*, vol. 12, pp. 88–98.

Raab, C. D. (1982a), 'Mapping the boundaries of education policy systems: the case of Scotland', *Public Administration Bulletin*, no. 39, pp. 40–57.

Raab, C. D. (1982b), 'The quasi-government of Scottish education' in A. Barker (ed.), *Quangos in Britain: Government and the Networks of Public Policy-Making* (London: Macmillan).

Rex, J. (1974), *Sociology and the Demystification of the Modern World* (London: Routledge & Kegan Paul).

Rhodes, R. A. W. (1985), 'Power-dependence, policy communities and intergovernmental networks', Public Administration Bulletin no. 49, pp. 4–31.

Rice, S. A. (1928), *Quantitative Methods in Politics* (New York: Alfred A. Knopf).

Richardson, J. J., and Jordan, A. G. (1979), *Governing Under Pressure* (London: Martin Robertson).

Rigby, T. H. (1968), *Communist Party Membership in the Soviet Union 1917–67* (Princeton, NJ: Princeton University Press).

Ripley, R. B. (1967), *Party Leaders in the House of Representatives* (Washington: Brookings).

Royal Commission on the Constitution, 1969–1973 (T973), Cmnd. 5460 (London: HMSO).

Rose, R. (1971), *Governing Without Consensus: An Irish Perspective* (London: Faber).

Schattschneider, E. E. (1942), *Party Government* (New York: Holt).

Schattschneider, E. E. (1960), *The Semi Sovereign People* (New York: Holt, Rinehart & Winston).

Scheuch, E. K. (1973), 'Soziologie der Macht', in H. K. Schneider and Ch. Watrin (eds), *Macht und Ökonomisches Gesetz*, Schriften des Vereins für Socialpolitik, vol. 73/II (Berlin: Duncker & Humblot).

Schmitter, P. (1979), 'Still the century of corporatism?' in P. Schmitter and G. Lehmbruch (eds), *Trends Towards Corporatist Intermediation* (London: Sage), pp. 7–52.

Schneider, J. E. (1979), *Ideological Coalitions in Congress* (Westport, Connecticut: Greenwood Press).

Schubert, G. A. (1964), *Judicial Behavior* (Chicago: Rand McNally).

Schumpeter, J. (1956), *Capitalism, Socialism and Democracy* (New York: Harper & Row).

Seidelman, R., and Harpham, E. J. (1985), *Disenchanted Realists: Political Science and the American Crisis, 1884–1984* (Albany: State University of New York Press).

Seldon, A., and Pappworth, J. (1983), *By Word of Mouth: Elite Oral History* (London: Methuen).

Shannon, W. W. (1968), *Party, Constituency, and Congressional Voting* (Baton Rouge: Louisiana State University Press).

Sheppard, D. (1983), *Bias to the Poor* (London: Hodder & Stoughton).

Sinclair, B. (1977), 'Party realignment and the transformation of the political agenda: the House of Representatives, 1925–1938', *American Political Science Review*, vol. 71, no. 3, pp. 940–54.

Sinclair, B. (1982), *Congressional Realignment 1925–1978* (Austin: University of Texas Press).

Sinclair, B. (1983a), *Majority Leadership in the US House* (Baltimore, MD: Johns Hopkins University Press).

Sinclair, B. (1983b), 'Purposive behaviour in the US Congress: a review essay', *Legislative Studies Quarterly*, vol. 8, no. 1, pp. 117–31.

Smith, S. S., and Deering, C. J. (1984), *Committees in Congress* (Washington: Congressional Quarterly Press).

Statistical Abstract of the US, 105th Ed. (Washington, D.C.: US Bureau of the Census, 1984).

Stokes, D. E., and Miller, W. E. (1962), 'Party government and the saliency of Congress', *Public Opinion Quarterly*, vol. 26, pp. 531–46.

Stone, C. N. (1984), 'New class or convergence?: competing interpretations of the impact of social complexity on the structure of urban power', *Power and Elites*, vol. 1, no. 1, pp. 1–22.

Suleiman, E. N. (1978), *Elites in French Society* (Princeton, N.J.: Princeton University Press).

Sundquist, J. L. (1981), *The Decline and Resurgence of Congress* (Washington: Brookings).

Suttles, G. D. (1972), *The Social Construction of Communities* (Chicago: University of Chicago Press).

Taubman, W. (1973), *Governing Soviet Cities: Bureaucratic Politics and Urban Development in the USSR* (New York: Praeger).

Thompson, K. (1970), *Bureaucracy and Church Reform* (Oxford: Clarendon Press).

Trotsky, L. (1965), *The Revolution Betrayed* (New York: Merit Publications).

Turner, J. (1951), *Party and Constituency: Pressures on Congress* (Baltimore: Johns Hopkins University Press).

Turner, J., and Schneider, E. V. (1970), *Party and Constituency: Pressures on Congress* (Baltimore: Johns Hopkins University Press).

Urio, P., Arigoni, G., Baumann, E., and Joyce, D. (1982), 'Elite interviewing amongst Swiss cantonal and federal higher civil servants – some methodological problems', ECPR Joint Sessions, University of Aarhus.

Utley, T. E. (1975), *Lessons of Ulster* (London: Dent).

Van Schendelen, M. P. (1984), 'Interviewing members of parliament', *Political Methodology*, vol. 10, no. 3, pp. 301–21.

Verba, S., and Nie, N. (1972), *Participation in America: Political Democracy and Social Equality* (New York: Harper & Row).

Voslensky, M. (1984), *Nomenklatura: An Anatomy of the Soviet Ruling Class* (London: Bodley Head). Originally published in German in 1980.

Wallis, R. (1976a), 'The moral career of a research project', in C. Bell and H. Newby (eds), *Doing Sociological Research* (London: Allen & Unwin).

Wallis, R. (1976b), *The Road to Total Freedom: A Sociological Analysis of Scientology* (London: Heinemann).

Weisberg, H. F. (1972), 'Scaling models for legislative roll call analysis', *American Political Science Review*, vol. 66, no. 4, pp. 1306–15.

Welsby, P. A. (1984), *A History of the Church of England, 1945–1980* (London: Oxford University Press).

Welsh, W. A. (1976), 'Elites and leadership in communist systems: some new perspectives', *Studies in Comparative Communism*, vol. 9, nos. 1 and 2, pp. 162–86.

Welsh, W. A. (1979), *Leaders and Elites* (New York: Holt, Reinhart & Winston).

White, S. (1979), *Political Culture and Soviet Politics* (London: Macmillan).

White, S. (1980), 'The effectiveness of political propaganda in the USSR', *Soviet Studies*, vol. 32, no. 3 (July), pp. 323–48.

Whiteley, P. (1978), 'The structure of democratic socialist ideology in Britain', *Political Studies*, vol. 26, no. 2, pp. 209–31.

Who's Who in America, 1980–81 Edition (Chicago: A. N. Marquis Co., 1980).

Wilde, A. W. (1978), 'Conversations among gentlemen: oligarchical democracy in Colombia' in J. J. Linz and A. Stepan (eds), *The Breakdown of Democratic Regimes* (Baltimore: Johns Hopkins University Press).

Wilson, W. (1885), *Congressional Government* (Cleveland: World Publishing).

Winkler, J. T. (1974), 'The ghost at the bargaining table: directors and industrial relations', *British Journal of Industrial Relations*, vol. 12, no. 2, pp. 191–212.

Winkler, J. T. (1975a), 'The two faces of capitalism', *The Director*, vol. 27, no. 7, pp. 91–6.

Winkler, J. T. (1975b), 'Company directors . . . or corporate knights?', *The Director*, vol. 27, no. 7, pp. 85–7.

Wolfe, T. K., and Johnson, E. W. (eds) (1975), *The New Journalism* (London: Picador).

Wolters, M. (1980), 'Strategic voting: an empirical analysis with Dutch roll-call data' in P. Whiteley (ed.), *Models of Political Economy* (London: Sage).

Wright Mills, C. (1956), *The Power Elite* (New York: Oxford University Press).

Young, H., and Sloman, A. (1982), *No, Minister* (London: British Broadcasting Corporation).

Young, H., and Sloman, A. (1984), *But, Chancellor* (London: British Broadcasting Corporation).

Young, K. (1977), ' "Values" in the policy process', *Policy and Politics*, vol. 5, pp. 1–22.

Young, K., and Mills, E., 'Public policy research: a review of qualitative methods' (London: Economic and Social Research Council, n.d.).

Young, K., and Mills, L. (1978), 'Understanding the "Assumptive Worlds" of governmental actors', a report to the Social Science Research Council panel on central/local government relations, Bristol.

Zinoviev, A. (1984), *The Reality of Communism* (London: Gollancz).

Zuckerman, A. (1977), 'The concept "Political Elite": lessons from Mosca and Pareto', *Journal of Politics*, vol. 39, no. 2, pp. 324–44.

Names Index

Subject Index